Contemporary Issues in Islam

The New Edinburgh Islamic Surveys
Series Editor: Carole Hillenbrand

TITLES AVAILABLE OR FORTHCOMING

Contemporary Issues in Islam Asma Afsaruddin
Islamic Astronomy and Astrology Stephen P. Blake
The New Islamic Dynasties Clifford Edmund Bosworth
Media Arabic (2nd Edition) Julia Ashtiany Bray and Nadia Jamil
Introduction to Persian Literature Dominic Parviz Brookshaw
An Introduction to the Hadith John Burton
A History of Islamic Law Noel Coulson
Medieval Islamic Political Thought Patricia Crone
A Short History of the Ismailis Farhad Daftary
Islam: An Historical Introduction (2nd Edition) Gerhard Endress
The Arabic Aristotle Gerhard Endress
A History of Christian–Muslim Relations Hugh Goddard
An Introduction to the Hadith Andreas Gorke
Medieval Islamic Science Robert Hall
Shi'ism (2nd Edition) Heinz Halm
Islamic Science and Engineering Donald Hill
Muslim Spain Reconsidered Richard Hitchcock
Islamic Law: From Historical Foundations to Contemporary Practice Mawil Izzi Dien
Sufism: The Formative Period Ahmet T. Karamustafa
Modern Turkish Literature Celia Kerslake
Islam in Indonesia Carool Kersten
Islamic Aesthetics Oliver Leaman
Persian Historiography Julie Scott Meisami
Pilgrims and Pilgrimage in Islam Josef Meri
The Muslims of Medieval Italy Alex Metcalfe
The Archaeology of the Islamic World Marcus Milwright
Twelver Shiism Andrew J. Newman
Muslims in Western Europe (3rd Edition) Jørgen Nielsen
Medieval Islamic Medicine Peter E. Pormann and Emilie Savage-Smith
Islamic Names Annemarie Schimmel
The Genesis of Literature in Islam Gregor Schoeler
Modern Arabic Literature Paul Starkey
Islamic Medicine Manfred Ullman
Islam and Economics Ibrahim Warde
A History of Islamic Spain W. Montgomery Watt and Pierre Cachia
Introduction to the Qur'an W. Montgomery Watt
Islamic Creeds W. Montgomery Watt
Islamic Philosophy and Theology W. Montgomery Watt
Islamic Political Thought W. Montgomery Watt
The Influence of Islam on Medieval Europe W. Montgomery Watt

www.euppublishing.com/series/isur

Contemporary Issues in Islam

Asma Afsaruddin

EDINBURGH
University Press

Edinburgh University Press Ltd
The Tun – Holyrood Road
12 (2f) Jackson's Entry
Edinburgh EH8 8PJ
www.euppublishing.com

Typeset in 11/13pt Monotype Baskerville by
Servis Filmsetting Ltd, Stockport, Cheshire,
and printed and bound in Great Britain by
CPI Group (UK) Ltd, Croydon CR0 4YY

A CIP record for this book is available from the British Library

ISBN 978 0 7486 3276 3 (hardback)
ISBN 978 0 7486 3277 0 (paperback)
ISBN 978 0 7486 3224 4 (webready PDF)
ISBN 978 0 7486 9575 1 (epub)

Contents

Acknowledgements

The impetus for writing this book came from Professor Carole Hillenbrand of the University of Edinburgh who invited me to undertake this project for The New Edinburgh Islamic Surveys series of Edinburgh University Press. My profound thanks to her for affording me this opportunity to reflect at greater length on topics that I have been regularly engaging with in my classes, in some of my research and in my 'public intellectual' activities. Additionally, I am grateful to Ellie Bush, Assistant Commissioning Editor at EUP, and to Lel Gillingwater, who provided critical assistance during the manuscript preparation and production phases.

I am most grateful to the following colleagues who took time out of their busy schedules to read portions of my manuscript: Fred Dallmayr, Ziad Elmarsafy, Roxanne Euben, and Nader Hashemi. Their feedback was very valuable. I would also like to thank the students over the years in my 'Islam and Modernity' class, both at the University of Notre Dame and at Indiana University, for their stimulating questions and discussions concerning many of the topics that are included in this book.

Gratitude is furthermore owed to the College Arts and Humanities Institute (CAHI) at Indiana University, Bloomington, which offered me a two-course release grant during the academic year 2012–13. This welcome turn of events enabled me to complete a bulk of the research then and start writing. During the following academic year 2013–2014 I was able to make considerable progress in my writing despite a hectic administrative schedule as chair of my department. By summer 2014, I was finally able to complete my manuscript.

During the book's gestation period and throughout the period of writing I was able to present selections from various chapters in the book to multiple audiences at a number of academic and professional association meetings, including those of the Middle East Studies Association, the International Society for Islamic Legal Studies, the American Academy of Religion, and the Building Bridges group, as well as at public colloquia and workshops sponsored over the years by the Foundation for Sciences and Arts, Istanbul, Turkey; the Prince al-Waleed Islamic Studies Program at Harvard University; the University of Westminster, England; the Center for the Study of Islam and Democracy, Washington DC; the Maurer School of Law and the Islamic Studies Program at Indiana University; the Woolf Institute and the Cambridge

Interfaith Programme at the University of Cambridge; the Oasis Foundation; the McDonald Agape Foundation at the University of Cambridge; and the Institut für Islamische Studien, University of Vienna. I benefited greatly from my interactions with these audiences, which provided valuable opportunities to rethink and reformulate parts of the book chapters.

At the University of Notre Dame, my undergraduate research assistant Laura Myers helped with an initial compilation of bibliography and source materials. My current graduate research assistant Michael L. Bevers at Indiana University provided valuable assistance in continuing to hunt down articles and books on the various topics included in this work, in checking bibliographic references, and in the preparation of the index. Finally, my family provided encouragement and support all along the way, expressing particular relief that I was finally writing on contemporary and therefore 'relevant' topics!

Asma Afsaruddin
Bloomington, Indiana
31 August 2014

Introduction

This book deals with certain contemporary issues in Islam that are often the focus of both scholarly and general public discussion. It seeks to place these issues within a larger historical context and discuss their contemporary significance. A key premise of this book is that the past can never be severed from the present; a fulsome understanding of the latter has to be firmly anchored in a longue-durée historical vision that deliberately undermines a myopic presentist perspective.

A main focus of this book is therefore upon the historical contextualisation of the evolutions and transformations that have taken place over time in the meanings and applications of certain key concepts and topics that are now very much current in public discourses about Islam and Muslims. Such topics include Sharia, jihad, the caliphate, women's roles, and the so-called 'Islamic State'. 'Islam' as a religious and sociocultural rubric continues to be essentialised in such public discourses, even sometimes in academic settings, and the Islamic tradition is more often than not presented as static and reified. This also has implications for policy-making in government circles and in fostering a certain kind of world-view that sees the Islamic and Western worlds as the antithesis of one another. By presenting Islamic thought as predictably monolithic and ossified, the 'clash of civilisations' thesis thus gains more credibility among the general populace, media pundits and many political scientists in the academy. In contrast, the historical, diachronic approach allows the reader to see the evolutionary nature of Islamic thought and the diversity within it, and to appreciate the resources within it for change and renewal.

Chapter One deals with Muslim attempts to negotiate modernity in its secular, Western form(s) and describes the emergence of distinctive Islamic 'modernism(s)' as a result of these dialectical encounters. Special attention is paid to the specific historical and political circumstances starting in the nineteenth century, the period of Western colonisation, which created the impetus for modernism in a number of Muslim-majority societies. The thought of key intellectuals, such as Jamal al-Din al-Afghani, Muhammad 'Abduh, Muhammad Iqbal and Fazlur Rahman, is discussed in this context and the continuing relevance of their ideas is indicated. This chapter further interrogates whether we can talk about a single phenomenon known as modernity or whether it is more appropriate to talk about 'multiple modernities' as plural phenomena inflected by the specific historical and cultural experiences of any given society.

Chapter Two discusses modern and contemporary rereadings of the Sharia based particularly on Qur'anic hermeneutics and explores the classical hierarchical relationship between the Qur'an and hadith. Qur'anic hermeneutics remains the key to formulating recognisably Islamic, and as some would say 'authentic', responses to specific issues of modernity, as becomes apparent in a majority of the chapters in this book. Competing theologies and ethical values based on scriptural interpretation undergird the debates between modernists and reformists on the one hand and hard-line or radical Islamists on the other, analysis of which is a critical component of our study of such discourses.

The verification of hadith – statements attributed to the Prophet Muhammad – has been the concern of scholars since the formative period of Islam. This issue has resurfaced in the modern period with a degree of urgency since many of the important legal and theological positions were and are predicated on hadith, some of which appear to contradict the letter and spirit of the Qur'an. The hadith, even 'sound' (sahih) hadiths, have thus come under the renewed scrutiny of modernist scholars in particular. Their method of hadith analysis and the responses it has provoked in traditionalist and Islamist circles are discussed in this chapter. What these hermeneutic stratagems developed by a cross section of modern Muslim thinkers augur for the future is briefly touched upon.

Chapter Three deals with the thorny issue of Islam and politics. It may be argued that the rise of political Islam was the most distinctive development of the twentieth century in a number of Muslim-majority countries. The historical factors contributing to this phenomenon – the debilitating effects of European colonialism and the abolition of the caliphate in 1924, among others – are explored and the main characteristics of political Islam are discussed. The chapter presents a spectrum of perspectives on the critical issue of Islam and its relation to politics, starting with the controversial views of 'Ali 'Abd al-Raziq on the caliphate in the early twentieth century and the rebuttals of two of his most trenchant critics, progressing to the documentation of views found among more recent scholars and ideologues. The concern with 'Islam's' ability to coexist with 'democracy' – the quotation marks emphasise the reified way in which these terms are usually invoked – has grown in significance, especially in the aftermath of the Arab Spring and is therefore a central concern of the chapter. One of the major conclusions that emerges from our discussion is that political, specifically democratic, trends are better explained by sociopolitical and economic variables in culturally specific contexts rather than through ahistorical pronouncements on religious or cultural essences, as unfortunately remains all too common in both scholarly and popular discourses.

One of the most fraught subjects in the contemporary period remains that of women and gendered identities in various Islamic societies, as is evident in Chapter Four. Modernists assert that women's equal social and legal status, in addition to religious, was a hallmark of early Islamic society, which became attenuated over time due to changing conceptions of women's societal roles. Traditionalists and Islamists mostly tend to maintain that legal and social practices towards women that are now regarded as discriminatory are an accurate reflection of early Islamic attitudes and mores. These debates will be delineated in some detail. The rise of 'Islamic Feminism(s)' that seeks to retrieve gender-egalitarian interpretations of key verses in the Qur'an through a distinctive feminist hermeneutics will form the bulk of our discussion in this chapter.

Chapter Five deals with the subject of war and peacemaking within the Islamic tradition, not merely as legal concepts, but also as ethical and socio-political concepts. The events of 11 September 2001 have foregrounded the concepts of jihad and martyrdom in relation to militant Islamists in particular and Muslims in general. While militant Islamists promote the military aspect of jihad, traditionalist and modernist Muslims emphasise primarily the non-violent aspects while not necessarily eschewing armed combat in restricted circumstances. Intra-Muslim debates regarding the legitimate purview of jihad and of the means that can be employed to carry out justified violence in defence of some higher ideal are conducted in print, online and in broadcast media all over the world. These intense dialectics are scrutinised particularly to establish their relationship to pre-modern juridical and ethical discussions about what constituted legitimate military jihad. The historical and political circumstances that accompanied these changing discourses over time are a critical part of this chapter.

Chapter Six deals with American Muslims and the expansion of the traditional Muslim community (umma) outside the traditional Islamic heartlands into the West (primarily Europe and North America). The burgeoning Muslim population in the West constitutes one of the most distinctive features of the last century that continues into the current one. The focus of this chapter is mainly on the United States with its diverse Muslim population of between three and six million (depending on the source), with occasional references to Europe for comparative purposes. How the increasing visibility of Muslims in the American public square and their political citizenship are recalibrating the salience of religion in the public sphere and changing the cultural landscape of America are dealt with in this chapter. Furthermore, how this expanding geographical purview of the traditional umma is affecting the self-perception and communal identity of Muslims is explored. The chapter also focuses on the challenges created by a changed historical reality after September 11th and the rise of a virulent strain of Islamophobia that have given rise to distinctive modes of 'coping' among American Muslims. Such modes include increased political mobilisation, the formation of advocacy groups, an emphasis on interfaith and intercultural dialogue and activities, and fashioning a distinctive 'jurisprudence of minorities' to address unprecedented legal and moral dilemmas confronting Western Muslims.

In an era of increasing globalisation, Muslims, like other groups, are world citizens in addition to being the citizens of individual countries and actors in their local environments. In this enlarged 'glocal' context,[1] they interact regularly with people of different faith and cultural backgrounds. Some ideologues warn of increasing tension and escalating irreconcilable differences in world-views as a result of these growing interactions, and suggest that nativists batten down the hatches and attempt to hermetically seal off their cultures from outsiders. Others welcome these increased opportunities for interfaith and intercultural conversations to facilitate better understanding of one another and to make room for the 'Other' in their multicultural and religiously plural environments.

Chapter Seven describes a number of these initiatives that have been launched, particularly after September 11th, as the quest for finding common ground between the world religions continues. Given the continued relevance of religious loyalties in the contemporary world, it is easy to agree with Hans Küng when he says, 'No peace among the nations without peace among the religions'.[2] The numbers of people currently engaging in such dialogic encounters remain small and they are often viewed with suspicion by members of their own communities and of others. Our account of some of the positive results that have already occurred in the wake of some of these initiatives is cause for optimism and establishes their necessity in our conflict-ridden world.

The book concludes with a brief Epilogue in which I ponder the possible future roles for Islam and Muslims in a rapidly globalising world. It provides the occasion for reflection on what the intellectual, theological, political and historical trends identified in the preceding chapters have to tell us regarding contemporary Muslims and their societies and what they may portend for the future. Such a future trajectory cannot be precisely determined in advance, of course, especially since so much depends on contingent external variables. It is, however, argued that it is the common responsibility of all, Muslim and non-Muslim, to shape this future in positive ways through a dialectical engagement with one another, a process that should prove, one hopes, to be mutually illuminating and transformative.

It bears repeating that throughout these chapters, I have attempted to link the present squarely with the past and to point out continuities and discontinuities whenever relevant. This longer, chronological view allows us to better understand the complexities of many of the issues confronting Muslims today in their variegated circumstances. An emphasis is placed on the use of primary sources to reconstruct a genealogy of the past and to investigate alternate rereadings of texts and of history that would impact our understanding of the present. These discrete essays are meant to stimulate further research and engagement on the part of the reader who is encouraged to understand that 'Islam' is constantly being reimagined and negotiated by Muslims as they, like other human beings, grapple with the uncharted waters of modernity. Given the topical and mercurial nature of some of the issues involved, I do not make the claim that the individual chapters provide exhaustive treatments of them or represent the final word on these matters. The expectation is rather that the historical overview and analysis undertaken in each chapter will provoke the reader into questioning endemic ahistorical treatments of these issues and into pursuing these topics further beyond the scope of this book.

A word about some conventions adopted in this book. Unless specifically stated otherwise, all dates are Common Era ones; the double dating system in general has not been adopted here. Arabic words are not fully transliterated; diacritics are used only to indicate the *'ayn* (') and the *hamza* (') in less-commonly used Arabic terms. Common words like Sharia, hadith, sunna, jihad, and umma are not italicised nor provided with any diacritics. It is expected that these simplified features will make the text more accessible and less distracting to a non-specialist readership.

Notes

1. 'Glocalization' refers to a synthesis of the global and the local; see, for example, Roland Robertson, 'Globalisation or Glocalisation?' *Journal of International Communication* 1 (1994): 33–52.
2. Hans Küng, *Islam, Past Present & Future* (Oxford: Oneworld, 2007), xxiii.

CHAPTER 1

Negotiating the shoals of modernity

Although most people tend to use the term 'modernity' as a concept with a fixed, recognised meaning, in reality there is no single universal definition of this phenomenon. 'Modernity' is a highly contested term with different inflections and implications in various societies of the world. In fact, it makes better sense to talk about 'modernities' in the plural to reflect the diversity inherent in this phenomenon.

In the singular, the term 'modernity', drawing upon European political history and sociological paradigms, is often used by social scientists in the Weberian positivist sense. Essential to this conception of modernity from this perspective are its two idealised components: rationalisation as assumed to be emanating from eighteenth-century European Enlightenment principles; and secularisation, which is understood to mandate a clear division between Church and State in the Western Christian context. If these traits constitute modernity, then their adoption is termed 'modernisation.'[1] These two key components of modernity require further elaboration as they are ubiquitous in the literature.

In his influential writings Max Weber (d. 1920) conceived of rationalisation as a metahistorical achievement that is uniquely Western and that is lacking in other parts of the world but available for emulation by others. Rationalisation, for Weber, meant a relentless historical movement towards a world in which 'one can, in principle, master all things by calculation'.[2] Thus modern capitalism represents a rational mode of economic existence because of its dependence on a calculable process of production. Rationalisation is furthermore a process occurring in different spheres of human life – in music, law, religion, art, and so on – with their own internal logic and directions, so that each one of these fields may be rationalised in terms of very different ultimate objectives and values. As a result of this process, 'irrational' customs and traditions, including religious ones, are replaced by conscious rational decisions based on the individual's self-interest. The calculability of these various spheres of human life inevitably leads to changes in moral, ethical, cultural and religious values and to the rise of a 'person of vocation' (*Berufsmensch*) with a distinctive rational type of personality. Modern scientific and technological development results from rational self-interest and intellectualisation, which has given the Western world an edge over the rest.[3]

Despite the general triumphalist tone of his thesis, Weber was quite ambivalent about the ethical and moral consequences of the rationalisation process. He was aware that, although on the one hand, the process of rationalisation contributes to the freedom of individuals by helping them to navigate through the complex network of institutions in order to realise the ends of their own choice, on the other, their agency and freedom are severely hampered when formal rationalisation leads to greater impersonality and a sense of being trapped in a bureaucratic 'iron cage' and reduced to mere cogs in the machine. Such a process leads to 'disenchantment', referring to the demystification of the world and loss of charisma.[4]

Weber's notion of rationality was later critiqued and modified by the German philsopher Jürgen Habermas as being too narrow and therefore incapable of generating a more nuanced and expansive notion of modernity. This failing he attributed at least in part to Weber's specific invocation of the Protestant Christian context as the backdrop against which he developed his rationalisation thesis. Habermas finds instead in rationality a medium for deliberation, communication and solidarity which allows him to develop concepts of democracy, civil society and the public sphere, which do not occur in Weber's theory. Habermas's conception of the public sphere, divided into a political and literary sphere, has become very influential in the context of modernity and civil society. The political sphere allows rational discourse to be carried out on matters of public policy while the literary sphere becomes the realm of cultural and aesthetic ideas and practices. It is the political public sphere which puts 'the state in touch with the needs of society'.[5]

As a consequence of the rational differentiation of the public sphere from the private, which allowed for a sharp bifurcation to be made between Church and State in the Western Christian context, secularisation emerged as a *sine qua non* of the modern nation state in Europe. This is another mandated feature of post-Enlightenment Western modernity that is then understood by its proponents to be universalisable, regardless of different historical trajectories and variegated political cultures in different parts of the world. It should be noted, however, that like modernity itself, secularism and secularisation are also highly contested concepts with different inflections in different societies.[6] The French understanding of secularism, as encoded in the term *laïcité*, for example, is quite different from the American understanding of the same. *Laïcité* has its roots in the French Revolution, which sought to wrest power away from the Catholic Church and vest it solely in the State; the tension between religion and politics frequently manifested itself in radical anti-clericalism (*laïcism*) within the French context. The American model of secularisation is closer to the European Protestant one which witnessed the relegation of religion to the private or associative sphere after the Treaty of Wesphalia (1648–9), but without the rise of French-style anti-clericalism. A simple but powerful difference between secularism in the American and French contexts can be distilled thus: in the former, religion is understood to need protection from the government while in the latter it is the government that needs to be shielded from religion. Although government sponsorship of a particular religion is officially forbidden, the American public sphere can hardly be described as being denuded of religious language, symbols and identity, especially in recent history, in contrast to French society where an almost militant aversion to certain kinds of (especially Muslim) public religious expression as a consequence of secularism has taken hold.

Until not too long ago, the possibility of a global resurgence of religion would have been unthinkable in Western academic and intellectual circles, so rooted was the conviction that modernity and religion were bound to part ways, especially in the public political realm.[7] As recently as the 1960s, sociologists of religion were convinced that modernisation would ineluctably lead to the occlusion of religion from the public sphere and that this would serve as the predominant global paradigm for social and political transformation. Most sociologists were also convinced that this would be a healthy and welcome development for humanity, for religion was largely understood to be a problem and an obstacle to human social advancement. Wesley J. Wildman, a scholar of philosophy of religion at Boston University, has identified the following three key aspects of this 'problem of religion' approach:

- Religion is understood to be dying whenever secular social orders thrive because religion is *about authority and social control*.
- Religion always retreats from intellectual confrontations or else engages it merely with reactionary authoritarianism because *religious beliefs can't compete on rational terms with scientific beliefs*.
- Flourishing, stable economies create lifestyles that render religion superfluous because *religion compensates for lack of perceived goods and needs poverty to make people willing to submit to its authority* (so-called deprivation theory).[8]

The last quarter of the twentieth century in particular has shown, however, that such views about the problematic essence of religion were over-generalisations; and, as events have turned out, the predicted demise of religion in public life was patently premature. The global resurgence of religion in many parts of the world, including in the United States, has clearly indicated that religion has not only not lost its salience in the public sphere today but remains an essential ingredient in the crafting of modern individual and communal identities in most societies.[9] The predominance of religion in American cultural and political life in particular belies much of what has been attributed to religion as a problem, as Wildman indicates above. After all, this approach fails to account for not only the survival, but also the flourishing, of religious belief and symbols in a highly industrialised society like the United States, with its scientific and technological advancements, its democratic political system and still abundant economic prosperity.

However, liberal political theory in general continues to accord inadequate space to religion, which in some quarters is now increasingly regarded as a serious methodological deficiency that retards its ability to grapple with contemporary political realities, especially on a global scale.[10] Peter Berger has underscored this theoretical myopia and insightfully observed, 'The world today, then, is massively religious, and it is anything but the secularised world that had been predicted (be it joyfully or despondently) by so many analysts of modernity.'[11] As a recovering secularist himself, Berger proceeds to interrogate the very premises of modernity confidently articulated by Western sociologists of the twentieth century who tended to see religious expression as a deviation from the behavioural norms of civil polities. He observes astutely:

> I think what I and most other sociologists of religion wrote in the 1960s about secularization was a mistake. Our underlying argument was that secularization and modernity go hand in hand. With more modernization comes more secularization . . . Most of the world today is certainly not secular. It's very religious. So is the U.S. The one exception to this is Western Europe. One of the most interesting questions today is not, How do you explain the fundamentalism in Iran? But, Why is Western Europe different?[12]

Disconcerting words from a sociologist that serve as a potent reminder that not too long ago even in the West, being religious in public and private was the normal and expected way to be in the world and to interact with one's fellow beings. As José Casanova has further observed, the phenomenon of public or what he calls 'deprivatised religion' – exemplified by the Iranian Revolution of 1978, the growth of the right-wing Christian evangelical movement in the United States, and Roman Catholic-inspired liberation theology movements in Latin America, for example – rapidly forced a revision of the secularisation thesis by the 1980s and has instead placed religion at the forefront of social and political developments in many parts of the world.[13]

The homogenising narratives of secular modernity and their underlying premises have been subjected to sustained critiques in recent times by a number of Western theorists, such as Robert Bellah, Alasdair MacIntyre, and Charles Taylor, from varying perspectives.[14] More recently, Habermas has coined the term 'post-secular society' to signal the fact that religion has begun to play an increasingly prominent role in the Western public sphere, deeply influencing popular debates on controversial issues such as environmental degradation, abortion, euthanasia and reproductive rights. Post-secular Western society would appear then to have moved beyond the Hegelian claim that religion should be bracketed from modern life because it no longer plays a role in the intellectual formation (*Gestalt des Geistes*) of individuals and societies.[15]

Resistance to the 'reinstatement' of religion in public discourses, however, continues in many Western countries, especially at the popular level, and especially when it concerns Islam. As Tariq Modood has observed, secularism is in flux in European countries, not least of all because substantial Muslim minorities who remain religiously observant pose a challenge to the dominant secular paradigms there.[16] In recent times, Western religious leaders have sometimes learned to their peril that to mount a public critique of secularism in order to carve out a space for religion – all religions, including Islam – in the public sphere can invite public condemnation of the most fervid sort. This was the fate in 2012 of the then Archbishop of Canterbury Rowan Williams when in a public speech in Great Britain he discussed the theological underpinnings of human dignity. In that speech he remarked that:

> a defence of an unqualified secular legal monopoly in terms of the need for a universalist doctrine of human right or dignity is to misunderstand the circumstances in which that doctrine emerged, and [to understand] that the essential liberating (and religiously informed) vision it represents is not imperilled by a loosening of the monopolistic framework.[17]

He also warned, 'what I have called legal universalism, when divorced from a serious theoretical (and, I would argue, religious) underpinning, can turn into a positivism as sterile as any other variety'.[18]

In brief, Williams made an impassioned appeal for recognition of the fact that notions like human dignity and human rights have deep theological roots and resonate within a number of religious traditions, not least of all the Abrahamic ones. When he went on to argue in essence that the best of Enlightenment values require that Islam and the Sharia be recognised in the British public square, as Christianity and Judaism (along with its legal code) already were, the resultant furore demonstrated that many had a skewed understanding of both the Enlightenment and the Sharia and, more broadly, of the role of religion in modern society.[19]

The reaction to Williams's lecture further indicates that Islam, more than any other religion currently, tends to be singled out for essentialising stereotypes in a particular strain of contemporary Western discourse that Mahmood Mamdani has dubbed 'Culture Talk'. According to the premise of this kind of 'Culture Talk', Muslims are inherently incapable of creating and living within democratic polities and of successfully adapting to modernity as conventionally defined. Their all-embracing Sharia, which supposedly regulates all aspects of their lives, leaves very little room for creativity and innovation, according to this particular strand of thinking. Mamdani observes astringently:

> According to some, our [Muslim] culture seems to have no history, no politics, and no debates, so that *all* Muslims are just plain bad. According to others, there is a history, a politics, even debates, and there *are* good Muslims and bad Muslims. In both versions, history seems to have petrified into a lifeless custom of an antique people who inhabit antique lands. Or could it be that culture here

stands for habit, for some kind of instinctive activity with rules that are inscribed in early founding texts, usually religious, and mummified in early artifacts?[20]

Arguably, essentialism of this sort is a necessary component of the homogenising discourse of secular Western modernity for it serves as

> the methodologically tempting sharp edge separating a view of civilization and modernity conceived as singular, and the counterview of civilization and modernity conceived as not only plural but also as inherently open to contact, interaction and exchange – however conflicted they be.[21]

It is useful to remember that such essentialising stereotypes that confer a state of 'otherness' on Muslims were similarly bestowed upon Catholics and Jews in an earlier period of American history. As Roy Mottahedeh has noted, distrust of Catholics was endemic in nineteenth-century Europe and the United States based on their presumed anti-liberal views and inability to participate in a democratic society. Mottahedeh references the remarks of the distinguished American Protestant theologian Reinhold Niebuhr in which the latter in 1944 bemoaned what he saw as the chasm 'between the presuppositions of a free society and the inflexible authoritarianism of the Catholic religion'.[22]

Jews were similarly regarded as congenitally afflicted with bad citizenship skills on account of their religious identity and thus ontologically incapable of assimilating into 'civilised' society. In 1843, Bruno Bauer, a German Protestant theologian commented:

> Human rights are the result of education, and they can be possessed only by those who acquire and deserve them. Can the Jew really possess them as long as he lives as a Jew in perpetual segregation from others, as long as he therefore must declare that the others are not really his fellow-men? As long as he is a Jew, his Jewishness must be stronger in him than his humanity, and keep him apart from non-Jews. He declares by his segregation that this, his Jewishness, is his true, highest nature, which has to have precedence over his humanity.[23]

Such attitudes towards Jews persisted at least until World War II in Europe and the United States and were displaced with great difficulty. The above statement by Bauer to imply a perpetual cultural warfare between Westerners and Jews can be recycled to apply *mutatis mutandis* to Muslims in the West today. The rhetoric of bigotry can be dismayingly unoriginal and easily transferable to the next targeted group.

The fear of Islam, and more broadly, the fear of religion and its outward expression, remains palpable in contemporary Western public spheres and evident in Western popular media. It even pervades the largely secular Western academy, where a general conviction exists that the study of religion should not make inroads into the curricula of the great educational institutions that had only recently sidelined it. This attitude has skewed the study of religion in the academy, even to the point of delegitimising it as a proper field of inquiry in certain circles. One may recall that in 2006, to much fanfare, Harvard University appointed a faculty committee to look into reforming its core curriculum. The faculty committee charged with overseeing this process was led by Louis Menand, the Pulitzer Prize-winning literary critic and professor of English, who made the case that undergraduate students should be required to take at least one course in a category called Reason and Faith. Such courses would explore big issues in religion, such as intelligent design, debates within and around Islam, and a history of American faith, for example. The Harvard evolutionary psychologist, Steven Pinker, however, led the charge against this proposed curricular reform, arguing that the primary goal of a Harvard education is the pursuit of truth through rational inquiry, and religion has no place in such an enterprise. In the end, Pinker prevailed, the committee backed down, and the matter was never put to a vote. This incident on the one hand indicates the genuine fear of religion that still exists in the secular academy; on the other, it points to the cautious recognition, as expressed by Louis Menand, that evacuating religion wholesale from the fundamental educational enterprise represents, at some critical level, a tragic truncation of it.

Against the backdrop of these contestations, Shmuel Eisenstadt's conception of 'multiple modernities' has received considerable attention as a much-needed corrective to the older univocal construction of modernity based on an uncompromising secularism. Eisenstadt notes that the twentieth-century expectation that Western-style modernity would spread uniformly did not materialise because, first, key institutional features of society, especially economic, political, and family structures, are constituted in different ways in different societies and in different stages of their development and, second, the cultural dimensions of modernisation are not intrinsically interlocked with the structural ones. The variegated sociohistorical factors at work have thus led to 'the development of several modern civilisations, or at least civilisational patterns'[24] creating 'a dynamics which gave rise both to political and ideological challenges to existing hegemonies, as well as to continual shifts in the loci of hegemony within Europe, from Europe to the United States, then also to Japan and East Asia'.[25] One of the most important consequences of the colonial, military and economic encounters between Western and non-Western societies, notes Eisenstadt, was that it allowed elites and intellectuals in non-European nations 'to participate actively in the new modern (that is initially Western) universal tradition, together with the selective rejection of many of its aspects and of Western "control" and hegemony'.[26] The 'new modern civilisation' became a site where non-Western actors could challenge its institutional realities and its fundamental premises and reconfigure them to accord with their own world-view and values. The term 'multiple modernities' therefore clearly implies that 'modernity and Westernisation are not identical' and that 'Western patterns of modernity are not the only "authentic" modernities'.[27]

Bridging the religious–secular divide: Islam in an age of globalisation

Eisenstadt's model of multiple modernities and its critique of the master narratives of secular modernity have been deepened by scholars from various disciplinary perspectives, particularly in relation to Islam and Muslim-majority societies. The influential anthropologist Talal Asad, for example, has written persuasive critiques of the Western project of secularism and its assumed universal and transferable character. The hermeneutics of asymmetrical power embedded in discourses of secularism have been skillfully analysed by him, in the course of which he lays bare what he clearly regards as some of the disingenuous and parochial claims made on its behalf. For example, one of the persistent myths that has been circulated concerning the secular liberal state is that it is the most effective system to ward off conflict, particularly of the religious and ethno-nationalist type, and to promote a tolerant, civil society. Asad disagrees. He states:

> The difficulty with secularism as a doctrine of war and peace in the world is not that it is European (and therefore alien to the non-West) but that it is closely connected with the rise of a system of capitalist nation-states – mutually suspicious and grossly unequal in power and prosperity, each possessing a collective personality that is differently mediated and therefore differently guaranteed and threatened.[28]

Secularism, he demonstrates, generates its own rigid orthodoxy and truth-claims; failure to acquiesce to them invites reprisal and political marginalisation. Today's concept of the secular, he notes,

> is part of a doctrine called secularism. Secularism doesn't simply insist that religious practice and belief be confined to a space where they cannot threaten political stability or the liberties of the 'free-thinking' citizens. Secularism builds on a particular conception of the world ('natural' and 'social') and of the problems generated by that world.[29]

This potentially hegemonic nature of secularism has sought to assert itself as an endemic feature of Western-style modernity, eliciting in its wake criticism from those who do not take kindly to having it imposed upon them. The particular historical encounters of specific people with modernity and secularism understandably colour their perspectives on both phenomena and create resistance toward homogenising narratives that do not match their own experiences and lived realities. This is certainly true of the Islamic world, where in the context of the modern dynamics of political power, Muslim intellectuals and political activists frequently forge, as John Esposito has observed, a connection between the secularist doctrine developed in Europe and European colonial expansion in the Muslim world with its legacy of non-democratic secular regimes in much of the Middle East and North Africa.[30]

The idealising narratives about secularism as a liberatory doctrine that have taken root in most of the West provide a striking contrast to the actual historical encounters of most Muslim peoples with forms of it that have brought in their wake political repression, cultural subjugation, and social instability. In this context, Khaled Abou El Fadl's remarks are apposite when he states that

> secularism has become an unworkable and unhelpful symbolic construct. In the Muslim world, secularism has been normally associated with what is described as the Western intellectual invasion, both in the period of Colonialism and post-Colonialism. Furthermore, secularism has come to symbolize a misguided belief in the probity of rationalism and a sense of hostility to religion as a source of guidance in the public sphere.[31]

The social and political crucible in which Muslims are engaging the modern world is thus historically specific to them; within the geographical swathe commonly referred to as the 'Islamic world', there is considerable diversity in the ways in which Muslim-majority countries are negotiating the shoals of modernity. Without doubt, as ample evidence can be marshalled, religion remains as relevant as ever in the various projects of modernisation undertaken by Muslims today. Ernest Gellner's observation in 1993 still applies today:

> In the social sciences, one of the commonest theses is the secularisation thesis, which runs as follows. Under conditions prevailing in industrial-scientific society, the hold of religion over society and its people diminishes. By and large this is true, but it is not completely true, for there is one major exception, Islam. In the last hundred years the hold of Islam over Muslims has not diminished but has rather increased. It is one striking counter-example to the secularisation thesis.[32]

Although the implicit charge of 'Islamic exceptionalism' in Gellner's remark seems primitive, especially since religious resurgence is abundantly evident today in other faith communities and non-Muslim societies as well, there is no denying the continued salience of religious belief, practices and identity in many Muslim-majority societies today. This is true even in countries where the post-colonial and modernising state has attempted to impose secularism on its population in recent history, as in Turkey, Tunisia and Algeria. As public opinion polls and surveys conducted in a number of Muslim-majority societies have repeatedly shown, an overwhelming majority of their inhabitants continue to express positive attitudes towards Sharia and democracy, for example, and advocate the implementation of both in their societies, regarding them as mutually reinforcing.[33]

The 'compatibility of Islam and modernity', as it is often simplistically and commonly phrased, has in fact been accepted since the eighteenth century by leading Muslim intellectuals and runs as a common leitmotif through modernist and reformist discourses down to the present day. Such thinkers typically 'saw the tension between Islamic faith and modern values as a historical accident, not an inherent feature of Islam'.[34] Modernisation from this perspective was/is also not wedded to secularism. Whereas secularism may be regarded as having been a necessary prelude for successful modernisation in Europe as a reaction against the centralised religious authority of the medieval Church and the considerable wealth and political power the priesthood had accrued, such a process is considered unnecessary in the Islamic milieu. The *'ulama'* (the religious scholars) in the pre-modern period (roughly before the seventeenth century of the Common Era) were, after all, not part of a powerful, centralised institution, and were usually not regarded as colluding in the oppression of the common people because of their frequent oppositional role to political rulers.[35] European post-Reformation scholars furthermore often portrayed the medieval Church as resistant to science and drenched in magic and superstition,[36] whereas science and rationality are generally understood by Muslims to be the hallmarks of medieval Islamic scholarship, particularly after the great translation movements of the ninth and tenth centuries.[37] The lack of an ordained priestly class within Islam as developed in Christianity has also typically allowed for a plurality of legal and ethical discourses to emerge within the Islamic tradition and has prevented the accrual of authoritarian political and ecclesial power in a privileged elite that claims an exclusive right to interpret the will of God.

Tradition, in the Islamic experience, is therefore not to be approached as an ossified corpus of beliefs and rituals which replicate authoritarianism and embrace conformity;[38] it is rather to be approached, as Asad has argued, 'as a discursive tradition that connects variously with the formation of moral selves, the manipulation of populations (or resistance to it) and the production of appropriate knowledges'.[39] It is this specific anthropological understanding of Islam as a discursive tradition that allows for tradition and change to be meaningfully welded to one another in the context of modernity. Asad continues:

> [M]any writers describe the movements in Iran and Egypt as only partly modern and suggest that it's their mixing of tradition and modernity that accounts for their 'pathological' character. This kind of description paints Islamic movements as being somehow inauthentically traditional on the assumption that 'real tradition' is unchanging, repetitive, and non-rational. In this way, these movements cannot be understood on their own terms as being at once modern and traditional, both authentic and creative at the same time. The development of politico-religious movements ought to force people to rethink the uniquely Western model of secular modernity. One may want to challenge aspects of these movements, but this ought to be done on specific grounds. It won't do to measure everything by grand conceptions of authentic modernity.[40]

Asad's observations are trenchantly apposite and allow for culturally and historically specific modulations of modernity to emerge within Islamic milieux. His work in recuperating a specific anthropology of Islam constituted by its own discursive practices and world-view and situating it within more malleable and heterogeneous conceptualisations of modernity is proving to be quite seminal.

Muslim critiques of Western-style modernity along the lines adumbrated by Asad and others may be regarded, as Nilüfer Göle has suggested,

> as a new stage in the process of the indigenization of modernity in non-Western contexts. The Islamic subject is formed both through liberation from traditional definitions and roles of Muslim identity and through resistance to a cultural program of modernity and liberalism . . . The search for difference and authenticity expresses a critical resistance to the assimilative strategies and homogenizing practices of modernity.[41]

The problem of modernity: narratives of authenticity and alterity

The pedigree of contemporary critiques of Western meta-narratives of modernity goes back to the nineteenth century during the heyday of Western colonisation of a broad swathe of the Islamic world. In the Arab world during this period, the leading and the most cogent voices of reform were those of Jamal al-Din al-Afghani (d. 1897) and Muhammad 'Abduh (d. 1905), the founders of Islamic modernism. Al-Afghani, 'Abduh's mentor and friend, was a somewhat enigmatic figure. He is believed to have been originally from Asadabad, Iran, according to many accounts. If these accounts are accurate (which are still debated), his Iranian origins would make him a Shi'i. By adopting the relational last name al-Afghani, he was clearly attempting to pass himself off as an Afghan Sunni. A peripatetic figure, al-Afghani travelled extensively through the Muslim world 'like a meteor from one country to another'.[42] He travelled to Egypt circa 1870 where he met 'Abduh, who became a lifelong disciple of his; a year later, al-Afghani would move to Egypt and live there until the British exiled him in 1879 for his 'dangerous' ideas of political reform. Like most Muslim thinkers of his time, al-Afghani was anguished by the European Christian colonial occupation of Muslim realms and attempted to galvanise his coreligionists to respond to the challenges posed by Western imperialism and scientific and technological advances. Al-Afghani bemoaned what he perceived to be the backwardness of Muslims during his time and promoted the revitalisation of learning and education as the most important means for ameliorating the situation. Like 'Abduh after him, he emphasised learning from the scientific achievements of Europeans while strengthening foundational Islamic values and promoting pan-Islamic unity. Al-Afghani stressed the compatibility between Islamic principles and reason and regarded a revitalised Islamic moral and intellectual tradition to be the basis for successful adaptation to modernity and its challenges; this became the typical modernist position. The magazine *al-'Urwa al-wuthqa* (The Firm Bond), which he established in Paris in 1884 and edited with 'Abduh who was exiled there at that time, became an influential medium for the dissemination of these ideas despite its short longevity. Al-Afghani died in Istanbul in 1897, where he had been summoned by the Ottoman sultan Abdulhamid II, and was buried there.

Al-Afghani's main ideas were passionately adopted by Muhammad 'Abduh. The son of peasants from lower Egypt, 'Abduh studied first at the Ahmadi mosque in Tanta and then enrolled at al-Azhar. Somewhat of a rebel, he was already highly critical of the traditional educational system, which he sought to reform later in life after being appointed as the Grand Mufti of Egypt. In his student years in Cairo, 'Abduh became greatly influenced by the Sufi Shadhiliyya order due to the advice of his first mentor, his uncle Shaykh Darwish. His second and most influential mentor, however, was al-Afghani. Al-Afghani exposed 'Abduh to Muslim classical works on theology, mysticism, logic, philosophy and astronomy, while being critical of traditional Islamic scholasticism. Between 1870 and 1879, before his expulsion from Egypt following the abdication of the Khedive Isma'il, 'Abduh taught at al-Azhar and at the Dar al-'Ulum in Cairo. He also wrote articles for the venerable newspaper *al-Ahram* in which he advocated many of the ideas he had picked up from al-Afghani – the unity of the Muslim umma in the face of Christian European aggression, the need for educational reform, the receptivity of Islam to the rational sciences and the role of the press in mass education. He later also wrote for the *Egyptian Gazette*, which he used as a medium for disseminating his modernist ideas, and to push for educational and political reform. Exiled in 1882 by the British, he eventually moved to Paris and edited the magazine *al-'Urwa al-wuthqa* there with al-Afghani. In this magazine, the two editors called for Muslims to return to the values of the pious forebears (*al-salaf al-salih*) in order to regenerate contemporary Muslim society. 'Abduh and al-Afghani are thus both counted among the early Salafiyya – which in its original signification referred to modernists and reformists who sought inspiration from the past in order to move forward in the present through the process of independent reasoning (*ijtihad*) and creative adaptation of Islamic principles to the exigencies of current circumstances.

Before proceeding further, we need to define the term 'modernist' as deployed in this study and usefully juxtapose it to the term 'Islamist', as will occur later in this work. 'Modernist' (who are also sometimes called 'reformist') Muslims refers in my usage to observant Muslims who, starting roughly in the eighteenth century, began to emphasise the inherent adaptability of Islamic principles and thought to modernity. For the most part, the terms 'modernists' and 'reformists' are used interchangeably here. Modernists typically argue that reinterpreted Islamic principles can reveal their congruence with modern liberal principles of democratic government, civil society, gender equality, and so on, without necessarily being identical to their formulations in the Western context. They stress the rereading of religious texts, primarily the Qur'an and hadith to arrive at interpretations appropriate to their historical circumstances without turning their backs on the classical heritage. They instead regard their hermeneutic enterprise as fostering a sense of a continuous critical and dynamic process of engagement with this heritage through education. 'Modernists' and 'reformists' are also called 'liberals' and 'moderates' by some.

The term 'Islamist' for our purpose refers to activist individuals and groups in various contemporary Muslim-majority societies whose primary wish is to govern and be governed politically only by Islamic principles, understood by them to be immutably enshrined in the Sharia or the religious law. Among these individuals and groups, I am using this term to refer primarily to particularly hard-line Islamists (also occasionally referred to as 'radical' or 'militant' Islamists), whose attitude towards modernity and its epistemic foundations can fairly be described as 'rejectionist'. There are also 'moderate' Islamists (as they are usually termed), who, while also committed to a highly politicised form of Islam, subscribe to democratic norms and embrace modern notions of gender equality and human rights to a considerable extent. The moderate Islamists are generally not included in my use of the term 'Islamist' in this discussion, unless specifically stated to the contrary.

To return to our narrative – 'Abduh returned to Cairo in 1888 and was appointed a judge by the Khedive Tawfiq Pasha and then later to the highest religious office of the Mufti of Egypt in 1899. In his various positions, he tried to effect legislative and administrative reforms. The sweeping educational reforms he advocated for al-Azhar would not be fully implemented until the time of his successor Mahmud Shaltut (d. 1963). Due to opposition to his proposed reforms, 'Abduh had to resign from his post on the Administrative Council which oversaw such projected reforms. But there is no doubt that without his pioneering work these reforms would never have been launched. During this period he also travelled extensively throughout the Middle East and Europe and became convinced that the two major problems facing Muslims globally were their ignorance of their own religious heritage and the corrupt rulers who exploited them. Many of these views were expressed in the new journal *al-Manar* (The Beacon) edited by his devoted student Rashid Rida.

'Abduh died on 11 July 1905. He left behind a rich corpus of influential writings, including the treatise *Risalat al-tawhid* (Essay on the Oneness of God) and the well-known Qur'an commentary *Tafsir al-manar*, which was continued after his death by Rida. He bequeathed a powerful but contested legacy of intellectual revival and promulgation of Islamic modernism. In the contemporary period it is impossible to discuss issues of reform and liberal thought within Islam without invoking 'Abduh's seminal contributions. Known for his towering intellect, profound spirituality and personal integrity, 'Abduh continues to exert considerable influence on contemporary Muslim thinkers. His thought and writings remain as relevant as ever to contemporary Muslim concerns and modernist world-views. We will encounter him again in the course of this book.

In the Indian subcontinent during the waning days of the Mughal empire and the onset of British colonialism, 'Abduh's older contemporary Sayyid Ahmad Khan (d. 1898) similarly emphasised Islam's embrace of rationality and scientific knowledge and the need for the Muslims of his time to learn from European scientific achievements. Not the profound, classically trained scholar like 'Abduh, Khan, however, made a deep impression on his contemporaries with his fervent advocacy of the regeneration of Muslim thought and civilisation through educational reform and a critical assessment of classical scholarship. He expressed a dim view of the Qur'an commentary literature in general, which he regarded as being full of unreliable traditions and fables drawn from the *Isra'iliyyat* (Tales from the Israelites) and other dubious sources. Thus he proceeded to start his own *tafsir* (Qur'an commentary) in 1879, which remained unfinished at the time of his death. The modernist orientation of the *tafsir* provoked strong resistance from the conservative religious scholars of the time. Khan, for example, strenuously rejected the possibility of miracles and tried to find a natural explanation for them. He remains best known for his founding of the Muhammadan Anglo-Oriental College in 1877 in the town of Aligarh, which in 1920, after his death, became known as Aligarh Muslim University, the equivalent of al-Azhar in South Asia.[43]

The gifted Indian Muslim philosopher of the next generation, Muhammad Iqbal (d. 1938) continued the project of revival and reform into the twentieth century. Trained in literature, law and philosophy, Iqbal earned academic degrees from Punjab University, Cambridge University and the University of Munich, where he completed his doctorate. With his enviable command of the principal Islamic and European languages, Iqbal was well poised to bridge Islamic and Western philosophic traditions. In what is generally regarded as his masterpiece *The Reconstruction of Religious Thought in Islam* published in 1930, Iqbal questions the intellectual foundations of Islamic philosophy and grapples with some of the same issues that had exercised the minds of a number of his modernist predecessors. In the sixth chapter of this book titled 'The Principle of Movement in the Structure of Islam', he argues for the necessity of innovation in Islamic thought through the hermeneutic tool of *ijtihad*. He inveighed against what he regarded as the 'state of immobility' to which Islamic law was understood to have been reduced after the formation of the classical schools of law. The Sharia, drawing upon the broad moral guidelines and principles of the Qur'an, was innately flexible, stated Iqbal, and adaptable to different historical and social circumstances. The Qur'an is not reducible to a legal code and the sunna may be understood as codifying the practices of generations past and is not literally binding on contemporary Muslims. The Muslims of his generation then had the responsibility of faithfully reconstructing Islamic thought in accordance with their needs through independent reasoning.[44] Iqbal's thought has been enormously influential on many thinkers after him, like 'Ali Shariati in Iran,[45] and his works have been translated into Arabic and other languages.

The forms of Islamic modernism subscribed to by the above thinkers may be regarded as having reached their culmination in the last quarter of the twentieth century in the thought of Fazlur Rahman, the brilliant and prolific Pakistani-American scholar of Islam who ended his days teaching at the University of Chicago. A specialist in Islamic philosophy and intellectual history, Rahman looms large in the field of Islamic modernism for his critical analysis of the current state of Islamic scholarship and for laying bare what he perceived to be its inability to revitalise itself. In a number of ground-breaking and thought-provoking works, Rahman essentially argued for a return to the Qur'anic text as a corrective to the legal and exegetical accretions that had over the years cumulatively masked the original purpose and signification of critical Qur'anic verses, creating in its wake a series of epistemological and spiritual crises for modern Muslims. In his seminal work *Islam and Modernity: Transformation of an Intellectual Tradition*, Rahman tellingly remarked, 'the first essential step . . . is for the Muslim to distinguish clearly between normative Islam and historical Islam.'[46] Furthermore:

> A historical critique of theological developments in Islam is the first step towards a reconstruction of Islamic theology. This critique . . . should reveal the extent of the dislocation between the world view of the Qur'an and various schools of theological speculation in Islam and point the way to a new theology.[47]

Rahman recognised the potential of the Qur'an to inaugurate endless social change and intellectual vitality when its text itself was the object of sustained study. Thus he lamented that

> a vibrant and revolutionary religious document like the Qur'an was buried under the debris of grammar and rhetoric. Ironically, the Qur'an was never taught by itself, most probably through the fear that a meaningful study of the Qur'an by itself might upset the status quo, not only educational and theological, but social as well.[48]

The old interpretive methods in relation to the Qur'an were no longer sufficient or relevant, according to Rahman; the modern era required a new hermeneutics that would result in reinterpretations based on 'a reworking and restructuring of sociomoral principles that will form the basis for a viable social Islamic fabric in the twentieth and twenty-first centuries'.[49]

A popular and renowned academic until his death in 1988, Rahman attracted students from all over the Muslim world who returned to their home countries to disseminate and build upon his ideas. Vilified in certain circles in his native Pakistan, Rahman's searing critique of a tradition that had veered away from its foundations was embraced by those who recognised the imperative to reconstruct Islamic thought in a credible and thoughtful manner within the matrix of modernity.

A vocal minority of radical ideologues within the Islamic world today may convey the impression that Islamic modernism and liberal thinking have been completely sidelined and rendered ineffectual. This volume, however, engages the views of a number of individuals in the contemporary period who would consider themselves as building upon the legacies of 'Abduh, Rahman, and others who are similarly mining the diverse Islamic tradition to craft carefully argued responses to modernity in an idiom that is recognisable and respected by many of their coreligionists. This process of the 'indigenisation of modernity', to borrow Göle's phrase, is strongly evident within learned Muslim discourses and praxes today; one of the overall purposes of this book is to describe the multiplicity of perspectives and contestations that this process has engendered. The impact of modernisation and the religious, intellectual and social ferment that it has instigated in many cases will be explored, particularly in relation to some of the most complex and burning issues of our time – Muslim re-engagement with the Sharia which entails above all the development of a modern Qur'anic hermeneutics and hadith criticism, democracy and democratisation, war and peace, and gendered identities, among others.

Notes

1. Marshall Hodgson, *The Venture of Islam: Conscience and History in a World Civilization* (Chicago and London: University of Chicago Press, 1961), 50.
2. H. H. Gerth and C. Wright Mills (eds), *From Max Weber, Essays in Sociology* (Oxford: Oxford University Press, 1946), 139.
3. A good discussion of Weber's *Berufsmensch* is found in the article by Arnold Eisen 'Called to Order: The Role of the Puritan Berufsmensch in Weberian Sociology', *Sociology* 13 (1979), 203–18.
4. Thus he laments in *The Protestant Ethic and the Spirit of Capitalism*, ed. T. Parsons (London: Routledge, 1992).
5. Jürgen Habermas, *The Stuctural Transformation of the Public Sphere: An Inquiry into a Category of Bourgeois Society*, tr. T. Burger (Cambridge, MA: MIT Press, 1989), 27 ff. These conceptualisations were not original on his part; Habermas was borrowing and refining many of these ideas from earlier Enlightenment thinkers like Marx, Hegel, Locke, Durkheim and Kant, in addition to Weber.
6. There is a prolific literature on this topic. For a concise treatment of these terms, see Janet R. Jakobsen and Ann Pellegrini (eds), *Secularisms* (Durham, NC: Duke University Press, 2008), especially 1–17.
7. It should be noted that 'religion' is also a contested concept, with some arguing that as a universal category, religion is specifically a construct of Western secular modernity; see Talal Asad, *Genealogies of Religion: Discipline and Reasons of Power in Christianity and Islam*

(Baltimore: Johns Hopkins University Press, 1993), 11. When referring specifically to Islam, I am using the term 'religion' as the equivalent of the Qur'anic Arabic term *din*, which connotes a holistic relationship between humans and a supernatural being that is understood to affect multiple spheres of life, including worship, ethics, morality, social and commercial relations. It is not reducible to a creed, identity, ideology and/or a program of socio-political activism, as invoked in certain quarters today.

8. Italics in original text; see Wesley J. Wildman, *Religious Philosophy as Multidisciplinary Comparative Inquiry: Envisioning a Future for the Philosophy of Religion* (Albany, NY: State University of New York Press, 2010), 238.

9. See John Micklethwait and Adrian Wooldridge, *God is Back: How the Global Revival of Faith is Changing the World* (New York: Penguin Books, 2010), 31–79, where the authors stress the important differences between European approaches to modernity versus the American; in the former, the tendency has been to emasculate religion and banish it from the public sphere while in the latter modernity remains entangled with religion in the public domain in noisy, contested ways.

10. This is the main premise of the book by Douglas Johnston and Cynthia Sampson (eds), *Religion: the Missing Dimension of Statecraft* (Oxford: Oxford University Press, 1995). Other notable works which explore this 'missing dimension' include J. Fox, 'Religion: An Oft Overlooked Element of International Studies', *International Studies Review* 3 (2001): 53–73; Elizabeth Shankman Hurd, *The Politics of Secularism in International Relations* (Princeton: Princeton University Press, 2008); and, specifically in regard to Islam, Sultan Tepe & Betul Demirkaya, '(Not) Getting Religion: Has Political Science Lost Sight of Islam?' *Politics and Religion* 4 (2011): 203–28.

11. Peter L. Berger, 'The Desecularization of the World: A Global Overview', in *Desecularization of the World: Resurgent Religion in World Politics* (1999), 9.

12. Peter L. Berger, 'Epistemological Modesty: An Interview with Peter Berger', *Christian Century*, 29 October 1997, 974.

13. José Casanova, *Public Religions in the Modern World* (Chicago: University of Chicago Press, 1994), especially 11–40.

14. For a good treatment of their views on secular modernity, see Roxanne L. Euben, 'Pre-Modern, Anti-Modern, or Post-Modern? Islamic and Western Critiques of Modernity', *Review of Politics* 59 (1997): 429–59.

15. Jürgen Habermas, 'Notes on Post-Secular Society', *New Perspectives Quarterly* 25 (2008): 17–29; see further Fred Dallmayr, 'Post-Secularity and Global Politics: A Need for Radical Redefinition', *Being in the World: Dialogue and Cosmopolis* (Lexington: University Press of Kentucky, 2013), 137–50.

16. Tariq Modood, 'Is There a Crisis of Secularism in Western Europe?' *Sociology of Religion* 73 (2012): 130–49.

17. Rowan Williams, 'Civil and Religious Law in England: A Religious Perspective', *Ecclesiastical Law Journal* 10 (2008): 273.

18. Ibid. 275.

19. Like 'Sharia' and 'religion' in general, the term 'Enlightenment' may also be understood as evading easy definition. As Peter Gay states in his study of the Enlightenment, 'The men of the Enlightenment were divided by doctrine, temperament, environment and generations. And in fact the spectrum of their ideas, their sometimes acrimonious disputes, have tempted many historians to abandon the search for a single Enlightenment'; see the preface to his *The Enlightenment: An Interpretation, the Rise of Modern Paganism* (New York and London: W. W. Norton, 1966; reissued 1995), x.

20. Mahmood Mamdani, *Good Muslim, Bad Muslim* (New York: Doubleday, 2005), 18.

21. Muhammad Khalid Masud et al. (eds), Islam and Modernity: Key Issues and Debates (Edinburgh: Edinburgh University Press, 2009), 14.

22. Reinhold Niebuhr, *The Children of Light and Children of Darkness: A Vindication of Democracy and a Critique of its Traditional Defense* (New York: C. Scribner's Sons, 1944), 319; cited by Roy P. Mottahedeh, 'The Clash of Civilizations: An Islamicist's Critique', in Emran Qureishi and Michael A. Sells (eds), *The New Crusades: Constructing the Muslim Enemy* (New York, Columbia University Press, 2003), 140.

23. Paul R. Mendes-Flohr and Jehuda Reinharz (eds), *The Jew in the Modern World: A Documentary History* (New York: Oxford University Press, 1980), 37; cf. Mottahedeh, 'Clash', 140.

24. Shmuel Noah Eisenstadt, *Comparative Civilizations and Multiple Modernities* (Leiden: Brill, 2003), 2:522.

25. Ibid. 2:525.

26. Ibid. 2:961.

27. Ibid. 2:536. This is a point that has been similarly emphasised by John O. Voll within an Islamic context; see his article, 'The Mistaken Identification of "The West" with "Modernity"', *American Journal of Islamic Social Sciences* 13 (1996): 1–6.

28. Talal Asad, *Formations of the Secular: Christianity, Islam, Modernity* (Stanford: Stanford University Press, 2003), 6–7.

29. Ibid. 81.

30. John Esposito, 'Rethinking Islam and Secularism', *ARDA Guiding Paper*, available at <http://www.thearda.com/rrh/papers/guidingpapers.asp>; last accessed on 20 July 2013.

31. Khaled Abou El Fadl, 'Constitutionalism and the Islamic Sunni Legacy', *UCLA Journal of Islamic and Near Eastern Law* 1 (2001): 9. For a different viewpoint stressing that the secular state is in better conformity with Muslim notions of governance and Sharia objectives, see Abdullahi Ahmed An-Na'im, *Islam and the Secular State: Negotiating the Future of Shari'a* (Cambridge, MA: Harvard University Press, 2010). For yet another variant perspective emphasising that the modern nation state is ultimately amoral and that an 'Islamic State' along such lines would constitute a betrayal of the Sharia's foundational ethical principles, see Wael Hallaq, *The Impossible State: Islam, Politics, and Modernity's Moral Predicament* (New York: Columbia University Press, 2012).

32. Ernest Gellner, 'Marxism and Islam: Failure and Success', in A. Tamimi (ed.), *Power-Sharing Islam?* (London: Liberty for Muslim World Publications, 1993), 36.

33. See, for example, the special report issued by the Gallup Center for Muslim Studies titled 'Islam and Democracy' by Dalia Mogahed, which collected data from ten predominantly Muslim countries whose inhabitants repeatedly asserted their desire for both democratic societies and religious values; available at <http://www.gallup.com/press/109693/Islam-Democracy.aspx>; last accessed on 3 July 2014.

34. Charles Kurzman, *Modernist Islam, 1840–1940: A Sourcebook* (Oxford: Oxford University Press, 2002), 4.

35. Richard Bulliet, *The Case for Islamo-Christian Civilization* (New York: Columbia University Press, 2006), 47–94.

36. Robert W. Scribner, 'The Reformation, Popular Magic, and the "Disenchantment of the World"', *The Journal of Interdisciplinary History*, 23 (1993): 475–94.

37. Josef van Ess compares and contrasts medieval Christian and Islamic intellectual traditions thus: 'Christianity speaks of the "mysteries" of faith; Islam has nothing like that. For Saint Paul, reason belongs to the realm of the "flesh"; for Muslims, reason, *'aql*, has always been the chief faculty granted human beings by God'; see his *The Flowering of Muslim Theology* (Cambridge, MA: Harvard University Press, 2006), 153–4. For an account of the

seminal translation movements of the ninth and tenth centuries, see Dimitri Gutas, *Greek Thought, Arab Culture: The Graeco-Arabic Translation Movement in Baghdad and Early Abbasid Society (2nd–4th/5th–10th c.)* (New York: Routledge, 1998).

38.   Contra G. E. von Grunebaum, *Modern Islam: the Search for Cultural Identity* (Berkeley: University of California Press, 1962), 209, where he describes 'the truth of Islam' to be 'one and indivisible' and also 'immutable; it is neither growing nor shrinking . . . This goes for doctrine and conduct as well as for their institutionalization'. Such Orientalist constructions still pervade the field of Islamic Studies and spill over into the popular, public arena.

39.   Talal Asad, *The Idea of an Anthropology of Islam,* Occasional Papers (Washington DC: Center for Contemporary Arab Studies, Georgetown, 1986), 7.

40.   Interview of Talal Asad by Saba Mahmood titled, 'Modern Power and the Reconfiguration of Religious Traditions', *Stanford Electronic Humanities Review* 5:1 (1996), available at <http://www.stanford.edu/group/SHR/5-1/text/asad.html>; last accessed on 20 July 2013.

41.   Nilüfer Göle, 'Islam in Public: New Visibilities and New Imaginaries', in Frederick Volpi (ed.), *Political Islam: A Critical Reader* (New York: Routledge, 2011), 226.

42.   Albert Hourani, *Arabic Thought in the Liberal Age, 1798–1939* (Cambridge: Cambridge University Press, 1983), 130.

43.   For a selection of Khan's writings and speeches, see Sayyid Ahmad Khan, *Writings and Speeches of Sir Syed Ahmad Khan*, ed. Shan Muhammad (Bombay: Nachiketa Publications, 1972). For a detailed recounting of Khan's interpretive project, see further Christian W. Troll, *Syed Ahmed Khan: A Reinterpretation of Muslim Theology* (New Delhi: Vikas Publishing House, 1978).

44.   For a selection of his writings and statements, see Muhammad Iqbal, *Speeches, Writings and Statements of Iqbal*, ed. Latif Ahmad Sherwani (New Delhi: Adam Publishers, 2006). For an analysis of his political thought, see John L. Esposito, 'Muhammad Iqbal and the Islamic State', in John L. Esposito and John Voll (eds), *Makers of Contemporary Islam* (Oxford: Oxford University Press, 2001): 175–90.

45.   See *Iqbal: Manifestation of the Islamic Spirit, Two Contemporary Muslim Views: Ayatullah Sayyid Ali Khamene'i and Ali Shariati*, tr. Mahliqa Qara'i and Laleh Bakhtiar (Markham, ON: Open Press, 1991).

46.   Fazlur Rahman, *Islam and Modernity: Transformation of an Intellectual Tradition* (Chicago: University of Chicago Press, 1982), 141.

47.   Ibid. 151–2.

48.   Ibid. 36.

49.   Ibid. 124.

CHAPTER 2

Engaging the Sharia: rereading the Qur'an and hadith

The Sharia – usually translated as 'Islamic Law' – is reflexively assumed by most Westerners to be inherently at odds with modernity. Such was after all the case with Christian (canon) law, which has largely been abandoned in modern Western legal systems. The Sharia, however, is a many-splendoured thing; it is in fact much more than Islamic law. Arabic dictionaries translate *al-Sharia* as 'the way' or more fully as 'the way/path to the watering hole (or spring)'. This definition points us in the direction of how Sharia in theological, ethical and legal contexts should be conceptualised. Rather than restricting its purview to 'law' as is generally understood in the positivist sense, Sharia is more accurately understood as referring to a wide-ranging moral and behavioural code and broad ethical principles of divine origin which are interpreted by humans to yield specific legal rulings (*ahkam*) and moral prescriptions. The study of law (jurisprudence) is termed *fiqh* in Arabic, which in its basic etymology means 'understanding' and 'discernment'. Jurisprudence is therefore a human intel-lectual activity and, by definition, leads to fallible and changeable results.

According to this more expansive conceptualisation of the legislative process within the Islamic tradition, Islamic legal rulings may be regarded as – at least theoretically – amenable to constant interpretation in accordance with the Sharia's foundational principles, known as the *maqasid* (objectives). Islamic law is frequently described as unchanging, however, because it is understood to be the equivalent of Sharia alone, whose principles and moral content are indeed constant and fixed though divine revelation. Human engagement with such revealed principles, however, may and does lead to multiple understandings of the same; hence the traditional internal plurality of the Islamic legal and intellectual tradition. In general usage, the English term 'Islamic law' subsumes Sharia and *fiqh*; in other words, both the divine and human (or jurists') law.[1] Understood this way, the purview of Islamic law was quite broad in the pre-modern period, covering many spheres of life. Today what is referred to as Islamic law, however, concerns itself primarily with personal status and family law (marriage, divorce, inheritance, and so on) in most Muslim-majority socie-ties, with the notable exceptions of Saudi Arabia and Iran.

The primary sources of the Sharia are the Qur'an and the sunna (practices and sayings) of the Prophet Muhammad. How the relationship between these two sources is configured has had enormous impact on how Islamic jurisprudence (*fiqh*) has been conceptualised and how specific legal rulings have been applied over the centuries. It is precisely this relationship between the Qur'an and the sunna that has assumed central importance in the modern period. New and unprecedented concerns that have emerged in the context of modernity require of today's scholars who are fundamentally concerned with Islamic thought and praxis to reassess the interaction of these two sources through time, taking into consideration not only their text but also their context.[2] The status of these two sources will now be discussed separately, followed by an examination of some of the ways in which the relationship between the two is being revisited and reformulated in the context of engaging the Sharia in the modern period.

Qur'an and hadith: a complex relationship of hermeneutics and hierarchy

The Qur'an: scripture and its authority

The Qur'an is Islam's foundational sacred scripture. As a document, it is believed by Muslims to contain the transcript of God's revelations to the Prophet Muhammad in the seventh century of the Common Era. It is *sui generis* – for Muslims, there is absolutely no other book like it, for no other religious text claims to be the faithful recording of God's direct communication with humankind. This belief is the central, bedrock tenet of Muslim faith and praxis. Without appreciating this fundamental truth-claim that is distinctive of Islam and which animates the believer's consciousness, one cannot fully appreciate the urgency with which faithful Muslims apply themselves to the study of the Qur'anic text and its interpretation today. A Muslim's personal connection with God is established through the very words of the Qur'an, which provide an essential window into the divine mind, as it were, and through the utterance of which humans feel transported into the divine presence, in so far as it is possible in this world. Moulding one's behaviour according to the Qur'an's moral guidelines and ethical precepts is to properly align one's physical state with the spiritual one. The Muslim's special, loving relationship with the Qur'an – in its actual physical manifestation as a book, in the melodic recitation and written rendering of its words, and in the performance of its commandments – can thus seem mystifying to the non-Muslim who does not share such an intense relationship with a book – any book. Even the Abrahamic scriptuary – Jew and Christian – who relates to a central, sacred text cannot fully share or comprehend the believing Muslim's reverence for and attachment to the Qur'an. Jews and mainstream Christians after all do not make the claim that the entire Bible is the faithful transcript of God's very words, as Muslims do about the Qur'an. In regard to their content and the history of their transmission and codification rather than in their status as Scripture, both the Hebrew and Christian Bibles better resemble the hadith corpus and biographical literature on the Prophet (*sira*), which record second-hand accounts of the details of Muhammad's life and narrate a sacralised history, viewed very much through an imperfect human lens.

So what is the implication of the Qur'an as divinely revealed text for today's Muslims who wish to remain grounded in their religious tradition while grappling with modernity? Non-Muslim, particularly Western, polemicists will make the charge that this particular truth-claim about the provenance of the Qur'an in itself prevents Muslims from successfully adapting to the modern world with its emphasis on reason.[3] Such polemicists, however, are merely projecting their own or their coreligionists' history of engagement with their scriptures onto the contemporary Muslim's relationship with the Qur'an. Those who are termed 'fundamentalists' in the Christian tradition after all are known for their literal readings of the Bible and their wariness of textual ambiguities. Such literal-mindedness has fostered on the part of these fundamentalists a general hostility towards and suspicion of the modern world. This development within the Christian tradition is then understood to be universally applicable to all religious traditions that have at their centre a sacred text. This conceit allows many Westerners from Christian backgrounds to assume *a priori* that a comparable Muslim belief in an inerrant scripture must of necessity hinder a positive engagement with modernity.

Regarding the Qur'an as the permanent and infallible word of God, however, has not prevented Muslims from developing multiple interpretations of many of its passages in different historical periods; one might even argue that the Qur'anic text itself has facilitated it. Taking seriously the Qur'an's assertion that true believers are 'Those who listen to the Word and follow the best [meaning] in it' (39:18), Muslim thinkers through time have tended to underscore the polysemy of the Qur'anic language and the perennial quest to retrieve the best possible meaning from the text in variegated historical circumstances.[4] Reform-minded Muslims in fact insist that it is precisely a return to the specific words of the Qur'anic text and reading them with fresh eyes that allows one to unearth relevant layers of meanings that are appropriate to one's time and circumstances. From a very early period, Muslim exegetes have typically emphasised the historical context of Qur'anic verses and engaged in various modes of interpretation: linguistic, rhetorical, historical, esoteric, mystical. Such diverse hermeneutical approaches to the Qur'an have militated against a literal 'fundamentalist' understanding of it and allowed for competing and complementary understandings of its text to emerge.

Subsequent chapters will indicate how reformist scholars are engaging three of the most persistent accusations hurled against Muslims today that presumably prevents them from 'modernising': that the Qur'an requires them to establish an authoritarian 'Islamic government' to which Muslims owe slavish obedience (taken up in the current chapter and in Chapter Three); that it mandates the subjugation of women to men (Chapter Four); and that it establishes violent military activity as a sacred duty to be undertaken against non-Muslims until the end of time (Chapter Five). In these chapters it becomes clearly evident that there are multiple, credible perspectives on these critical topics among Muslim thinkers engendered by varying interpretations of relevant Qur'anic verses reflecting contemporary sociopolitical concerns. When we engage in a diachronic comparison of these interpretations linked to their historical circumstances, we often see that early exegetical views tended to remain close to the prima facie meaning of the Qur'anic passages in question. As we advance through the era of conquests and the expansion of Muslim territorial borders, the establishment of imperial dynasties, changing demographics, contestations of self- and communal identities, and growing violence directed against Muslims by external enemies down to our very own time, understandings of the Qur'anic text frequently became mediated through these contingent sociopolitical concerns. Consequently, the resultant interpretations in the later period sometimes tended to veer away from the obvious significations of specific Qur'anic locutions, even to the extent of occasionally subverting and eliding them, especially through the hermeneutic tool of *naskh* or abrogation. Understanding a number of these interpretations as authoritative for all time, uninflected by their specific historical milieu, has led to a number of epistemological problems within contemporary Islam that are increasingly being subjected to critical scrutiny by modern reform-minded Muslims.

The hermeneutics of political authority and citizenship: Qur'an 4:59

It is possible to illustrate a number of these hermeneutical trajectories and principles by focusing on a specific Qur'anic verse that is frequently cited in political discourses, generated by both Muslims and non-Muslims, to establish the existence of a pre-determined sociopolitical order presumably sanctioned by the Sharia. The Qur'anic verse invoked in this context is 4:59. Some modern scholars have gone so far as to say that this verse precludes the possibility of a dynamic political and democratic culture from emerging in Muslim-majority societies.[5] It should be noted that in some Muslim medieval political treatises composed after the ninth century, this verse is indeed often deployed as a prooftext to promote political quiescence and a culture of obedience to legitimate political authority. However, it is patently wrong to assume, as some have, that this was an uncontested interpretation whose genealogy goes back to the very inception of Islam, rather than a historically conditioned organic development in response to specific external political circumstances.

In order to illustrate this point and provide a case study of how a single, critical Qur'anic verse can generate multiple interpretations in different historical contexts with considerable implications for the understanding of Sharia today, especially in regard to its role in the moral and political ordering of society, we will now proceed to look at a broadly representative sampling of exegeses of this verse through time. This diachronic, historicising approach is helpful in undermining the essentialist understanding imposed by some on this verse and exhumes instead a broader repertoire of interpretations that are not restricted to the political sphere alone.

Qur'an 4:59 states, 'O those who believe, obey God and the Messenger and those who possess authority among you' (*Ya ayyuha alladhina amanu, ati'u Allah wa-ati'u al-rasul wa-uli 'l-amr minkum).*

The Arabic phrase *uli 'l-amr* as occurs in this verse has in particular given rise to various interpretations in different historical contexts. When the earliest significations of this verse available to us are compared with later, including modern, interpretations, certain important evolutionary transformations emerge.[6] We will start with a discussion of pre-modern exegeses of this verse followed by modern interpretations.

Pre-modern exegetical works
The earliest published work of exegesis we have at our disposal is the one by the late seventh century exegete Mujahid b. Jabr (d. 722). In his *Tafsir*, Mujahid states that this verse was revealed in reference to 'those possessing critical insight into religion and reason' (*uli 'l-fiqh fi 'l-din wa'l-'aql*). A second variant report recorded by Mujahid relates that the phrase refers to 'those possessing critical insight, knowledge, [sound] opinion and virtue' (*uli 'l-fiqh wa'l-'ilm wa-'l-ra'y wa-'l-fadl*). Both of these reports are attributed to the Companion 'Abd al-Rahman b. 'Awf.[7] Particularly noteworthy in these glosses is the emphasis on knowledge, independent reasoning, and critical discernment as the distinctive characteristics of the *uli 'l-amr*, who are not identified with any particular group of people or occupational category.

Another early exegete from the eighth century, Muqatil b. Sulayman al-Balkhi (d. 767), records in his Qur'an commentary that the key phrase *uli 'l-amr minkum* was revealed specifically in reference to the military commander Khalid b. al-Walid in a particular historical context, and more broadly refers to the commanders of military contingents (*saraya*).[8] Significantly, Muqatil considers Qur'an 4:59 to have an analogue in Qur'an 24:51–2, which helps to further elucidate the meaning of the former verse. The verses Qur'an 24:51–2 state:

> When the believers are invited to God and His messenger so that He may judge between them, they say, 'we hear and we obey;' these are the successful. For those who obey God and His messenger and fear God and heed Him, they are the ones who are victorious.

In comparison with these verses, Muqatil thus understands Qur'an 4:59 to be prescribing obedience to God and His messenger only, with the *uli 'l-amr* excluded.

These two interpretations find reflection in the early *tafsir* work of 'Abd al-Razzaq al-San'ani (d. 827) who reports on the authority of the famous Successor al-Hasan al-Basri (d. 728) that 'those possessing authority among you' refers to 'the learned people' (*al-'ulama*), and on the authority of Mujahid that the phrase refers to 'people of insightful understanding and knowledge' (*ahl al-fiqh wa-'l-'ilm*). 'Abd al-Razzaq provides valuable corroboration that in the first two centuries of Islam, the phrase *uli 'l-amr* was understood primarily to refer to (a) learned people in general, and, on the basis of a report from Abu Hurayra, to (b) the Prophet's designated military commanders in specific circumstances.

The celebrated late ninth century Qur'an commentator al-Tabari (d. 923) gives an account of the various meanings attributed to this phrase and gives us a sense of the evolution in its interpretation. He cites several early authorities who understood the *uli 'l-amr* as a reference to diverse groups of people. According to Ibn 'Abbas and the early exegete al-Suddi (d. 744) the phrase referred to various military commanders during the lifetime of the Prophet.[9] Interestingly, in another report recorded by al-Tabari, Ibn Zayd, from the second genera-tion of Muslims (Successors), quotes the Companion Ubayy b. Ka'b as saying that the verse was a reference to the political rulers (*al-salatin*).[10] *Al-salatin* is an interesting, anachronistic usage in this context here since sultans did not rise in the Islamic world until about the ninth century, well after the time of the Companions.[11]

However, al-Tabari then goes on to refer to a considerable number of authorities[12] who understood this verse as referring to 'the people of knowledge and insightful understanding' (*ahl al-'ilm wa-'l-fiqh*). Other variants of this report which identify the *uli 'l-amr* as 'the possessors of insightful understanding in religion and of reason' (*uli 'l-fiqh fi 'l-din wa-'l-'aql*); 'people of insightful under-standing and religion'; 'people of knowledge'; and 'the possessors of knowl-edge and insightful understanding', are recorded on the authority of various sources.[13] Another cluster of reports identifies the *uli 'l-amr* as 'the perspicacious and learned people'. All these variant terms together refer in general to people who possess unusual discernment and knowledge.[14] Other early commentators like Mujahid were inclined to understand this verse as referring to all the com-panions of Muhammad (*ashab Muhammad*).[15] Al-Tabari's fulsome commentary therefore corroborates for us that the earliest strand of exegesis on this critical verse did not impute political authority to the *uli 'l-amr* but rather an epistemic one, predicated as it is on superior knowledge and understanding of matters.

The twelfth-century exegete Fakhr al-Din al-Razi (d. 1210) offers a detailed exposition of this verse and its various interpretations. He lists the various inter-pretations already current by his time, which are now familiar to us. He notes additionally that various exegetes have been of the opinion that *uli 'l-amr* indi-cates the Rightly-Guided Caliphs; others regarded the phrase as referring to the various military commanders, among whom were 'Abd Allah b. Hudhafa, and

Khalid b. al-Walid during the Prophet's time. Finally, he records the interpretation of the Qur'an commentator al-Tha'labi (d. 1035) who had related from the Companion Ibn 'Abbas that the phrase refers to the scholars 'who make legal pronouncements regarding the religious law and instruct the people in their religion'.[16]

Al-Razi then indicates his preferred interpretation and asserts that the phrase *wa-uli 'l-amr minkum* is a reference to scholars who are also termed *ahl al-hall wa-'l-'aqd* (literally 'the people who loosen and join') in the juridical literature. This conflation of terms establishes that only the jurists are to be included in the *uli 'l-amr*, for he remarks that 'this type of scholar' has the exclusive ability to command and prohibit on the basis of the religious law. Interestingly, he maintains that the theologian (*al-mutakallim*), the exegete, and the hadith scholar who cannot deduce legal principles from the foundational texts are not to be included in the *ahl al-hall wa-'l-'aqd*, and, therefore, not to be counted among the *uli 'l-amr*.[17] Al-Razi's exposition is a clear indicator of the primacy of *fiqh* (jurisprudence) and of the pre-eminent position of the jurists in the religio-intellectual circles of his own time.

Another late medieval exegete, Ibn Kathir (d. 1373) records the various interpretations of this verse in his influential exegetical work, documenting both its earliest interpretation as referring to 'people of discernment and religiosity' (*ahl al-fiqh wa-'l-din*) and/or to specific military commanders during the Prophet's lifetime.[18] However, it is clear that Ibn Kathir himself is inclined to accept the view predominant in his time (the Mamluk period) that the Qur'anic term *uli 'l-amr* refers primarily (if not exclusively) to those who have political authority. He enlists as proof-texts a disproportionate number of hadiths which enjoin obedience to the political ruler in general and counsel the faithful to maintain stoic forbearance during the reign of an unjust ruler, since the latter is bound to be punished for his excesses in the next world. The text of the hadiths, however, betray no connection to Qur'an 4:59; that is to say there is no indication within the reports themselves that the Prophet may have uttered them in direct explication of this verse.

It seems clear from this survey of Qur'anic exegeses so far that once the word *amr* came to be understood as primarily referring to political authority by sometime after the ninth century, prophetic reports (of varying degrees of reliability according to the criteria developed by the medieval hadith scholars) that advised against causing social upheaval (*fitna*) by engaging in political rebellion would be associated with Qur'an 4:59. These reports would then be marshalled as religious warrants for promoting political quietism and authoritarianism. One such hadith annexed for this purpose is derived from the Prophet's sermon delivered at the conclusion of the last pilgrimage of his life in 632 CE. In this sermon, the Prophet addresses the crowd of pilgrims and advises them to 'Obey and listen, even if an Abyssinian slave with a head like a raisin were to rule over

you'. It is noteworthy that this hadith has generally been understood to underscore the egalitarian nature of the Islamic polity and to point to the primacy of
requirements such as personal piety and moral excellence in selecting a leader
for the polity. According to this prophetic utterance, race, ethnic background
and social class were to exert no influence, so that even a lowly slave, on account
of his greater moral excellence, could be regarded as being more worthy of the
leadership of the polity than a high-born, free Arab who was less morally excel-
lent. Ibn Kathir appropriates this hadith in this context, however, to more firmly
anchor the notion of practically unqualified obedience to the ruler, regardless
of whether he was deemed agreeable or not, it would seem, by the general
populace.

In this section of his exegesis, Ibn Kathir is, however, careful to include the
customary caveats against obeying the ruler who is guilty of violating God's
commandments (ma'siyat Allah), thus imposing a critical condition on what
otherwise would appear as an absolute entitlement on the part of the political
ruler.[19]

Pre-modern political treatises in relation to Qur'an 4:59

The interpretive differences we see between early and later commentaries (produced after the tenth century) are similarly replicated in political treatises that
deal with Qur'an 4:59. That is to say, we similarly see a progressive evolution
from an emphasis on the epistemic authority of scholars to the political authority
of rulers in explications of the term uli 'l-amr in these texts.

This is quite evident when we compare the treatise Risalat al-'Uthmaniyya of
the celebrated medieval belletrist and polymath 'Amr b. Bahr al-Jahiz (d. 869)
to the later political work of Ibn Taymiyya (d. 1328). In the ninth century, the
Risalat al-'Uthmaniyya preserves the full gamut of the meanings ascribed to this
phrase in the early works of tafsir and also provides new insights into the early
trajectory of this term. Al-Jahiz indicates the range of possible interpretations
of this verse thus: some Qur'an exegetes, he says, have understood the phrase
ulu 'l-amr to have a restricted application and to apply only to specific agents
('ummal) of the Prophet, to his specific delegates or representatives (wulat) and/
or to specific commanders of his armies. Others have understood it to refer to
political rulers (salatin; umara'). Yet others have interpreted this phrase to refer
more broadly to the Companions of the Prophet as a group, and/or to Muslims
in general.[20]

In tandem with the exegetical works discussed earlier, al-Jahiz's political
treatise composed in the early ninth century still does not show a preference for
the meaning of amr as 'political authority'. His work instead continues to document the broad range of meanings that were ascribed to the word in the first
three centuries of Islam. The last exegetical gloss recorded by al-Jahiz would
invest the entire Muslim community (or, at the very least, its righteous members)

with moral and political authority.[21] Interestingly, this range of meanings given by al-Jahiz is more in accordance with recent, modernist interpretations of this verse (as we will see below in the case of Rashid Rida and his expansive view of 'the people who loosen and join') than with the interpretations of most late medieval exegetes who seem not to have favoured such semantic and exegetical inclusiveness.

The standard and better-known political treatises of the later period do, in fact, increasingly begin to restrict the term *uli 'l-amr* to the political rulers of the various Muslim communities. The well-known political theorist al-Mawardi (d. 1058) in his classic *al-Ahkam al-Sultaniyya wa 'l-Wilaya al-Diniyya* ('Governmental Ordinances and Religious Administration') refers to Qur'an 4:59 and explicates it as ordaining virtually unquestioning obedience on the part of Muslims to their appointed leaders. He cites in this case a hadith narrated by Abu Hurayra in which the Prophet states:

> After me there will be rulers/governors (*wulat*), the righteous (*al-barr*) with his righteousness and the corrupt (*al-fajir*) with his corruptness; listen to them and obey them in what is in accordance with the truth (*al-haqq*). If they should rule wisely or justly then it counts in your and their favour. And if they should act unjustly, then it counts in your favour and against them.[22]

It is pertinent to note that this hadith counselling political quietism is attributed to Abu Hurayra, whose reputation as a hadith transmitter is mixed at best, and which reputation should impel us to regard the reliability of this report (and others like it attributed to him) as less than completely assured.

In the fourteenth century, the well-known Mamluk jurist and theologian Ibn Taymiyya (d. 1328) in the collection of sermons entitled *Fatawa*, refers to Qur'an 4:58–9 and interprets these verses as enjoining obedience to God and His Messenger. He goes on to paraphrase *uli 'l-amr* as *wulat al-'amr* (political leaders/administrators), thus clearly understanding the Qur'anic phrase in a politicised sense. These *wulat al-'amr*, he maintains, are also due obedience tempered by solicitation on their part of good advice from those he rules over.[23]

In his political treatise *al-Siyasa al-Shar'iyya*, Ibn Taymiyya asserts that Muslims must discharge their duties to the ruler (*al-sultan*) to the fullest, 'even though he may be corrupt (*fajir*)'.[24] He does not, however, invoke Qur'an 4:59 at this point in the *Siyasa* to underscore an assumed religiously mandated duty of practically unconditional obedience to the ruler. In the alarming world he lived in, besieged by ferocious invaders (the Crusaders and, more immediately, the Mongols), unconditional loyalty to the ruler (or, as we would say today, 'rallying around the flag') was a given. His emphasis at the same time on the Qur'anically prescribed duty of consultation among the faithful (Qur'an 3:159; 42:38), which on implementation serves as a check on arbitrary, strongman rule (*istibdad*), is noteworthy. In these two works, we thus observe Ibn Taymiyya's attempt to effect a rapprochement between what he regards as a religious responsibility to offer good counsel to the ruler as a check on his absolute authority and real-politik which required loyal obedience to the ruler on the part of his subjects, regardless of his personal qualities, in times of crises.[25]

Modern/ist exegetical works on Qur'an 4:59
We will now skip ahead several generations and consult the early twentieth century exegete Rashid Rida's important Qur'an commentary *Tafsir al-Manar* and his treatment of this critical verse. Rida concurs with al-Razi that the phrase *uli 'l-amr* refers to 'the people who loosen and join' among Muslims and they are the *umara'* (whom he understands to be the political rulers), the judges, the religious scholars, the chiefs of the army and the rest of the rulers and leaders upon whom, he says, people rely for their general welfare.[26] In this work, the term *amir* or *umara'* is explained as referring exclusively to political leaders and rulers, since Rida clearly distinguishes the *umara'* from military leaders whom he terms *ru'asa al-jund*. In this he departs from the classical and medieval understanding of *umara'* as referring predominantly to military commanders, at least as evident in exegetical works.

Rida also warns, however, that Qur'an 4:59 does not call for obedience to the *uli 'l-amr* but only to God and His Messenger, the reason being that the verse continues with 'And if you should differ with regard to a matter, then refer it to God and His Messenger'. If the *uli 'l-amr* rule according to the precepts of God and the sunna, then obedience is due to them; if they do not and in fact resort to tyranny and oppression (*zulm*), then obedience is no longer an obligatory duty but is rather forbidden.[27] He continues by saying that the actions of the temporal, political rulers are bound by the legal opinions of the scholars, for the latter are in fact 'the leaders of the leaders' (*umara' al-umara'*).

In this interpretation, Rida is echoing in part the exegesis of the eighth-century commentator Muqatil b. Sulayman, who had similarly understood the verse as enjoining obedience to God and His messenger only, and not to the *uli 'l-amr* as well. The *uli 'l-amr* in Rida's conceptualisation have primarily a consultative role; their counsel is to be solicited when the Qur'an and the sunna do not provide categorical answers in certain matters. Acting upon the *uli 'l-amr*'s recommendations is consequently a discretionary option, rather than binding. These conclusions are implicit in Muqatil's exegesis but more explicitly formulated in Rida's.

Further on, Rida, who equates the *uli 'l-amr* with the 'people who loosen and join' as did al-Razi before him, broadens the description of this group of people in a modernist vein. The 'people who loosen and join' include all those in whom the Muslim community (the umma) places its trust: they would include the scholars, the leaders of the army and the leaders of various sectors of society who promote the general well-being of the people. Among these sectors are trade, industry and agriculture. Therefore, labour union leaders, political party leaders, members of the editorial boards of respectable newspapers and their chief editors are all included in the category of the 'people who loosen and join'. Rida asserts that obedience to them constitutes obedience to the *uli 'l-amr*.[28]

We cannot help but notice that al-Rida's exegesis, once again, echoes the interpretations of the early exegetes. As we recall, the late seventh-century exegete Mujahid, like al-Rida, had defined the *uli 'l-amr* broadly. Mujahid had described them as people endowed in general with critical insight into religious matters and reasoning, without restricting them to specific occupational categories, as would later commentators like al-Razi. The latter, as we saw, was of the opinion that among all categories of scholars, only the jurists, because of their ability to engage in legal reasoning, could be regarded as constituting the *uli 'l-amr*. Rida's understanding of this locution is as broad as Mujahid's but he also identifies specific occupational groups peculiar to the modern world, who, in addition to the traditional groups of scholars, jurists and theologians, contribute to the general welfare and guidance of society as well, through their specialised learning and professional expertise which are not religious in nature.[29]

The Islamist thinker and Qur'an commentator Abul A'la Mawdudi (d. 1979) in his exegetical work *Tafhim al-Qur'an* (Comprehension of the Qur'an) echoes Rashid Rida's broad understanding of *uli 'l-amr* as referring to 'intellectual and political leaders of the community, as well as to administrative officials, judges of the courts, tribal chiefs and regional representatives'.[30] Mawdudi counsels obedience to them in general, with the caveat that this obedience is contingent on the *uli 'l-amr* being believers themselves and on their being obedient to God and the Prophet. In the event that a Muslim is commanded to carry out a deed that would be in contravention of God's laws, he or she must not obey such a command.

In this context, Mawdudi goes to some length to explain a sound hadith recorded by al-Bukhari in which the Prophet describes to his Companions the situation after his death during which time there would be rulers, both just and unjust. Some of the Companions asked if they should fight against the unjust rulers and the Prophet counselled them to desist 'as long as they [that is the rulers] continue to pray'. Mawdudi refers to another hadith, recorded not by al-Bukhari but, among others, by Muslim (d. 875) and al-Tirmidhi (d. 892), in which the Prophet advises his Companions in response to a similar question not to rise up against oppressive rulers, 'as long as they establish Prayer [sic] among you'.[31] Mawdudi considers the second report as providing further clarification of the purport of the first report cited: that the rulers are to be obeyed not because of their personal observance of the duty of prayer but because they have established congregational Prayers as a regular feature in the collective life of Muslims. He states further that '(t)his concern with Prayer is a definite indication that a government is essentially an Islamic one'.[32]

Mawdudi's argument, it should be noted, is a rather disingenuous one. His argument hinges particularly on the Arabic verb *aqama*, which in specific contexts may refer 'to establish' something. The usual meaning of this verb in connection with prayer is simply 'to perform' and 'to carry out'. The Qur'an frequently uses this word in relation to prayer, and often in reference to the individual believer and his or her personal obligation to pray (for example, 2:177). Even if one were to understand the verb as 'to establish', it still would not a priori convey the meaning of 'to establish something publicly'. One may infer this meaning, if one is so inclined, but this meaning is not explicit in the verb itself. Consistent with his politicised understanding of a number of Qur'an verses, however, Mawdudi finds this particular meaning to be the most conveniently appropriate.

And, finally, on to Sayyid Qutb (d. 1966), whose religiopolitical thought on 'Islamic government' and 'divine sovereignty' (*al-hakimiyya*) continues to have considerable influence on those whom we call Islamists today. In his exegetical work *Fi Zilal al-Qur'an* ('In the Shade of the Qur'an'), Sayyid Qutb does not dwell as much on the phrase *uli 'l-amr* itself as one might have expected him to, but regards the 'people possessing authority' as being practically subsumed under the commandment to obey God and His messenger. At two points, he glosses the term *uli 'l-amr*. In the first instance, he says: 'as for the phrase '*uli 'l-amr*' the text [that is the Qur'an] distinguishes who they are; that is, they are those believers in whom the condition of faith and the precepts of Islam . . . are realised'. [33] He continues by stating that these precepts have to do with obedience to God and to the Messenger, and with divine sovereignty – *al-hakimiyya* – and the right to legislate for the people from the very outset on the basis of the Qur'an and the sunna alone. Slightly earlier in his *tafsir*, Sayyid Qutb makes clear that sovereignty belongs to God alone and governs every aspect of human life, for God had prescribed His law as contained in the Qur'an. [34]

In the second instance, he says that the phrase *uli 'l-amr* refers to 'believers who stand upon the law of God (*Shariat Allah*) and the sunna of the Messenger', [35] which is a more succinct rephrasing of his first gloss.

In effect, Sayyid Qutb's highly politicised understanding of verse 4:59 with its linkage to the novel term *al-hakimiyya* represents the culmination of Mawdudi's vision of a hegemonic political Islam. In his exegesis of Qur'an 4:59, Qutb does not include the customary caveat, common in exegetical works composed by the earliest authors down to Mawdudi, against obeying the ruler if his actions or dictates are deemed to be in violation of the religious law. His brief explication of this critical verse also leaves little room for consultation with the people at large and solicitation of their advice (*munasaha*), a procedure Ibn Taymiyya had insisted upon. [36] A dangerous determinism appears to undergird Qutb's schema for an Islamic government. The *uli 'l-amr*, that is, those who have political authority, are clearly to be obeyed along with God and His messenger, since they are tautologically understood to be the best equipped to interpret and apply Qur'anic injunctions and the sunna on account of their status as *uli 'l-amr*. Clearly, such an assumed providential arrangement brooks little or no opposition from those who might see things differently.[37]

And yet, as we know from his other works, Sayyid Qutb also advocated the application of the Qur'anic principle of *shura* (consultation), and his utopian Islamic community is comprised of Muslims who infer (practically infallibly) the will of God from the Qur'an and sunna and implement it in active and respectful consultation with one another. The disjunction between these two positions may be resolved by bringing in Qutb's concept of *al-tali'a* (the vanguard) which, since it perfectly comprehends God's will, is in charge of spearheading the worldwide Islamicising movement.[38] Before the final establishment of the Islamic utopia, this vanguard consists of a minority of rightly-guided individuals adrift in a sea of misguided people, imbued with the reckless and godless notions of the pre-Islamic era (*al-jahiliyya*). Under such circumstances, the vanguard is not required to consult with the larger community; in fact, it is forbidden to do so. It must instead close ranks and strive to bring everyone into line with their manner of thinking. Although Qutb does not make this connection explicitly in the works surveyed here, the *uli 'l-amr* of his conception are none other than the vanguard of his coming revolution.

Concluding remarks: Qur'an 4:59 and its bearing on political authority
Our diachronic survey thus categorically establishes that political thought in the later period described above represents a dramatic departure from early Muslim conceptualisations of legitimate political and religious authority. Modernist Salafis like Rashid Rida, in truth, are far closer in their thinking and understanding of the term *uli 'l-amr* to the first and second generation of Muslims, according to our extant sources, than are Islamists who claim to be reviving the thought and practices of the earliest Muslim community. Modern Islamist thinkers, as we saw, have appropriated Qur'an 4:59 to construct their so-called theo-democratic government founded on the notion of 'divine sovereignty'. They claim that this notion goes back to the formative period of Islam, being completely unaware of or deliberately ignoring the diverse and primarily non-political understandings of this verse that were paramount through at least the first three centuries of Islam, as can be retrieved from early sources.

To a large extent, modern, particularly Western, scholarship on political and religious authority in Islam has focused primarily on late medieval works which present a conception of the Muslim polity along authoritarian lines, often invoking Qur'an 4:59 as undergirding this formulation. This position is not tenable. As our survey establishes, political expediency rather than any kind of an assumed scriptural mandate allowed for the notion of practically unqualified obedience owed to the ruler to progressively gain ground (but not without opposition) in certain quarters.

It is not surprising, therefore, that reform-minded and modernist Muslim thinkers typically emphasise going back to the Qur'anic text as the primary point of departure for rethinking the Sharia and consequently, the ethical, intellectual, political and legal traditions that are understood to have emanated from it. Our survey above of the exegesis of a highly significant verse that has been deployed in varying historical contexts to legitimise a particular moral and political ordering of society brings to the fore the polysemy of concepts like *uli 'l-amr* and their malleability within the Muslim ethical/political lexicon. A fundamental point that frequently emerges in modernist discourses is that one must always have recourse to the Qur'an's explicit wording and that the exegetical tradition that has developed around it through time must be recognised for what it is – a record of historically contextualised discourses that does not exhaust the potential meanings latent in the original Qur'anic text. Since the first source of the Sharia is the Qur'an, this conclusion further allows for the Sharia to be conceptualised as the fount of ethical and legal norms that, outside of matters concerning worship, are continuously open to a range of interpretive possibilities.

Hadith: the second source of the Sharia

As our discussion of Qur'an 4:59 above clearly indicates, hadiths – sayings attributed to the Prophet Muhammad – were frequently used to refine and elaborate upon the meanings of many verses in the Qur'an. This is known in Arabic as *tafsir bi al-ma'thur* (explanation of the Qur'an by means of transmitted reports) in contrast to *tafsir al-qur'an bi-l-qur'an* (explanation of the Qur'an by means of the Qur'an). The former mode of interpretation became highly popular from the ninth century on and distinctly impacted the understanding and deployment of critical verses in the Qur'an that has a bearing upon a whole range of issues: political governance, gendered roles, waging of the military jihad and interfaith relations, among others. These are all critical topics today, engagement with which is regarded as practically a *sine qua non* in the transition to modernity – however that may be specifically conceptualised.

Reformist/modernist critiques of a number of traditional, Sharia-based exegetical and juridical positions on these four topics in particular frequently (if not for the most part) are grounded in their ambivalent attitudes towards the hadith corpus and towards the classical scholarly methods for determining the reliability of individual prophetic statements. These critiques are writ large in the works of a number of scholars from the eighteenth century to our own period. We now proceed to discuss the views of some of the most prominent of these thinkers on the topic of the relation of the hadith corpus to the Qur'an and the necessity of resorting to independent reasoning (*ijtihad*) to reassess the juridical tradition which often relied on the use of hadiths as proof-texts.

One of the giants among such modernist thinkers was Shah Wali Allah Dihlawi (d. 1762), a prominent Muslim scholar and reformer in the Indian sub-continent who was widely regarded as the centennial renewer (*mujaddid*) of the eighteenth century. He launched a critique of classical legal scholarship as part of his overall project to reject *taqlid* (imitation of past precedent) and inaugurate a new phase of *ijtihad* (independent reasoning).[39] The historical backdrop to Shah Wali Allah's reformist agenda was the disintegration of Muslim political power under the Mughals during this period at the beginning of British colonisation. During such a phase of insecurity and political decline, Shah Wali Allah took a profound interest in fostering the unity of Muslims through a reform of Islamic thought and education. The scholars therefore had an important role to play in the social and political regeneration of the Muslim community.[40] In his envisioned project of reform and revival of the Islamic sciences, Shah Wali Allah emphasised the importance of hadith studies from a 'proper' perspective, which would lead to an appropriate reform of the classical legal tradition.[41] Emphasis upon the sunna of the Prophet was meant to provide a corrective to parochial and absolutist interpretations of the law; religious scholars, according to him, should have equal expertise in the hadith sciences as well as jurisprudence. He stressed that the Sharia can only be known through authentically transmitted texts (*naql*); after the Qur'an, therefore, the scholar must concern himself with the study and scrutiny of *hadith*s in order to establish their reliability.[42] From today's perspective, Shah Wali Allah's views on the whole appear quite conservative in regard to the hadith literature and his critique of classical scholarship is rather mild. But in his principled and forceful rejection of *taqlid*, he laid the groundwork for future scholars to continue further down the same path.

In the early nineteenth century, another prominent Muslim reformer Muhammad al-Shawkani (d. 1834) in the Yemen did just that. Like Shah Wali Allah, he was highly critical of non-reflective adherence to legal precedents (*taqlid*) in regard to the classical legal schools of thought and stressed the right of modern scholars like himself to resort to independent reasoning (*ijtihad*). In his well-known work, *Nayl al-awtar: sharh muntaqa al-akhbar* (The Attainment of the Objectives: Explanation of Select Reports), al-Shawkani makes the case for more rigorous scrutiny of weak hadiths that had entered into legal texts. An important qualification of a true *mujtahid* (a scholar who exercises *ijtihad*) is his mastery of the hadith sciences, he says, which included knowledge of the reliability of hadith transmitters (*jarh wa ta'dil*), in addition to his superlative command of the Arabic language. Like Shah Wali Allah, al-Shawkani used hadith criticism as a way of undercutting the consensus of the jurists of the traditional schools of law (*madhahib*) and to assert the right of modern scholars like himself to reinterpret the law.[43] For his emphasis on *ijtihad* and contributions to reform of religious thought, al-Shawkani has been widely recognised as the centennial renewer of the nineteenth century.

In the latter part of the nineteenth century, the redoubtable Egyptian scholar and reformer, Muhammad 'Abduh, affirmed the importance of the sunna, specifically in the sense of prophetic practice, as a source for explaining the Qur'an and points of law. But like a number of his reform-minded predecessors, he was at the same time critical of using solitary (*ahad*) hadiths as proof-texts, even those which occurred in authoritative collections, and primarily accepted *mutawatir* or widely disseminated reports as reliable. According to his student Rashid Rida, 'Abduh was highly critical of the *isra'iliyyat* (Israelite tales of Biblical origin that were often fanciful) and tended to be dismissive of eschatological (*fitan*) reports on account of their historically dubious content. 'Abduh was also critical of hadiths that were at variance with the clear meaning of Qur'anic passages and/ or that defied reason and common sense. He stated that a Muslim was only required to accept the reliable, widely disseminated (*mutawatir*) reports; as for the non-*mutawatir* reports, he or she was free to either act on them or disregard them. No one could be declared a disbeliever for rejecting the latter. [44]

These views on hadith, particularly concerning the *ahad* and *mutawatir* reports, continued to be propagated by 'Abduh's disciple, Rashid Rida, and by influential reformers like the later rector of al-Azhar, Mahmud Shaltut (d. 1963), Rida's student Abu Rayya (d. 1970) and another Azhar scholar Muhammad al-Ghazali (d. 1996), among others. These scholars affirmed that solitary (*ahad*) reports – the majority of hadiths – could only generate at best probable and not certain knowledge and therefore were not reliable as proof-texts in the case of essential doctrinal beliefs.[45] Abu Rayya stands out among the modernists for having impugned the general reliability of Abu Hurayra, the most prolific transmitter of reports from among the Companions in his work titled *Adwa' 'ala al-sunna al-Muhammadiyya* (Light upon the Prophetic Custom). Abu Rayya stresses that Abu Hurayra was not known as a man of learning, was regarded as an opportunist by some and was partial to Israelite tales of dubious origins. Furthermore, numerous reports are attributed to him even though he joined the Muslim community a mere three years before the death of Muhammad.[46] Criticism of Abu Hurayra has also been mounted by the Moroccan feminist scholar Fatima Mernissi for many of the same reasons.[47]

A general scepticism towards hadiths that are not well documented or widely disseminated (*ahad*) and whose content appears to be at variance with Qur'anic prescriptions became a hallmark of modernist criticism of classical religious scholarship. It is in the second half of the twentieth century that we find a systematic and more trenchant critique of the general reliability of particularly those hadiths whose texts were at variance with specific Qur'anic passages and which were deployed as proof-texts to mandate an understanding of the law that directly contravened relevant Qur'anic injunctions. This school of thought is best represented by the previously encountered Pakistani-American scholar Fazlur Rahman, who in his seminal work *Islam and Modernity* argued for the retrieval of the fundamental world-view of the Qur'an. He regarded this world-view as having been obfuscated by the rise of Sunni orthodoxy, especially in its Ash'ari form.[48]

Rahman was furthermore highly critical of what he considered to be the undeserved superior status of hadith in Islamic law and ethics vis-à-vis the Qur'an, a status that had gradually evolved in pre-modern Islamic scholarship, thanks in large measure to the efforts of the famous jurist al-Shafi'i (d. 820). Thus Rahman deplored the 'proliferation of hadiths [which] resulted in the cessation of an orderly growth in legal thought in particular and in religious thought in general';[49] as a consequence of which

> the need for a critical study of our intellectual Islamic past is ever more urgent because, owing to a peculiar psychological complex we have developed vis-à-vis the West, we have come to defend that past as though it were our God. Our sensitivities to the various parts or aspects of this past, of course, differ, although almost all of it has become generally sacred to us. The greatest sensitivity surrounds the Hadith, although it is generally accepted that, except the Qur'an, all else is liable to the corrupting hand of history. Indeed, a critique of Hadith should not only remove a big mental block but should promote fresh thinking about Islam.[50]

This 'Rahmanian' view has strongly permeated modernist discourses after him, since many of his students, like Nurcolish Madjid in Indonesia and Amina Wadud in the United States, have gone on to implement this perspective in their own writings. This call for a return to the Qur'an is particularly evident in the writings of modern Muslim feminists (as we will soon see in Chapter Four) who have sought to retrieve the gender-egalitarian élan of the Qur'an by stripping away the masculinist exegetical tradition that they understand to have effectively cloaked it. This modernist hermeneutic enterprise is thus rightly to be viewed as quite subversive of parts of the classical tradition and legal status quo. It is liberatory and revolutionary in so far as it seeks to foreground the foundational principles of equality, justice and compassion which modernists stress are at the foundation of the Qur'anic message, with no regard for social privilege and gendered differences.

Rahman significantly posits a critical difference between the hadith and sunna of the Prophet, whose continuing importance and organic connection with the Qur'an he recognised. The sunna, which he described as 'the ideal legacy of the Prophetic activity',[51] is a living, dynamic one which can be creatively engaged and interpreted by Muslims to meet the needs of their time. The hadith corpus, on the other hand, has to be used with caution since over time it had incorporated a number of beliefs and concepts for which there is no basis in the Qur'an.[52] The Qur'an was without doubt the final arbiter in such matters. To derive benefit from the hadith corpus, it needs to be subjected to stringent historical criticism and its content analysed with the Qur'an as reference.

Rahman was therefore deliberately challenging two key conceptions of the status of hadith that became standard after the time of al-Shafi'i (d. 820): that (a) sunna is to be conflated with hadith, so that it becomes reduced to the authenticated sayings of Muhammad; and (b) it is to be regarded as unrecited revelation (*wahy ghayr matlu*), which differs from the recited Qur'anic revelation (*wahy matlu*) only in form, not in substance.[53] Al-Shafi'i's position is understood to be corroborated by a report contained in Ahmad b. Hanbal's hadith collection which states: 'Gabriel used to descend to the Prophet with sunna just as he descended with the Qur'an',[54] establishing the sunna's infallibility on par with that of the Qur'an.

Despite his highly critical attitude towards the hadith corpus, it should be pointed out that Rahman never advocated that it be completely jettisoned as a source in Islamic scholarship. He recognised the historical value of hadith and its indispensable value for elucidating many details having to do with the Prophet's life and therefore providing necessary contextualisation for many Qur'anic verses. Thus he observes, 'For, if the Hadith *as a whole* is cast away, the basis for the historicity of the Qur'an is removed at one stroke'.[55] Rahman is rather proposing, as are most reformists, that individual hadiths be appraised for their veridicality and either retained or abandoned as valid proof-texts based on how they stand up to such scrutiny.

More recently, Khaled Abou El Fadl, the scholar of Islamic law at the University of California at Los Angeles has written works that criticise the uncritical acceptance of the hadith corpus and the tendency in conservative quarters to, as he phrases it, 'hurl hadith' as a way of trumping positions contrary to their own. Like many of his modernist predecessors, Abou El Fadl traces the contemporary crisis within the Islamic intellectual tradition to an excessive and unreflective over-reliance on hadith as a body of text that is to be literally applied, sometimes at the expense of the Qur'anic text and the rich interpretive literature that has grown up around it. Abou El Fadl makes a critical distinction between the 'authoritativeness' of the religious text and 'authoritarian' methodologies developed by those he labels as the 'puritans' for interpreting it and thus for co-opting alternate methodologies of engaging the same. Such a seamless hermeneutics is intended to generate a single normative understanding of the text in the puritans' understanding. As Abou El Fadl remarks:

> According to the puritans, not only does the text regulate most aspects of human life, but also the Author of the text determines the meaning of the text, while the reader's job in engaging the text is to understand and implement, as if the meaning of the text is always clear. In the puritan paradigm, subjectivities of the interpreting agent are irrelevant to the realization and implementation of the Divine command, which is fully and comprehensively contained in the text. Therefore, the aesthetics and moral insights or experiences of the interpreting agent are considered irrelevant and superfluous.[56]

Here, in this depiction, we see the close resemblance between the puritan's approach to the text of the hadith or the Qur'an and that of the Christian fundamentalist in his or her approach to the Bible as an inerrant text capable of generating only a single authoritative reading. Within Islam as in Christianity, this scriptural literalism is a largely modern phenomenon that is a reaction to the anxieties of the modern world with its accompanying erosion of the old certitudes and the rise of moral relativism. Imposing a single uncontested interpretation on the text offers the assurance of constancy even as the world continues to change dramatically around the reader. As Abou El Fadl warns, such hermeneutic rigidity has dire consequences for religious and intellectual traditions that thrive on polysemy and pluralist readings. He observes:

> Texts that are unable to become liberated from their authors or unable to challenge the reader with levels of subtlety or tease with nuances of meaning have a nasty . . . habit of becoming predictable, dull and closed. Texts that remain open stay alive, relevant and vibrant.[57]

In many ways, this receptivity towards textual polyvalence or lack thereof remains the ultimate divide between the 'fundamentalist' and the 'non-fundamentalist' mindset. In broad strokes we may be able to say that while the former seeks certitude in univocality and firm, irrevocable boundaries, the latter revels in the multitude of meanings that the text in its porosity may legitimately yield through a faithful and imaginative engagement with it in variegated circumstances.

Revisiting the Sharia: implications for the twenty-first century and beyond

In the view of modernists then, the revitalisation of the Sharia, understood holistically as a collectivity of broad moral guidelines and ethical prescriptions that shape the Islamic way of life rather than more narrowly as law, depends on recovering this hermeneutic dynamism and interpretive pluralism by Muslims who critically engage the sources of their religious tradition. Their restoration to the Qur'an of its primacy in ethical deliberations and legal adjudication reverses what became the standard relationship between the Qur'an and the hadith corpus from after the ninth century CE in which the latter frequently mediated and elaborated upon the meaning of the former. The modernist project of revisiting the Sharia is consequently two-pronged – requiring first, a return to the Qur'an as the most authoritative arbiter of ethical and legal matters; and, second, subjecting the hadith corpus to renewed scrutiny and evaluating the legal prescriptions that have emanated from the hadith in light of what the Qur'an pronounces. Both methods are strongly apparent in the writings of the prominent liberal Egyptian thinker and prolific scholar Jamal al-Banna (d. 2013), the younger brother of Hasan al-Banna (d. 1948), the founder of the

Muslim Brotherhood. Jamal al-Banna was fundamentally concerned with revisiting the classical relationship that had been established between the Qur'an and sunna and the legal–ethical positions generated by this relationship through time. We focus next on one such important work by him.

Return to the Qur'an and critique of the hadith corpus

In his work titled *Return to the Qur'an* (*al-ʿAwda ila al-Qur'an*), Jamal al-Banna dwells at length on what he describes as the 'suspension of the Qur'an' (*taʿtil al-Qur'an*) at the hands of traditional scholars through the centuries, a state of affairs that began during the time of the Companions and continues, he says, among the contemporary Azhari elite.[58] This 'suspension of the Qur'an' has occurred in a number of ways, says al-Banna. It has occurred through the phenomenon of *naskh*, so that between a hundred and five hundred verses of the Qur'an have been declared to be abrogated by various scholars. It has occurred through the relegation of the Qur'an in judicial reasoning to a secondary source (*farʿ*) as opposed to a primary one (*asl*), and through recourse to dubious methods derived from scholastic theology and philosophical inquiry to determine the meanings of the Qur'an. It has furthermore occurred through the interpretation of Qur'anic verses which contradicted both their letter and their spirit and reflected rather the influence of the political and social milieu of the commentators.[59]

The worst consequence of this 'suspension' has been the betrayal of the spirit that animates the Qur'an during the juridical process of extrapolation of laws from its text, continues al-Banna. The Qur'an in its fundamental élan invites to justice (*ʿadl*) and condemns all forms of oppression (*zulm*), which is considered to be the equivalent of attributing partners to God (*shirk*), the worst possible transgression in Islam. The Qur'an refers to justice in its social, political and economic aspects, urges people to be equitable and ethical in their business transactions with one another, and expresses the greatest solicitude for the weakest members of society – slaves and women. However, al-Banna remarks ruefully, when one reads the books of jurisprudence, one is struck by the lack of this glorious spirit of liberation and mandate for justice and excoriation of oppression that characterise the Qur'an. Instead one finds legal rulings in these juridical tomes which sometimes flagrantly contradict the spirit and the intent of the Qur'an.[60]

This contradiction is nowhere more apparent than in the case of women. Al-Banna directs the attention of the reader to the inclusive language of the Qur'anic text with regard to men and women and the assertion of their equal moral and human agency in general. He cites as proof-texts Qur'an 9:71, which states, 'The believing men and women are allies of one another; they command good and forbid wrong . . .'[61]; Qur'an 16:97 which states, 'Whoever commits a good deed, male or female, while a believer, we will grant them a pleasant existence'; and Qur'an 4:124, which similarly affirms, 'Whoever carries out a good deed, male or female, while a believer, they will surely enter Paradise'. He further refers to the much-cited Qur'an 33:35, which asserts the ontological equality of women and men.[62] Other verses come to the defence of the female and confer on her specific reciprocal legal rights vis-à-vis the male, particularly within the context of the family (Qur'an, Chapter Four).[63] The implications are clear: in their adjudications concerning the legal status of women, the jurists frequently imposed extraneous restrictions on the conduct and rights of women based on prevailing social norms and cultural sensibilities which violated the spirit and intent of these verses.

Jamal al-Banna also turns his attention to the issue of apostasy, one of the most controversial and hotly debated topics within modern Islam, and one of the most obvious examples of legal divergence from the letter and spirit of the Qur'an, primarily on the basis of one influential hadith recorded by al-Bukhari in his *Sahih*. This hadith, narrated by 'Ikrima from Ibn 'Abbas, states, 'Whoever changes his religion, put him to death.' In contrast to the text of this hadith, notes al-Banna, there are more than one hundred verses in the Qur'an which affirm freedom of conscience and religion and signify acceptance of a plurality of religions and ways of life. On the question of apostasy specifically, several verses in the Qur'an undermine the command in the previously cited hadith. For example, Qur'an 2:108 states, 'Whoever substitutes unbelief for belief has certainly missed the straight path'; another verse Qur'an 2:217 states, 'Whoever among you retreats from his religion and dies an unbeliever, they are those whose actions are in vain in this world and the next'. Other verses (Qur'an 47:25; 16:109; 24:55) similarly criticise relapse into unbelief and warn of divine retribution in the next world but prescribe no worldly punishment. To those who would respond that this is an example of a case where the Qur'an is silent and the sunna provides the requisite answer and necessary specification (*min majalat ikhtisas al-sunna*), al-Banna identifies the following problems inherent in this position:

1. The Qur'an does in fact identify a punishment for apostasy;
2. This punishment, however, is postponed to the next world and is not the prerogative of any human being;
3. The Qur'an categorically states that no human being, including the Prophet, has the right to forcefully impose religious belief on another human being.

Furthermore, the hadith itself does not qualify as an unimpeachable proof-text for the following reasons: first, it is one of the solitary reports (*ahad*) which are not admissible as proof-texts in matters of doctrine, since by their paucity of nar-rators and of chains of transmission, they do not conduce to certainty but only to presumption and conjecture. Second, there is no evidence that the Prophet ever put anyone to death for mere apostasy. The evidence instead shows that only when apostasy was coupled with treason and sedition was it considered a punishable offence. Third, the language of the hadith is imprecise, since it does not indicate in which direction the conversion went. With more than a touch of irony, al-Banna remarks that the hadith could potentially be used by priests in churches to proscribe conversion to Islam! The fourth reason is that the hadith is related by 'Ikrima, who, although one of the most prominent narrators from Ibn 'Abbas, was held in low esteem by Muslim b. Hajjaj, who transmitted only one report from him concerning the pilgrimage. On such a weighty matter concerning belief and doctrine, it would be more prudent, counsels al-Banna, to not place one's reliance on a narrator with less than sterling credentials. The fifth and the final reason is that the larger context invoked for this hadith is 'Ali's alleged campaign against the *zanadiqa* (roughly 'heretics') whom he is said to have put to death by burning. When news of this purported event reached Ibn 'Abbas, he is reported to have disavowed the legitimacy of this action because the Prophet had forbade punishing anyone in this manner. The problem, al-Banna notes, is that the term *zanadiqa* is clearly being employed here anach-ronistically since it was not in circulation until well after the time of Ibn 'Abbas during the waning days of the Umayyad dynasty. Also it is hardly likely that 'Ali, a close Companion of the Prophet, would not have been aware of the prophetic proscription against burning anyone – all of which create a cloud of suspicion around this report. And finally, attribution of the report to Ibn 'Abbas is in itself doubtful, given the fact that Ibn 'Abbas was a mere child during the lifetime of Muhammad, yet almost 1600 reports are attributed to him, many of which were recorded by al-Bukhari and Muslim in their highly respected hadith collections.[64] Once again, such a fact does not invite much credibility in this presumed proof-text in favour of capital punishment for the mere renunciation of one's faith.

Al-Banna's treatment of the contested issue of apostasy is reproduced at some length above as an illustration of the critical vein in which many reformist and modernist Muslims approach the hadith and classical legal and interpretive literature. As demonstrated persuasively by al-Banna, pre-modern scholars were either sometimes not overly concerned with context and did not exercise due diligence in determining the reliability of the content of hadiths, as opposed to their chain of transmission; or, alternatively, their texts were read by poster-ity in an ahistorical matter, which facilitated the rise of interpretations among modern Muslims that demonstrably militate against both the letter and spirit of the Qur'an, a situation that was not always intended by the classical scholars. Against this backdrop, one can appreciate the modernist emphasis on a return to the text of the Qur'an and to wield it as the final arbiter over all other non-Qur'anic literature, regardless of how authoritative they have been deemed to be through the centuries. From this vantage point, a true hermeneutic and epistemic transformation of the modern Muslim condition is possible only through this restoration of the Qur'an's primacy over all other texts and discourses and rediscovering its humane and just message through careful consideration of its own words, as stressed by Rahman, al-Banna, and other reform-minded Muslims in the modern period.[65]

The Qur'anists and their approach to the hadith literature

The scepticism with which many modernists view the hadith corpus stops considerably short of dispensing with it altogether. As Fazlur Rahman had remarked, the hadith literature remains an indispensable source for Muslims for understanding the larger context of the Qur'an and for illuminating many details concerning religious observances and acts. From this perspective, it is necessary to spend the time and energy to winnow out the reliable, widely disseminated hadiths from within the corpus, for such reports remain valuable sources for deriving ethical principles and for legal reasoning. This position was clearly articulated by 'Abduh's student, Rashid Rida, as follows:

> The pillar of the faith is the Qur'an and the customs (sunan) of the Prophet which are transmitted through mutawatir traditions; these are the sunan 'amaliya (the applied customs), as for example the prayer ritual (salat) and the pilgrimage ceremonies (manasik), and some of the Prophet's sayings (ahadith qawliya), which most of the worthy ancestors have accepted. The remaining traditions with one or only a few isnads (ahad), the transmission of which is doubtful or which do not specifically indicate anything, are subject to independent judgment (ijtihad).[66]

There is, however, a very small group of Muslim thinkers and activists who consider themselves solely as 'people of the Qur'an' (ahl al-Qur'an) or Qur'anists as they are often called in English, who reject the hadith corpus in its entirety. Their name and views hark back to the Ahl-e Qur'an movement in the Indian subcontinent in the early twentieth century, a movement that was spearheaded by 'Abdallah Chakralawi (d. 1930)[67] and Khwaja Ahmad Din Amritsari (d. 1936). These early Qur'anists argued that Islamic doctrine and legal rulings should be derived only from the Qur'an since the hadith corpus is not reliable. This is a position that continues to be subscribed to by later Qur'anists who maintain that many hadiths undermine and contradict the just and liberatory teachings of the Qur'an and it is no longer possible to reliably determine which hadiths represent the true speech of Muhammad. They argue that the hadith literature – as a human product – has been the source of misogyny, intolerance and lack of religious freedom among Muslims, whereas the Qur'an espouses the equality of men and women, acceptance of religious minorities and non-coercion in religious matters. Although small, this group is not without some influence and their criticism of hadith is shared by other Muslim reformists to a certain degree, although not to the extent of advocating for the abandonment of the entire hadith corpus.

The Qur'anists' dismissal of hadith continues to be regarded as extreme and intellectually unwarranted by the majority of scholars of Islam, who regard the former as too quick to denounce a religious corpus about which they do not have deep knowledge nor wish to engage critically. Popular reaction to some of the vocal proponents of the Qur'an-only position has ranged from benign neglect to violence in some instances. Among the best-known Qur'anists from the latter half of the twentieth century are Rashad Khalifa, an Egyptian émigré to the United States who founded a mosque in Arizona; Ahmad Mansour, also an Egyptian who was trained as a scholar of Islamic history at al-Azhar University and then emigrated to the United States, where he founded the organisation Ahl al-Qur'an: the International Qur'anic Center; and Edip Yüksel, a Turkish political and religious activist who also settled in the United States and published the *Reformist Qur'an* which eschews hadith in its translation and commentary on the Muslim scripture. These Qur'anists claim to derive their hostility to the hadith directly from the Qur'an itself, which they regard as the true sunna of Muhammad. Khalifa, for example, described his opposition to the entire hadith corpus as Qur'anically mandated, grounding his position in Qur'an 6:114–15 which state, 'Shall I seek as a source of law any other than God, when He has revealed this Book to you with full details? . . . The word of your Lord is complete in regard to truth and justice.' Khalifa's uncompromising position raised the ire of a number of Muslims. In January 1990 he was murdered at the mosque he founded in Tucson, Arizona by an unnamed assailant who was never found.[68] Mansour and Yüksel, however, continue to run active websites in the US dedicated to promoting their particular views.

Ultimately, the disinclination of the Qur'anists to take part in the kind of rigorous hadith analysis that modernists typically engage in makes them vulnerable to the criticism of 'throwing out the baby with the bathwater'. Their reluctance to engage in a sustained scholarly appraisal of the hadith literature results in adopting the convenient shortcut of dismissing in its entirety an otherwise historically valuable source. Given the sometimes deeply visceral reaction to their position, it is very doubtful that the extreme Qur'anist perspective will gain much traction in the near future. It is also doubtful that the Qur'anists will simply disappear altogether, since scepticism towards hadith in some form or another will remain a hallmark of modernist critiques of the Islamic tradition as it developed in history. A much more likely future scenario is the emergence of a middle site where the necessity of a thorough reappraisal of the hadith corpus is acknowledged by all reformists without its wholesale rejection. This modus vivendi may result in an attendant diminution in the normative status of even the so-called 'canonical' reports contained in the six authoritative Sunni hadith compilations, whose reliability would be tested against the Qur'an and the

Qur'an alone. This would not result in the wholesale nullification of the hadith corpus, and might even allow for the rehabilitation of parts of it as constituting a firmly reliable source of legal and ethical deliberation among the adherents of the Qur'an-only school.

It should be noted that scepticism towards the 'canonical' hadith is not a perspective that is radically new within the history of Islamic scholarship but rather builds upon the pre-modern science of hadith criticism (*'ulum al-hadith*) that continued to subject the hadith compilations, including the famous two *Sahihs* (*al-Sahihayn*) of al-Bukhari and Muslim, to critical re-examination through the late medieval period. As Jonathan Brown has noted, 'Even scholars who actively employed the *Sahihayn* canon occasionally criticized a hadith from the two books if it contradicted the doctrines of their school of law or theology.'[69] Such scholars included prominent mainstream authorities, such as the well-known hadith scholar al-Daraqutni (d. 995), who criticised seventy-eight reports in al-Bukhari's revered collection and one hundred in Muslim's.[70] Such criticism grew progressively less after the tenth century but was still continued by highly regarded scholars like al-Bayhaqi (d. 1066), Muhammad b. 'Ali al-Mazari (d. 1141), and the famous Hanbali jurist Ibn al-Jawzi (d. 1200). Ibn al-Jawzi subjects at least two reports from al-Bukhari's *Sahih* to rigorous *isnad* criticism in his *Kitab al-Mawdu'at* (Book of Fabrications).[71]

The 'middle site' alluded to above may already be emerging with the new hadith reappraisal project recently completed by Turkish religious scholars under the jurisdiction of the Presidency of Religious Affairs and the Religious Charitable Foundation of Turkey. In a formal statement released to the press in 2008, the objectives of this hadith project were described as follows:

> The aim of the study is to offer the contemporary audience the Prophet's message in a comprehensible language while taking into account the interpretations concerning hadith narrations, making necessary amendments in cases of misconceptions and omitting the issues and interpretations which do not have current value. In preparing the project, the Traditions are explained within the context of the unity of Hadith and the Quranic verses; throughout the course of evaluating the Tradition, attention is given to the reciprocal connection of the basic religious texts and the existing internal coherence between them. Above all, the closeness among the Koran and Hadith is continually reflected in the texts . . .
>
> While the Hadith project seeks to establish a connection between Hadith narrations and current thinking and scientific data, it has avoided judging the past on the basis of today's categories and stayed away from extreme interpretations.[72]

In this vein, Mehmet Görmez, one of the eighty-five scholars drawn from various Faculties of Theology in Turkey to participate in the project, points to the hadith which prohibits women from travelling for more than three days without their husband's permission. He states that such a report should be weighed along with another narration in which the Prophet is quoted as saying that he longs for the day when women may be able to travel alone. Comparison of the two texts allows one to arrive at the conclusion that the restriction on women's travel suggested by the first report is not religious in nature but prompted rather by concerns for their physical safety when travelling long distances alone in a social and historical milieu in which their security could not be guaranteed. This approach to the hadith literature reveals that the scholars involved in the project are engaging in a holistic study of the hadith corpus grounded in hermeneutic historicism which consciously avoids the atomistic wielding of individual hadiths as proof-texts, divorced from a larger historical context.

The Turkish diyanet-sponsored hadith project, published as a seven-volume encyclopedia in 2013, however, neither signals the onset of a Protestant-style reformation as breathlessly proclaimed by some of the Western media[73] nor the continuation of the conventional form of solely transmitter-based analysis of the pre-modern period. With its focus on the content of prophetic reports and declared intention of building on past Islamic intellectual tradition, the project marks something of a milestone in the ongoing critical engagement of Muslim scholars with the hadith corpus to establish its continued relevance in contemporary re-fashionings of Muslim self- and communal identities.

Conclusion

I have described and analysed above how certain modern Muslim scholars are rereading the Qur'an and hadith literature and revisiting the relationship between the two. The results are potentially transformative and already suggest reinterpretations of the Sharia that are occasionally dramatically different from the understandings that certain pre-modern Muslim scholars arrived at. Such a project is still very much a work in progress. The rereadings that have been discussed here are still strongly contested today in traditional juridical circles and are probably not about to be widely accepted any time soon. But modest and progressive inroads continue to be made, as noted throughout this volume; their cumulative effect over the years is bound to make a difference. In the meantime, in the full light of history, we have underway the reform and renewal of a major world religion, whose consequences will be with us for a goodly long time.

Notes

1. Khaled Abou El Fadl, *The Great Theft: Wrestling Islam from the Extremists* (New York: HarperOne, 2007), 150. For an account of modern reformist approaches to this distinction between Sharia and *fiqh*, see further Aziz Azmeh, *Islams and Modernities* (London: Verso, 2009), 125 ff.; Ziauddin Sardar, *Reading the Qur'an: The Contemporary Relevance of the Sacred Text of Islam* (Oxford: Oxford University Press, 2011), 283–91. The distinction between Sharia and *fiqh* is particularly critical to Muslim feminist hermeneutics, since traditional

Muslim family law is susceptible to reform as an instance of changeable, human-generated *fiqh*; see Chapter Four in this volume. This traditional conflation between Sharia and *fiqh* is being increasingly interrogated by reformist Muslims as a prelude to instigating legal reform.

2. This point has been made most forcefully by Tariq Ramadan in his *Radical Reform: Islamic Ethics and Liberation* (Oxford: Oxford University Press, 2009). Ramadan states, 'Traditional religious scholars, the "text scholars" (*'ulama' al-nusus*), must be placed on no more than an equal footing with "context scholars" (*'ulama' al-waqi'*) in a reconfigured landscape of epistemic and moral authority for the Islamic Universe of reference;' ibid. 4. This fundamental consideration of text along with context is stressed by Ramadan as a necessary hermeneutic step for a genuine transformation to occur in Islamic epistemology and for the retrieval of a holistic Islamic ethics from foundational texts.

3. For example, Sam Harris, *The End of Faith: Religion, Terror and the Future of Reason* (New York: W. W. Norton, 2005), 109–10.

4. Asma Barlas stresses this point strenuously in her '"Holding Fast by the Best in the Precepts": the Qur'an and method', in Kari Vogt et al. (eds), *Changeable and Unchangeable: New Directions in Islamic Thought and Practice* (London: I. B. Tauris, 2008), 17–22.

5. Among Orientalists, Bernard Lewis has brashly asserted that Qur'an 4:59 teaches that 'the primary and essential duty owed by the subjects to the ruler is obedience'. He further comments, 'The duty of obedience to legitimate authority is not merely one of political expediency. It is a religious obligation, defined and imposed by Holy Law and grounded in revelation'; see Bernard Lewis, *The Political Language of Islam* (Chicago: University of Chicago Press, 1988), 91; cf. Elie Kedourie, *Democracy and Arab Political Culture* (London: Routledge, 1994), 7.

6. This section draws heavily on my previous essay 'Obedience to Political Authority: An Evolutionary Concept', in Muqtedar Khan (ed.), *Islamic Democratic Discourse: Theory, Debates, and Philosophical Perspectives* (New York: Lexington Books, 2006), 37–60.

7. Mujahid b. Jabr, *Tafsir Mujahid*, ed. 'Abd al-Rahman al-Tahir b. Muhammad al-Surati (Islamabad: Majma' al-buhuth al-islamiyya, n.d.), 1:162–3.

8. Muqatil b. Sulayman, *Tafsir Muqatil* (Cairo: Mu'assasat al-halabi wa-shuraka'uh, 1969?), 1:246.

9. Al-Tabari, *Tafsir al-Tabari*, also known as *Jami' al-bayan fi ta'wil al-qur'an* (Beirut: Dar al-kutub al-'ilmiyya, 1997), 4:151.

10. Ibid.

11. See the article 'Sultan', in G. E. Bosworth et al. (eds), *Encyclopedia of Islam*, new edition (Leiden: Brill, 1997; henceforth abbreviated as *EI²*), 9:849–51.

12. The authorities include Jabir b. 'Abd Allah and Mujahid.

13. Al-Tabari, *Tafsir*, 4:152.

14. This is how the Arabic terms *al-fuqaha' wa-'l-'ulama'* employed in these instances should be translated for the early period. Understanding these terms to refer to the later occupational categories of jurists and scholars (from the ninth century on) would be clearly anachronistic here.

15. Ibid. 4:152.

16. Al-Razi, *al-Tafsir al-kabir* (Beirut: Dar ihya' al-turath al-'arabi, 1999), 4:113.

17. Ibid.

18. Ibn Kathir, *Tafsir al-qur'an al-'azim* (Beirut: Dar al-jil, 1990), 1:490–1.

19. Ibid.

20. Afsaruddin, 'Obedience to Political Authority', 46.

21. Ibid. 46.

22. Al-Mawardi, *Al-Ahkam al-Sultaniyya wa-'-wilayat al-diniyya*, ed. 'Isam Faris al-Harastani and Muhammad Ibrahim al-Zaghli (Beirut: al-Maktab al-islami, 1996), 13–14.
23. Ibn Taymiyya, *Majmu'at al-fatawa*, ed. 'Amir al-Jazzar and Anwar al-Baz (Riyad: Maktabat al-'ubaykan, 1998), 18:7.
24. Ibn Taymiyya, *Al-Siyasa al-shar'iyya fi islah al-ra'i wa 'l-ra'iya* (Cairo: Dar al-kutub al-'arabi, 1951), 161-64.
25. Afsaruddin, 'Obedience to Political Authority', 47.
26. Rashid Rida, *Tafsir al-qur'an al-hakim,* known as *Tafsir al-manar,* ed. Ibrahim Shams al-Din (Beirut: Dar al-kutub al-'ilmiyya, 1999), 5:147.
27. Ibid. 5:150.
28. Ibid. 5:152.
29. Afsaruddin, 'Obedience to Political Authority', 43.
30. Abul A'la Mawdudi, *Towards Understanding the Qur'an,* tr. and ed. Zafar Ishaq Ansari (Leicester: Islamic Foundation, 1988), 51.
31. Ibid. 51.
32. Ibid. 52.
33. Sayyid Qutb, *Fi zilal al-qur'an* (Cairo: Dar al-shuruq, 2001), 2:691.
34. Ibid.
35. Ibid. 2:692.
36. See above p. 33.
37. Afsaruddin, 'Obedience to Political Authority', 45.
38. See Qutb's *Ma'alim fi 'l-tariq* (Beirut: Dar al-shuruq, 1982), 11–12. This work is further discussed below.
39. This position is explained in great detail in his legal treatise *'Iqd al-jid fi ahkam al-ijtihad wa al-taqlid* (Cairo: al-Matba'a al-Salafiyya, 1385 AH); translated by Marcia Hermansen in her work *Shah Wali Allah's Treatises on Islamic Law* (Louisville, KY: Fons Vitae, 2011).
40. Shah Wali Allah, *Hujjat allah al-baligha* (Cairo: Dar al-turath, 1936), 1:120; 2:150. For an English translation of this work, see Marcia Hermansen, *The Conclusive Argument from God: Shah Wali Allah of Delhi's Hujjat Allah al-Baligha* (Islamabad: Islamic Research Institute, 2003).
41. Shah Wali Allah, *Hujjat allah,* 1:130.
42. Ibid. 1:2. For useful discussions of Shah Wali Allah's thought in the context of eighteenth-century reformist and revivalist trends, see Ahmad Dallal, 'The Origins and Objectives of Islamic Revivalist Thought, 1750-1850', *Journal of the American Oriental Society* 113 (1993): 343–9; Daniel Brown, *Rethinking Tradition in Modern Islamic Thought* (Cambridge: Cambridge University Press, 1996), 22–5.
43. For a detailed study of al-Shawkani's thought, see Bernard Haykel, *Revival and Reform in Islam: The Legacy of Muhammad al-Shawkani* (Cambridge: Cambridge University Press, 2003). For his specific views on the sources of jurisprudence, see Rudolph Peters, 'Ijtihad and Taqlid in 18th and 19th Century Islam', *Die Welt des Islams* 20 (1980): 131–45.
44. Jonathan Brown, *Hadith: Muhammad's Legacy in the Medieval and Modern World* (Oxford: Oneworld, 2009), 253–4; Daniel Brown, *Rethinking Tradition,* 37.
45. Brown, *Hadith,* 254–6.
46. Abu Rayya, *Adwa' 'ala al-sunna al-Muhammadiyya* (Cairo: Dar al-ta'lif, 1958), 151ff.; Brown, *Hadith,* 246–8.
47. Fatima Mernissi, *The Veil and the Male Elite: A Feminist Interpretation of Women's Rights in Islam,* tr. Mary Jo Lakeland (Abingdon: Perseus Books, 1991), 65–81.
48. For the theological school known as the Ash'ariyya, see *EI²,* 1: 696
49. Fazlur Rahman, *Islam and Modernity: Transformation of an Intellectual Tradition* (Chicago: University of Chicago Press, 1982), 26.

50. Ibid. 147.

51. Fazlur Rahman, 'Sunna and Hadith', *Islamic Studies* 1 (1962): 1–4; also his 'Social Change and Early Sunnah', *Islamic Studies* 2 (1963): 206.

52. Abdullah Saeed, 'Fazlur Rahman: a framework for interpreting the ethico-legal content of the Qur'an', in Suha Taji-Farouki (ed.), *Modern Muslim Intellectuals and the Qur'an* (Oxford: Oxford University Press in association with The Institute of Ismaili Studies, London, 2004), 54–8. Cf. Fazlur Rahman, *Islamic Methodology in History* (Karachi, Pakistan: Central Institute of Islamic Research, 1965), 30–1; 44–5.

53. Al-Shafi'i, *Al-Risala fi usul al-fiqh*, ed. Ahmad Muhammad Shakir (Cairo: al-Halabi, 1940), 110.

54. Ahmad b. Hanbal, *Musnad* (Cairo: n. p., 1895), 4:126.

55. Fazlur Rahman, *Islam* (Chicago: University of Chicago Press, 1979), 66.

56. Abou El Fadl, *Great Theft* (New York: HarperOne, 2007), 96.

57. Khaled Abou El Fadl, *Speaking in God's Name: Islamic Law, Authority and Women* (Oxford: Oneworld, 2001), 264.

58. Jamal al-Banna, *al-'Awda ila 'l-qur'an* (Cairo: al-Ittihad al-islami al-duwali li 'l-'amal, 1984), 9ff.

59. Ibid. 18–22.

60. Ibid. 25–31.

61. See our discussion of this verse in Chapter Four.

62. See further Chapter Four of this book.

63. Al-Banna, *'Awda*, 34–45.

64. Ibid. 122–130.

65. It should be noted that similar questions have been raised about stoning for adultery, for example, of which there is no mention in the Qur'an. The punishment is based rather on hadiths found in authoritative collections, which is understood by some to betray biblical influence since the Hebrew Bible does prescribe stoning adulterous couples.

66. Quoted in G. H. A. Juynboll, *The Authenticity of the Tradition Literature: Discussions in Modern Egypt* (Leiden: Brill, 1969), 22–3.

67. For his thought, see the article by Ali Usman Qasmi, 'Towards a New Prophetology: Maulwi 'Abdullah Cakralawi's Ahl al-Qur'an Movement', *The Muslim World* 99 (2009): 155–80.

68. Aisha Musa, *Hadith as Scripture: Discussions on the Authority of Prophetic Traditions in Islam* (New York: Palgrave Macmillan, 2008), 87–105.

69. Jonathan Brown, *The Canonization of al-Bukhari and Muslim: the Formation and Function of Sunni Hadith Canon* (Leiden: Brill, 2011), 191.

70. Ibid. 117.

71. Ibid. 292–7.

72. For the full text of the declaration, see <http://www.islamonline.net/servlet/Satellite?c=Article_C&pagename=Zone-English-News/NWELayout&cid=1203757550116>; last accessed on 1 May 2010.

73. See, for example, the article by Robert Pigott, 'Turkey in radical revision of Islamic texts', published by BBC news, 26 February 2008; available at <http://news.bbc.co.uk/2/hi/7264903.stm>; last accessed on 8 March 2014. For a more sober and accurate assessment, see the article by Tom Heneghan, 'Turkey presents Prophet's sayings for the 21st Century', published by Reuters, 22 May 2013; available at <http://www.reuters.com/article/2013/05/22/turkey-islam-hadiths-idUSL6N0E00KE20130522>; last accessed on 8 March 2014.

CHAPTER 3

Islam and politics

It has become a truism to state that in Islam, religion and politics are inextricably bound together and this feature is one of its distinctive hallmarks. This apparently essential and irreducible feature of Islam is then understood to have prevented Muslims and Muslim-majority societies from successfully adapting to Western-style secular modernity and from partaking of the usual fruits of political and economic progress (as conventionally defined). This is in striking contrast to Western Christendom, which is understood to be unburdened by a fusion between church and state, and as a consequence, provides the ultimate model for an enlightened political culture and socio-economic development.

The above confident master narrative endemic in many Western circles (primarily in the United States and Europe) appears to have sharpened, at least for some, the cultural fault lines assumed to exist indelibly between 'Islam' and 'the West'. This is a scenario made popular by the late academic Samuel Huntington in his provocative 'Clash of Civilizations' thesis. Although Huntington recognised several civilisational blocs at odds with the West, Islam received disproportionate attention and was fingered as representing the most obvious antithesis of the West and the values it is assumed to uniquely hold dear, especially democracy. The thesis is rife with historical inaccuracies and shot through with a dangerous Manichean world-view that pits an assumed monolithic Islamic world against a monolithic West. However, since it had the imprimatur of a prominent political scientist at Harvard University, cultural warriors in the West have willingly embraced it as a blueprint for dealing with the 'regressions' of particularly Arab societies as key representatives within the Islamic world.

The atrocities of September 11th were believed by a considerable number of influential policy-makers during George W. Bush's two presidential terms (2000–08) to have vindicated this thesis and inaugurated a new era of conflict along civilisational lines. Such a belief was notably articulated by Bernard Lewis who, after the Twin Tower attacks, remarked ominously to an interviewer, 'I have no doubt that September 11th was the opening salvo of the final battle [between Islam and the West].'[1] Underlying such intractable views is Lewis's unshaken belief, as later adopted and purveyed by Huntington and like-minded colleagues, that democracy and Islam – always reified in such discourses – are fundamentally incompatible. Islam has more than just an autocratic streak in it, he would have us believe; its foundational texts themselves mandate slavish obedience on the part of its adherents to their rulers, who govern them with divine fiat.[2] Totalising statements of this kind about Islam and Muslims are fairly commonplace in the contemporary American public sphere and even in academia and are infrequently challenged.

The concern with 'Islam's' ability to coexist with democracy has therefore not gone away in the first quarter of the twenty-first century; if anything, the debates concerning this issue have intensified in the last decade. 'Islam and Politics' remains a hotly debated issue, especially in the aftermath of the Arab Spring, and the relation between the two continues to generate lively discussions in the academy and the public sphere.

The politics of a theology of governance

There are a number of people – Muslim and non-Muslim – who attempt to read into the Qur'an a distinctive mandate for the creation of a particular political culture and even a specific form of government. Most notable among them are modern Islamists who claim to derive a wholesale political system based on scripture and who regard its establishment as the most urgent priority of Muslims in the modern period. Interestingly, a number of Orientalist scholars would support their assumption that there is a distinctive political theology within Islam and that the Qur'an itself imposes upon Muslims a religious, charismatic mode of leadership. Official Sunni histories that project a different, more mundane image and role for the ruler of the Muslim polity are assumed by such scholars to deliberately obfuscate early political trends and subvert the Qur'anic ideal of legitimate leadership. Among the more recent Orientalists who have argued in favour of this position has been Wilferd Madelung. In his 1998 book *Succession to Muhammad: A Study of the Early Caliphate*,[3] Madelung affirms that the Shi'i conception of dynastic charismatic leadership restricted to the descendants of the Prophet Muhammad is the original and authentically scripture-based model of governance decreed for Muslims. He comes to this conclusion partly on the basis of a particularist reading of several verses in the Qur'an which speak highly of the *ahl al-bayt* – the members of the Prophet's household. Even though these verses contain no explicit mention of who exactly these members are (hence their contested interpretations in the exegetical literature) and prima facie have nothing to do with the issue of succession to Muhammad, Madelung discerns a scriptural prescription in them in favour of hereditary leadership for the blood relatives of the Prophet.

Other Orientalists have regarded the caliph/imam as similarly shrouded in a religious aura and projected this construction back to the earliest period of Islam as an authentic depiction of the way things must have been then.[4] From this perspective, the official histories had to be wrong and guilty of deliberately covering up the true state of affairs. The strong conspiratorial tone to these revisionist narratives is unmistakable and on that account have garnered quite a bit of attention and criticism.

Remarkably, modern hard-line Islamist views on the nature of 'Islamic Government' and the all-important 'Islamic State' are not that far from these determinist Orientalist positions. Islamists typically claim that their notion of 'divine sovereignty' (al-hakimiyya) is derived from the Qur'an itself and that this concept imposes upon Muslims the obligation to set up a 'theo-democracy' as the most authentic realisation of Islamic administrative principles. Like some of the Orientalists, they too project this political arrangement back to the foundational period of Islam and reject the idea that government in any Islamic milieu might be purely concerned with worldly and pragmatic notions of statecraft and have nothing to do with an assumed divine mandate. Once again, religion and state are assumed to be fused together and both conjoined spheres are therefore governed by immutable scriptural directives.

Like most truisms, this particular one concerning the religious provenance of mandatory governance within Islam – whether it emanates from Orientalists or the Islamists – bears little resemblance to the historical reality that may be reconstructed based on what the extant sources have to say about the earliest Islamic period. Our earliest document is the Qur'an itself, which contains no reference to the issue of prophetic succession nor does it contain explicitly political terms. This, however, has not prevented later Muslims from reading political meanings back into specific Qur'anic terms, such as *amr*, *khalifa*, and *hukm*. Our extended discussion in Chapter Two of the phrase *uli 'l-amr* as it occurs in Qur'an 4:59 illustrated how we can trace this process of transformation through a close, diachronic study of Qur'an commentaries, among other sources. Similar transformations occurred in relation to the terms *khalifa* and *hukm*, so that their apolitical significations in the Qur'an became transmuted into primarily political ones by the third century of Islam (ninth century of the Common Era).[5]

The desirability of good governance and the necessity of establishing some form of government or another is both an old and new issue within Islamic thought. Various idealised and contested conceptualisations of the institution of the caliphate (also referred to as the 'imamate') exist in medieval sources. Classical Sunni, Shi'i and Khariji views differ dramatically on the requirements and parameters of the office. Some, especially Mu'tazili, thinkers were of the opinion that the whole office could be dispensed with; the righteous Muslim society is after all capable of self-governance, equipped as it is with the necessary moral and ethical directives through revelation.[6]

However, after the first three centuries of Islam, the majority of Muslim political thinkers (but not all) came to endorse the caliphate as a necessary, even divinely mandated institution that legitimately governed the properly constituted Islamic polity. The Sunnis would stress historical precedent and pragmatism to establish this claim while the Shi'a emphasised the notion of *nass* – prophetic designation of a successor who constituted the legitimate imam, and who in turn would designate his legitimate successor. For the majority of the Shi'a (Ithna 'Ashari or Twelver), this imamic line was terminated in 941CE with the occultation of the twelfth legitimate Imam, who will return as a messianic figure at the end of time. Ayatollah Khomeini's 'guardianship of the jurist' (*velayet-i faqih*) in the twentieth century marks a radical and pragmatic departure from this classical Shi'i theory of governance.[7] For Sunnis, the caliphate ended only in 1924 at the hands of the Republican Turks, a cataclysmic event whose repercussions are still with us today. Today's hard-line Sunni Islamists have taken it upon themselves to revive this historical caliphate in some form or another, which they recognise as the only legitimate form of government for Muslims. It should be noted that this has not prevented more centrist Islamists from embracing modern democratic procedures for instituting legitimate governments that would uphold Islamic principles, as they choose to define them, in contrast to the hardliners who eschew the ballot box as an illegitimate and foreign procedure for establishing the desired Islamic State.[8]

In the contemporary period, there is therefore a mélange of perspectives and discourses on what constitutes good governance and what institution(s) are required to implement it in Muslim-majority societies. On one point, however, it appears that a majoritarian consensus is crystallising in the contemporary period. Large-scale surveys and polls conducted in Muslim-majority societies, such as the one conducted by the Pew Research Center's Global Attitudes Project in 2012,[9] repeatedly affirm that a majority of Muslims want democratic governments in their countries which may be deemed to be consistent inter alia with Islamic principles of *shura* (consultation) and *bay'a* (the offering of allegiance by the people to legitimate political authority). The heated debates concerning the necessity of the caliphate in the first half of the twentieth century have become somewhat of a dim memory for the average Muslim. Yet it is these very debates that encapsulate for us what is at stake for Muslims in the modern world when they argue noisily among themselves about proper governance and its compatibility with the Sharia. The ascent of Islamist parties to political prominence in the aftermath of the Arab Spring in Tunisia and Egypt (and as of the writing of this book, the fall of the Muslim Brotherhood in Egypt in a military coup) has once again made these debates urgently relevant to the contemporary Arab and Muslim world. We now therefore turn to one key thinker and his provocative *oeuvre* in the first quarter of the twentieth century that reopened this particular 'can of worms', the dust from which (to deliberately mix metaphors) has still not fully settled in our own time.

Theorising about politics and the state in the modern period

In the aftermath of the dissolution of the caliphate in 1924 by the Republican Turks, an Azhar-trained Egyptian religious scholar 'Ali 'Abd al-Raziq (d. 1966)[10] wrote a work which questioned the mandatory nature of the office of the caliph. The work titled *al-Islam wa-usul al-hukm* (Islam and the principles of governance) was published in 1925 and exploded like a bombshell in the Islamic world, adding (as must have appeared to many) insult to injury. The book essentially argued that the caliphate was not a religiously mandated institution and that Muslims are under no obligation to establish or re-establish this office. Published against the backdrop of widespread dismay ensuing from the peremptory end to the Ottoman caliphate, 'Abd al-Raziq's work created a firestorm of controversy. Some of his detractors regarded it as an attack upon Islam itself through the author's attempts to devalue a long-standing institution within historical Islam.[11] While 'Abd al-Raziq's views have received some scholarly mention in the context of Islamic modernism, the counter-arguments of his critics have not received similar attention. A detailed understanding of both 'Abd al-Raziq's and his critics' perspectives is, however, essential for reconstructing an important religious–intellectual debate about leadership and Muslim communal identity in the early twentieth century. These early modern debates about the assumed religious necessity for institutionalising political authority continue to exert considerable influence on contemporary Muslim discourses about the parameters of legitimate governance and the construction of political authority. They are thus deserving of renewed attention.

Our discussion below begins with the salient features of 'Abd al-Raziq's treatise and then proceeds to present the refutations of two of his trenchant critics – the Egyptian scholar Muhammad Bakhit al-Muti'i (d. 1935), who was the Grand Mufti of Egypt at the time, and the Tunisian scholar Muhammad al-Khidr Husayn (d. 1958), who became the Shaykh al-Azhar in 1952.[12] A detailed analysis of the doctrinal and legal arguments crafted by these authors to argue their respective positions concerning the caliphate will allow us to dwell on the larger ramifications of this critical debate on the subject of organising and governing Muslim-majority societies which continues until today.

Views of 'Abd al-Raziq

'Abd al-Raziq begins his controversial treatise by discussing the etymology of the word *al-khilafa* and its meanings. He refers to the explanation of the eleventh century scholar al-Raghib al-Isfahani (d. c.1060) who concluded that *khilafa*, like its synonym, *imama*, signified leadership (*riyasa*) concerning matters of religion and the world as a deputy of (*al-niyaba 'an*) the Prophet Muhammad.[13] He further references the views of the Qur'an commentator Nasir al-Din al-Baydawi (d. c.1286) who defined *imama* as a position held by 'an individual serving as a successor to the Messenger, peace and blessings be upon him, in establishing the religious law and in preserving the territory of the Muslims, so that it becomes incumbent on the Muslim community to follow him'.[14] 'Abd al-Raziq also notes Ibn Khaldun's (d. 1406) opinion that the caliph represented the Prophet in 'safeguarding religion and the administration of the world, according to the principles of the Sharia'.[15]

According to such prevalent views, the caliph by virtue of his office is therefore understood to succeed the Prophet who received the revealed religion from God and proceeded to implement and defend its precepts, just as he was entrusted with the proclamation of the faith and summoning people to it. In emulation of this prophetic example, the caliph is concerned with both religious and worldly, political matters.[16] The Arabic term *khalifa* by itself – or in the longer collocation *Khalifat Rasul Allah* – points to his role as Muhammad's representative to the Muslim community. The variant title – *Khalifat Allah* – is controversial and deemed permissible by some but not by others. Abu Bakr is known to have repudiated this designation, continues 'Abd al-Raziq. The caliph's other common appellation – imam – indicates that his position is equivalent to that of a prayer leader.[17] According to this conceptualisation, the caliph is owed complete obedience (*ta'a tamma*) by the Muslim community and he exercises broad powers (*al-sultan al-shamil*), including the carrying out of the *hudud* punishments and other requirements of the law. In return, Muslims are required to love and revere him as the deputy of the Prophet who safeguards their religion, since, our author comments, 'religion (*al-din*) is the most precious to Muslims of what they know in this world.'[18]

According to this traditional depiction of the office of the caliph, which requires Muslims to obey their leader in all matters, 'disobeying the imams is tantamount to disobeying God.' Giving good counsel to the imam (*nash al-imam*) and obedience to him is regarded as a religious obligation (*fard wajib*), so much so that one's faith and submission to God are only perfected through him. The imam is 'God's Protection' (*hima allah*) in his realm, and 'His shadow' covering his subjects. All other forms of worldly authority derive from his authority and he shares his authority with none.[19] This conceptualisation of the caliphate, notes our author, proceeds from the assumption that the caliph always holds himself accountable to the restrictions imposed on his authority by the law and never oversteps these bounds and that there is only one uniform and unambiguous way to govern. It is also assumed that the pedigree of this mode of governing goes back to the time of the Prophet who had painstakingly explained its details, and which mode is defined by the Qur'an, the sunna, and the consensus of the Muslims.[20]

While in general scholars had a dim view of rebellion against a legitimately appointed ruler, 'Abd al-Raziq acknowledges that there were those who were of the opinion that if the caliph was unjust or tyrannical, he could be removed from office. On this account, they made a distinction between the caliphate and kingship (al-mulk), as Ibn Khaldun had discussed. Kingship was deemed to be of two types, according to Ibn Khaldun: 'Natural kingship' (al-mulk al-tabi'i) which arises for the achievement of worldly desires and ambition; and political kingship (al-mulk al-siyasi) which is constituted for rational reasons so as to attain worldly benefit and ward off harm. The caliphate, however, is constituted for religious considerations. According to this criterion, Ibn Khaldun considered the ideal caliphate to have existed only during the time of the Rightly-Guided Caliphs.[21]

After the period of the Rightly-Guided Caliphs began the era of kingship, during which tribal solidarity ('asabiyya) and the sword became dominant, and only in the pursuit of religion and truth could the vestiges of the legacy of the ideal caliphate be discerned. This was the situation during the Umayyad period and the first part of the 'Abbasid period. After the time of 'Abd al-Malik, the caliphate existed only in name and there was mere kingship, characterised by political ambition and struggle for domination and control. The caliphate in fact became indistinguishable from kingship as it existed in Persia and the East.[22]

There are, however, two schools of thought regarding the caliph's source of authority during the medieval period. One maintains that the caliph derived his authority (sultan) and power (quwwa) from God's authority and power – and this is a position held by most scholars and the general run of Muslims.[23] The other (by default minority) school subscribes to the view that the caliph derives his authority from the community of Muslims and is selected by them for his office.[24] 'Abd al-Raziq implies, but does not state explicitly, that the first majoritarian position reinforces the notion of the caliphate as equivalent to absolute kingship with religious roots.

Apostleship vs political mission

Arguably the most critical question for 'Abd al-Raziq is, as he phrases it: 'Was Muhammad, peace and blessings be upon him, one of those for whom God combined apostleship (al-risala) and politics (al-hukm), or was he only an apostle and not king (malik)?'[25] He notes such a question had not previously been for-mulated so explicitly and therefore no unambiguous answer to this question exists. Nevertheless, it is possible to state that the average Muslim more or less inclines to the view that Muhammad was both an apostle and a king, since he had founded a political civil state in Medina for the sake of Islam which he ruled as its king and head of state. This is a view, 'Abd al-Raziq speculates, that is also prevalent among the majority of Muslim scholars who regard Islam as a trope for political unity (wahda siyasiyya), emanating from the state founded in Medina by Muhammad.[26] Once again, 'Abd al-Raziq references the views of Ibn Khaldun who had stated that the term khilafa, indicating the conjoining of religious and worldly duties, encompassed kingship or political rule (al-mulk).[27]

'Abd al-Raziq next proceeds to critique these prevalent assumptions about early modes of governance among Muslims, a summary of which follows. He concedes that there were elements of political governance and aspects of kingship apparent in 'the Prophet's government', especially when he carried out the military jihad against his adversaries. But it is clear that these military campaigns were carried out to protect Islam and expand the political realm of Islam and not for the purpose of propagating Islam or to coerce people into believing in God and His messenger. The propagation of religion (da'wat al-din) is a summons to God; such an activity, whose purpose is the guidance of hearts and purification of beliefs, can only be accomplished through persuasive speech and appeals to the heart and human emotion – not through force and coercion. During the time of Muhammad, no one is known to have embraced Islam at the tip of the sword and no military campaign was carried out to forcibly convert people to Islam. This is after all in conformity with Qur'an 2:256 which asserts that there is no compulsion in religion and Qur'an 16:125, which proclaims 'Summon to the path of your Lord with wisdom and beautiful counsel, and engage their arguments with what is better.' Other verses underscore Muhammad's primary role as a 'warner' (mudhakkir, compare with Qur'an 88:21) and his primary obligation to convey the divine message (compare with Qur'an 3:20).[28]

In the course of administering the Medinan polity, the Prophet also had to deal with financial affairs pertaining to the state treasury and the collection of taxes and revenues. Furthermore, he had to appoint governors and other officials to administer other regions, such as the Yemen, Najran and others. All of these may be regarded as features of a formal state and government.[29] The key question that our author next proceeds to pose in this context is: Was Muhammad's establishment of the Medinan polity part of his prophetic mission or extraneous to it? Our author's response is: even though the view that the Prophet's political actions were separate from his prophetic role as summoner to Islam is not an accepted position, it is a view worthy of serious consideration, the expression of which does not constitute unbelief (kufr) nor blasphemy (ilhad). No historical authority had maintained that apostleship required a political dimension except for Ibn Khaldun, who had deemed this to be the singular characteristic of Islam.[30]

This latter Khaldunian position, according to 'Abd al-Raziq, is untenable, for it 'negates the meaning of prophethood'.[31] Furthermore, if the Prophet had intended to legislate concerning the founding of a political state, why had he not issued detailed instructions concerning the appointment of judges and governors or discussed the specifics of a political system or explained the rules of consultative decision-making (qawa'id al-shura)? Why, he asks in exasperation, would the Prophet have refrained from explaining such critical details if part of his mission was to found a political system?[32] The hadith transmitters after him have also failed to convey to us such details. If they had indeed transmitted such information, it is no longer available to us.[33] It is more reasonable to conclude, continues our author, that such matters are deliberately concealed from us for our benefit and it is the responsibility of scholars to undertake the task of pursuing these matters through scholarly inquiry rather than through transmitted reports. 'In that,' he says, 'is the life of knowledge and its growth.' [34]

In fact, many of the political conventions and terminologies that arose over time are accidental and not essential in the formation of what many tend to regard as 'pristine government' (hukumat al-fitra), our author continues.[35] The application of some of these political conventions in the contemporary period would constitute a hardship for Muslims, and the Prophet had always advised against assuming unnecessary burdens and counselled adopting the easier path.[36] Some of the actions he took that were of a political nature were tied specifically to his apostleship and not meant to be emulated by ordinary mortals. [37] This is borne out by a number of verses in the Qur'an which assert that Muhammad was not sent as a guardian (hafiz or wakil) over the people (Qur'an 4:80; 6:107; 42:6, and so on) and that he had not been sent as a mighty ruler (jabbar; compare with Qur'an 50:45) nor to exert control over people (musaytir; Qur'an 88:22). If one is not any one of the above types, then one is not a king, says 'Abd al-Raziq, since control and political might are among the prerogatives of the king.[38]

The Qur'an furthermore attests profusely that Muhammad was no more than a warner (nadhir) and a messenger (rasul).[39] Similarly in various hadiths, the Prophet affirmed that 'I am neither a king nor a tyrant' (lastu bi-malik wa-la jabbar) and explicitly repudiated the role of a prophet–king for himself.[40]

Positing religious unity (wahda diniyya) is one thing – and acceptable – continues our author, but political unity (wahda siyasiyya) is another and 'has nothing to do with the will of God'. In the realm of politics, humans have been given free rein to act according to their rational dictates, their knowledge and their benefit. This position is borne out in Qur'an 5:48, for example, which indicates that God had deliberately not fashioned 'a single community' (umma wahida) out of all humanity.[41] All of these proof-texts should suffice to show that Muhammad's authority was solely derived from his apostleship and was untainted by any connection to politics.[42]

With regard to the title Khalifat Rasul Allah adopted by Abu Bakr, 'Abd al-Raziq says we cannot be sure of the reasons for his adoption of this specific title. According to the sources, he approved of it and used it in his correspondence with others. As Muhammad's successor, Abu Bakr was assuming the administrative and political functions of the former only. There are those, however, who have conflated this title with Khalifat Allah, even though Abu Bakr is on record as having expressed displeasure at this designation.[43]

Different perceptions of Abu Bakr's authority emerge in variant interpretations of the ridda wars. Those who subscribe to a religious conception of the caliphate view the ridda wars as a consequence of the renunciation of Islam by the rebel tribes, while those who view the caliphate as strictly a political office understand the *ridda* wars to be a manifestation of purely political rebellion by those who remained Muslims. In the latter case, fighting these rebels constituted an attempt by Abu Bakr to shore up the fledgling Medinan government and maintain the political unity of the polity. Malik b. Nuwayra, one of the rebels, is on record as having told Khalid b. al-Walid that he remained a Muslim but refused to pay *zakat* to Abu Bakr's government. The so-called *ridda* wars then were not fought 'regarding the fundamentals of religion nor regarding tenets of faith'.[44] However, the predominant view became that the *ridda* wars were religious in nature. The caliphate thereby acquired religious trappings so that it was deemed to be the equivalent of the Prophet's deputyship, to the extent that disobedience to the caliph was understood to constitute disobedience to God.[45]

'Abd al-Raziq concludes by asserting that despite these historical trends, the truth of the matter is that the office of the caliph is extraneous to Islam and all the functions pertaining to it are strictly political and have no religious purpose. Administrative matters – establishing cities, running the treasury and the military, and so on – are purely temporal which emanate from pragmatic concerns and are decided through rational deliberation. There is nothing therefore preventing Muslims from turning their back on the past and inaugurating new ways of governance in accordance with the dictates of reason and human experience.[46]

A critique of al-Islam wa-'l-Hukm: *the* Haqiqat al-Islam wa usul al-hukm *by Muhammad Bakhit al-Mutiʿi*

Al-Mutiʿi begins his treatise, published in 1926, by engaging 'Abd al-Raziq's discussion of the etymology of *khilafa* and concludes, that according to the majority of Muslims, the *khalifa* is one who acts as the Prophet's deputy so that 'he assumes his place in preserving the good reputation of Islam, the implementation of [its] laws and the governance of the Muslim polity, according to the requirements of the law of the Prophet, peace and blessings be upon him'.[47] The term *khalifa* may be understood to refer specifically to the one who succeeded Muhammad as leader after his death or, more generally, to the one who succeeds his immediate predecessor as leader. In the first sense, only Abu Bakr was the successor of the Prophet. The rights of the caliph, according to the majority of Muslims, are founded upon the fact that 'God has ordained for us obedience to him' and prohibited disobedience, continues al-Mutiʿi. Furthermore, the caliph is bound by administrative rules (*bi-'l-qawanin al-siyasiyya*) based upon the religious law and the rules promulgated by the Prophet. The caliph derives his authority from the Muslim community, which in turn is delegated to the 'people of loosening and joining' (*ahl al-hall wa al-ʿaqd*). The caliph does not derive his legitimacy from God except for the fact that everything ultimately emanates from and returns to God.[48]

Al-Muti'i notes that 'Abd al-Raziq accepts the comparison between *khilafa* and 'natural rule' (*al-mulk al-tabi'i*), following Ibn Khaldun's taxonomy, but then errs by severing 'political governance' (*al-mulk al-siyasi*) from the caliphate. Rather, al-Muti'i proceeds to say, the caliphate is to be regarded as a specific type of 'political governance', since the latter rubric includes intellectual and legal forms of administration.[49] He takes strong exception to 'Abd al-Raziq's assertion that the precise nature of the early caliphate and the reasons for setting up the caliphate are not clearly known to us. Not so, he says, because according to the information recorded in various sources, well known among all scholars, the office of the caliph is consequentially related to prophecy (*al-nubuwwa*) and is established for the 'protection of religion and administration of worldly affairs' (*fi hirasat al-din wa siyasat al-dunya*). The caliphate represents a pact (*'aqd*) concluded between the holder of the office and the 'the people of loosening and joining' on behalf of the Muslim community, whereby the caliph undertakes the task of protecting their religion and administering their affairs in accordance with the relevant prescriptions in the Qur'an and sunna or with what is authoritatively extrapolated from them based on consensus (*ijma'*) and 'correct analogical reasoning' (*qiyas sahih*). Should someone install himself as an imam by force and against the popular will, such an individual may be recognised as the leader if Muslims acquiesce in his appointment, out of fear of causing civil discord and bloodshed, as long as they are not compelled to disobey their religious laws (*fi ghayr ma'siya*).[50]

Al-Muti'i stresses that the imam derives his authority solely from the 'people of loosening and joining' who stand in for the Muslim community, which empowers him to appoint his governors, judges, agents and others, who in turn derive their legitimacy from their association with him. After the death of the Prophet, the Muslims gave their allegiance to Abu Bakr, thereby establishing normatively for the first time 'that it is the Muslim community that is the source of all authority'. It is the community that chooses its ruler, in accordance with what has been prescribed by Islam and its laws. When a ruler imposes himself by force upon the community, he is in violation of these laws that determine the proper method of electing an imam. Even if such a tyrant (*ja'ir*) is eventually accepted by the community, he is merely 'a leader out-of-necessity' (*imam darura*), states al-Muti'i, whose position is not sanctioned by the laws of Islam and is attributable only to the weakness of the community. Such a situation represents a grave infraction of the commandments of God and is to be regarded as reprehensible and unjust.[51] The Umayyads were such tyrannical usurpers under whom the caliphate became transformed into 'kingship' (*al-mulk*). A proper caliphate would be governed by religious principles and would protect the rights of the people, in which case it is a noble and mighty office and represents a great blessing from God.[52]

Not surprisingly, it is 'Abd al-Raziq's assertion that Muhammad was primarily the Messenger of God, not a king, and that the Qur'an, the sunna, and the overall gestalt of Islam (*tabi'at al-islam*) undermine the notion that he was a political ruler (*hakim*) that irks al-Muti'i. He proceeds to refute this assertion in the following manner.[53]

First of all, he says, the author of *al-Islam wa usul al-hukm* is denying what 'Muslims have categorically affirmed': that Islam is a divine revelation with both missionary and practical dimensions. Religious and political authority is combined in Islam, a feature that does not occur in any other religion. In contrast to what 'Abd al-Raziq states, al-Muti'i affirms that the Qur'an and the sunna both provide detailed practical and procedural directives concerning matters of religion and state, which the Prophet and the Muslim community implemented, particularly through exhorting the faithful to follow the revealed law and in undertaking jihad. Does not the Qur'an (59:7) warn after all: 'Whatever the Messenger has brought to you, adhere to it and desist from whatever he has forbidden?' All religions are predicated on belief in God and His messengers, says al-Muti'i, and all religious laws are founded on five universal principles (*al-kulliyat al-khams*) – the preservation of life, intellect, property, lineage and honour. Each religion has its own set of laws which uphold these principles, as indicated in Qur'an (42:13): 'Prescribed for you of religion is what we prescribed for Noah.' Islam, he continues, has based itself upon the pursuit of political power and earthly rule in order to promulgate its own divinely revealed laws in repudiation of all other laws which contradict it.[54]

Al-Muti'i finds untenable the following conclusions reached by 'Abd al-Raziq: that Muhammad's main function as a prophet was the delivery of the divine message (*al-risala*) that he was entrusted with, and not the assumption of political office (*hukm*); that he was sent to establish religion, not a state (*din la dawla*), and that he was an apostle, not a king. If by the latter assertion 'Abd al-Raziq meant that the Prophet was not called 'king', that would indeed be correct – such a nomenclature would be objectionable because, first, it usually indicates tyrannical rule when applied to humans, and second, as a definite noun (*al-malik*), the term is reserved only for God in the Qur'an. It would, however, be wrong to claim that the king's authority was not subsumed in Muhammad's prophethood. Moreover, the Qur'an (4:105) after all says, 'Indeed we have revealed to you the Book in truth so that you may judge (*li-tahkuma*)[55] among the people according to what God has shown you.' Such proof-texts indicate that there must be a government for the Muslim community – who then, asks al-Muti'i, was the head of this government, if not the Prophet?[56]

Al-Muti'i is similarly scandalised by 'Abd al-Raziq's statement that the very nature of Islam (*tabi'at al-islam*) militates against such a politicised understanding of its mission, which is fundamentally one of propagation of the faith (*da'wa*). So outrageous is this assertion, declares our author, that the mind reels at it and one feels overpowered by astonishment. Does not one encounter verses in the

Qur'an which exhort the faithful to strive to 'raise the word of truth and religion', which are then understood to decree that Muslims should struggle to strengthen Islam, contain dissension and spread their rule over others, even to the point of fighting when others resist? Muslims must not succumb to the rule of others; this message is further bolstered through relevant hadith and the prophetic *sira* and is not doubted by anyone who is a true believer, asserts al-Muti'i.[57]

Second critique: the Naqd kitab al-Islam wa usul al-hukm *by Muhammad al-Khidr Husayn*

Husayn, like al-Muti'i, is also concerned with attempting to debunk 'Abd al-Raziq's assertion that Muhammad is to be regarded primarily as a prophet/apostle and not a 'political ruler/king'. However, he is less scandalised by this assertion than al-Muti'i for he goes on to comment that to state this against the consensus of scholars through time is not an act of innovation (*bid'a*) or an aberration (*shudhudh*), since this statement has nothing to with matters of doctrine but is rather a matter of intellectual inquiry into the religious sciences. Husayn begins by criticising 'Abd al-Raziq's use of the term *malik*, which he says Muslims are not accustomed to applying to their prophet and that he would proceed to isolate the significations of this term that are in accordance with prophethood and those that are not, as follows.[58]

Husayn defines *mulk* as the rule/sovereignty exercised by one who commands and prohibits matters pertaining to his subjects and who implements laws. If such a ruler behaves in accordance with the dictates of justice and the general well-being of his people, then his reign is to be praised and deemed honourable. This is the kind of rulership granted by God to His prophets, as is indicated in Qur'an 38:35, in which Solomon asks God to 'grant me power/kingdom [*mulkan*] which no one else after me will enjoy', and in Qur'an 12:21, in which Joseph expresses gratitude to God for having granted him 'political power' and the interpretation of speech. (It is noteworthy that Qur'an 12:21 actually states: 'We had likewise strengthened/firmly established Joseph on earth' [*wa-kadhalika makkanna li-yusuf fi 'l-ard*]; Husayn clearly understands this act of 'strengthening' to be political in nature). If such a ruler's conduct is based on caprice and wilfulness leading to tyranny and misery, continues Husayn, then such a type of political rule is objectionable and has nothing to do with the prophets and is completely divorced from apostleship. All the prophets initiated 'just political administration' (*al-siyasa al-'adila*), and this is the only kind of political rule that is intended when one states that the Prophet Muhammad 'held fast to the reins of power'. Despite this aspect of apostleship, people have refrained from calling prophets 'kings' or 'rulers' because the term 'apostle' or 'prophet' is far nobler and indicative of just behaviour than the term 'king' which is applied equally to the just or unjust ruler.[59]

'Abd al-Raziq's attempts to dissociate political rule from apostleship represent an unprecedented departure from what the Qur'an, the continuously transmitted sunna, and Muslims in general and the scholars in particular have affirmed, declares Husayn. The last group has categorically affirmed that Muhammad was a 'messenger, a prophet and a political legislator (*mushri'an siyasiyyan*)' and unanimously agreed that the sum total of his legal decisions and adjudications in matters pertaining to the state constitute irrefutable proof of his political role. In the face of this insurmountable evidence, 'Abd al-Raziq's casual dismissal of Muhammad's role as prophet–king does in fact constitute 'lies' (*uftiyat*) against Islam.[60] Whoever espouses the point of view that the Prophet was not a political administrator 'has flung the Book of God behind his back, wrangled with the Messenger, and followed what is not the path of believers', he asserts.[61]

Husayn criticises 'Abd al-Raziq's citation of several Qur'an verses to support his contention that Muhammad was primarily a warner and summoner to Islam and that the Qur'anic injunction 'There is no compulsion in religion' prevents his apostleship from being understood as more than the peaceful propagation of faith. Husayn counters by saying that the military jihad carried out by the Prophet was in fact part of summoning to Islam 'through wisdom and good counsel', as commanded in Qur'an 16:125. The sword may not transform the hearts of unbelievers but it can guide people into leading orderly lives in societies organised by revealed laws, as happened with the idol-worshippers. From this perspective 'Abd al-Raziq skews the Qur'anic evidence by citing only those verses that were revealed in the Meccan period, says Husayn, before fighting became permissible.[62]

Husayn goes on to state that among the fundamental objectives of Islam is the foundation of a state, not for the sake of attaining worldly power and for the enjoyment of this life, but for two primary purposes: (1) the implementation of the just legal system of Islam in order to ensure the good life, which only the individual who believes in its wisdom and has imbibed its spirit can undertake; and (2) to protect the honour and dignity of Muslims so that they are not ruled by those who would trample on their rights and demean them. He points, not surprisingly, to Qur'an 4:59 ('O those who believe, obey God and the Messenger and those who possess authority [*uli 'l-amr*] among you'), and Qur'an 9:8 ('How [can there be a treaty with the polytheists] when, if they gain power over you, do not observe in regard to you any pact of kinship or covenant of protection') as proof-texts from which these objectives may be inferred. Denying that Muhammad had exercised political authority and that such authority proceeded from 'the essence of religion' (*jawhar al-din*) and had nothing to do with apostleship further contradicts what we know from the biography of the Prophet. His military campaigns, his collection and distribution of the obligatory alms and other forms of revenue – in other words all his administrative functions – were guided by divine revelation and were therefore an inalienable part of his prophetic mission.[63] To deny this causes one to 'stumble into the morass of heresy' (al-wuqu' ila hama' al-ilhad).[64]

'Abd al-Raziq is furthermore wrong, continues Husayn, in maintaining that the Sharia and the prophetic sunna do not provide directives for political conduct and administration, for such directives may be rationally inferred from broad religious precepts. One example of such a seminal directive is the principle of consultative decision-making, which is easily traceable to the Qur'anic pronouncement (42:38): 'Their matters are decided by consultation (shura) among them.' The verse clearly intended to put an end to tyranny (al-istibdad) and provides the imperative for rulers to confer with 'those who loosen and join' when making decisions. At the same time the principle of shura in Qur'an 42:38 allows these learned decision-makers to resort to their own reasoning in the actual deliberation of political matters and in making their views known regarding the best course of action for the community, whether it be through 'secret or open vote, by writing, raising the hand or standing'.[65]

Similarly with regard to the appointment of judges and governors, the Sharia adumbrates broad principles of justice and mandates the protection of people's rights but leaves specific legislative activity to the discretion of the jurist who uses his intelligence and independent reasoning to judge cases, according to the specificities of sociohistorical circumstances and consideration of the common good.[66] Husayn concludes by criticising 'Abd al-Raziq for what appears to him the latter's deficient knowledge of particularly the sunna of the Prophet and expertise in the traditional hadith sciences. What else may one expect from someone who belongs to 'the category of those people who transmit hadiths from the Kamil of al-Mubarrad?' he asks derisively.[67] People of this ilk cannot be deemed scholars of the Sharia 'even though they place turbans on their heads' and offer legal judgements.[68]

Analysing the hermeneutics of prophethood and political authority

'Abd al-Raziq and his critics all claim to be basing their respective arguments firmly on the foundational texts of Islam –the Qur'an and hadith – and particularly in the case of his critics, on the classical Islamic theological and legal tradition. While their sources overlap, their approach to the relevant texts and their interpretive strategies are often quite different. An analysis of these different reading strategies is highly revealing of the process of constructing competing views of the past, especially as they relate to conceptions of prophethood and political governance, as becomes evident below.

'Abd al-Raziq's treatise is fundamentally concerned with the deconstruction of the classical views of the imamate that had emerged roughly after the tenth century. As mentioned above, the key question for him is whether the establishment of the Medinan polity is to be regarded as an integral part of Muhammad's prophetic mission or as an extraneous, contingent development that occurred in response to specific historical developments. 'Abd al-Raziq mounts his critique of the standard juridical and theological position that the Prophet was both prophet and head of state (or 'king' as he phrases it) and that the latter position was a natural consequence of the former by assessing its congruity with primarily the Qur'an and, to a lesser extent, with the hadith literature. If these dual roles are scripturally mandated, where are the evidentiary texts, he asks? Instead, he argues, the Qur'an emphasises Muhammad's role as a warner (*nadhir, mudhakkir*) and a messenger (*rasul*) and categorically disavows any role for the Prophet as a guardian over the people (*hafiz* or *wakil*) or a powerful ruler (*jabbar*) who seeks to impose his rule over the people. A king (or head of state) in the usual sense must possess all these attributes; the Qur'an's disavowal of them in relation to Muhammad unambiguously establishes the apolitical nature of his apostleship. This unambiguous nature is further established through the invocation of relevant hadiths in which the Prophet denies the ascription of kingship and political power to himself.

Aspects of Muhammad's roles in Medina that do appear overtly political are, according to 'Abd al-Raziq, either accidental and completely divorced from his apostleship or are tied exclusively to his mission and not meant to be replicated by ordinary Muslims after him. These included his activities of revenue collection, the appointment of governors and judges, and the carrying out of the military jihad; the latter in particular had to do only with defence of the Medinan polity and had no religious function, especially in the activity of summoning to Islam. If any of these activities were religiously mandated as opposed to being pragmatic responses to specific time-bound circumstances, the Prophet would have left detailed instructions concerning their implementation, in addition to having endorsed a specific political system, maintains 'Abd al-Raziq. In the absence of such directives, one must logically assume that none of these political and worldly matters have theological implications and are not religiously binding on Muslims; to assert this consequently is not an act of heresy.

Classical jurists nevertheless went on to articulate the contrary position –that specific political institutions, particularly the caliphate, and certain political processes were religiously binding upon Muslims in order to unite them politically. 'Abd al-Raziq's rejoinder to such arguments is that the juridical desideratum of political unity (*wahda siyasiyya*) is actually contrary to God's will, since it is clearly articulated in the Qur'an that He had deliberately refrained from creating a single human community (Qur'an 5:48). The juridical consensus on such political matters is therefore merely the result of rational and pragmatic responses to specific events during the medieval period that threatened to and indeed did fracture the Muslim community. Recognition of the historically circumscribed nature of such a consensus leaves the door wide open for a new consensus to emerge among Muslims through similar rational processes of deliberation regarding modes of governance that are appropriate to their changed circumstances in the modern period. Islam desires ease for its followers – replication of antiquated social and political processes would constitute hardship for contemporary Muslims and the imposition of such a hardship would therefore violate the spirit of the Qur'an. In 'Abd al-Raziq's hermeneutics, the point of departure is without doubt the Qur'anic text above all, which should be understood on its own terms. The resulting understanding of the scriptural text unmediated by later human exegeses should serve as a corrective to the ultimately human, fallible and contingent interpretations of the jurists and theologians through time.

The counter-arguments of al-Muti'i and Husayn show, not unexpectedly, a great deal of convergence. Both are after all essentially in agreement that it is the classical theological and juridical tradition that emerged after the third century of Islam which establishes the correct and comprehensive paradigm for instituting political processes and institutions. It is from this vantage point that they then proceed to interpret what they understand to be relevant proof-texts culled from the Qur'an and hadith. Thus, al-Muti'i invokes Qur'an 4:105 ('Indeed we have revealed to you the Book in truth so that you may judge among the people according to what God has shown you') as creating a scriptural mandate for conjoining political office to prophethood and to establish the imperative for continuing such political office after the demise of Muhammad. As is to be expected in such a context, the Arabic verbal collocation – *li-tahkuma* – occurring in the verse is understood by al-Muti'i to unambiguously refer to 'rule' in the political sense rather than to 'judge' in the broadest and most basic sense. This politicised understanding is connected to Muti'i's conviction that the obligation to summon to Islam (*da'wa*) must be fulfilled by a state and its military apparatus, for Muslims must spread their rule over others and resist being subjugated by Muslims. This interpretation, favoured by a number of the classical jurists from al-Shafi'i onward, is imposed by al-Muti'i on the Qur'an itself. Such an enterprise then requires an organised political entity that is to be entrusted with this duty, the obligatory nature of which is inferred through this circuitous reasoning rather than through any explicit scriptural mandate. Husayn similarly tends to work backwards from juridical pronouncements to the Qur'an and sunna, all of which for him also represents a seamless whole. Thus the conjoining of apostleship with political power is understood to have been categorically established mainly on the basis of the scholarly consensus which affirmed that Muhammad was 'a messenger, a prophet and a political legislator.' Such a position is subsequently understood to be consonant with a Qur'anic and sunnaic understanding of Muhammad's roles. Husayn basically agrees with 'Abd al-Raziq that this position is inferred from the above sources rather than explicitly mentioned. However, whereas the latter then went on to say that such a historically deductive process frees contemporary Muslims to engage in renewed interpretation of relevant texts, the former states the exact opposite – that since scholarly consensus had invested this historical process and its resulting conclusions with normativity, Muslims are not at liberty to overturn this consensus by similarly studying and understanding foundational texts in light of their own circumstances.

Neither Husayn nor al-Muti'i deal at length with the verses foregrounded by 'Abd al-Raziq in which the Prophet is described primarily as 'a warner' and 'a reminder' or with the hadith in which Muhammad himself disavows any function as a prophet–king. Husayn cites Qur'an 4:59 which asks believers to obey God and His prophet and those possessing authority among them, as emphasising political obedience to Muhammad and his successors, even though the nature of that authority is not specified in the verse. Later exegetes and jurists, however, did impose primarily a political understanding on this verse (as we saw already in Chapter Two), and it is to this exegetical development that Husayn is indebted for making his case against 'Abd al-Raziq.

The politicised understanding of the Qur'an and sunna eventually became the predominant one among religious scholars and jurists, creating a scholarly consensus – *ijma'* – which came to be regarded as inerrant, and which also became firmly established as a fundamental juridical principle. Ultimately for both Husayn and al-Muti'i, it is this consensus of scholars and jurists through the centuries on political matters which trumps the rereading of the Qur'an and hadith in isolation from the classical juridical and exegetical tradition, as 'Abd al-Raziq attempts to do. As a consequence, they are both resorting to what is known in German as *Hineininterpretieren,* an exercise in retrospective exegesis which allows one to deduce scriptural justification for legal rulings considered a priori appropriate.[69]

For 'Abd al-Raziq and other modernists like him, ascribing normativity to a purely historical process represents a dangerous conflation of contingent – and ultimately imperfect – human understanding of the divine will with the divine will itself. 'Abd al-Raziq's relative obscurity and continued unpopularity in conservative circles today[70] reminds us that throughout history, in complex religious–intellectual traditions, this conflation has remained a fraught and highly contested issue, especially within the crucible of religion and politics.

Implications for twenty-first-century conversations on religion and politics

'Abd al-Raziq's position in favour of a separation between religion and politics resonates strongly among modernists as an accurate reflection of the traditional bifurcation between religious and political authority already characteristic of Islam's formative period. Such a position is misleadingly characterised as 'secular' – with the implication of being irreligious – by his detractors. The work *al-Islam wa usul al-hukm* reveals its author as drawing firmly upon the Qur'an, relevant hadith and early history to make a plausible case for his perspective – not exactly the approach of secularists.[71] Muti'i's and Husayn's rebuttals are very close, if not identical in parts, to contemporary conservative Islamist arguments for establishing the 'Islamic State' as a prelude to the revitalisation of the umma, which do not draw upon the Qur'an to affirm its necessity (because it cannot) but rather primarily upon the juridical consensus that emerged on this point well after the first three centuries of Islam. Neither of his interlocutors satisfactorily respond to 'Abd al-Raziq's question that ultimately has to do with hermeneutics – if pre-modern Muslims could deduce credible positions concerning political administration appropriate to their contexts through a rational engagement with their foundational texts, what prevents Muslims today from undertaking a similar task of extrapolating answers from the same texts that are more in tune with their contemporary circumstances? It is clear that modernists consider the hermeneutical process itself to be replicable in the modern period, but not the conclusions from the pre-modern period since they were historically contingent; whereas conservative/traditionalists and now hard-line Islamists conversely regard the conclusions themselves as normatively binding and the hermeneutical process to have effectively ended in the medieval period.

'Abd al-Raziq's discussion also brings to the fore the process of politicisation of certain Qur'anic terms by post-classical Muslim authors, which in their original context do not have overt political connotations. Both his detractors freely draw upon these post-classical sources to make their case. Besides *'amr* (which has been fulsomely discussed in Chapter Two), the term *hukm* is understood by Muti'i and Husayn to refer to political rule rather than the more obvious meaning of 'judgement', specifically divine judgement of humans in the next world. This politicised meaning has been fully embraced in the writings of the prominent Islamist ideologue of the twentieth century – Abul A'la Mawdudi. Proceeding from this politicisation of the meaning of Qur'anic *hukm*, Mawdudi in his works coined the term *al-hakimiyya* or divine sovereignty, which, as conceptualised by him, is opposed to the notion of democracy since the latter is predicated on popular sovereignty.[72]

Mawdudi's views represent a further development of the political conservatism evident in the thought of al-Muti'i and Husayn in the aftermath of the abolition of the caliphate. In his writings, Mawdudi presents *al-hakimiyya* as a concept that has always informed Muslim political culture and thought. This is, of course, a clear anachronism; *al-hakimiyya* is in fact a term that was coined only in the twentieth century and represents a rupture from mainstream Sunni political thought.[73] The Qur'an, to be sure, emphasises God's suzerainty and refers to God's dominion over all 'the heavens and the earth' (Qur'an 24:42). The word used in this context is *mulk*, while elsewhere it is *malakut* (36:83). *Hukm* is not used at all in the sense of divine dominion or sovereignty in the Qur'an (6:57;

12:40) but to refer to divine judgment of human actions, particularly in the next world. The term *hukm* otherwise does not have an early political genealogy. This is confirmed by the fact that early commentators on the Qur'an, like Muqatil b. Sulayman, understand *hukm* and its derivatives to refer primarily to God's (moral) judgment (*qada'*) of human beings, in this world and the next. When the term is used in relation to humans, it also refers to legal adjudication and conveys no intrinsic this-worldly political signification.[74] Two of the Qur'anic verses (Qur'an 5:44–5) that Mawdudi cites in his works to link the notion of divine political sovereignty to the Arabic verbal root *hukm* and its derivatives are addressed in fact to Jews, entreating them to uphold the laws of the Torah and 'to judge' (*yahkum*) by them. The occurrence of the Arabic verb *yahkum* in Qur'an 5:45 clearly means 'to judge' rather than 'to rule' in this context, since the reference is to the *lex talionis* in the Bible.[75]

Mawdudi's notion of *al-hakimiyya* was adopted by Sayyid Qutb in his political writings and became entrenched in many Islamist circles as the religiously mandated mode of governance acceptable to true Muslims. In his fiery, revolutionary work, *Ma'alim fi al-tariq*, Qutb indicts contemporary Muslim-majority societies for having failed to have established just and righteous governments along the lines he envisioned and thereby having lapsed into *jahiliyya* or an age of barbarism. The only way forward for Muslims, he counsels, is to establish a government in accordance with the principle of *al-hakimiyya*. Such a government is theoretically consultative in nature and led by the morally irreproachable vicegerent of God (*khalifat allah*), who apparently is privy to all the right answers. This era of righteous governance can only be ushered in by the vanguard (*al-tali'a*) of the revolution to come (in which of course Qutb is included). Such terminology is highly reminiscent of the socialist utopian movements (specifically Leninism) of the 1960s when Qutb was active and harks back to darker European ideologies of political authoritarianism current at that time. Qutb's conception of the ideal Islamic government, based on Mawdudi's original notion of a 'theo-democracy' has in fact no precedent in classical Islamic political thought and represents a bricolage of ill-digested ideas of eclectic origins. When he does use Islamic terminology such as *jahiliyya*, he often invests it with a new meaning that reflects presentist concerns rather than any continuity with classical understandings of the same.[76]

As Yousef Choueiri has compellingly argued, the genesis for this semantic development in regards to the term *jahiliyya* must be sought in the European totalitarian thought of the twentieth century that Qutb had access to, particularly that of Alexis Carrel, a Nobel prize-winning French Catholic biologist and philosopher, accused of collaborating with the fascist government of Vichy France. Carrel bemoaned the lapse of Western culture into crude materialism and moral degradation that he regarded as constituting a state of barbarism, a situation that could only be remedied by the appearance of an enlightened, elite cadre that would guide the Western world back to the path of self-redemption. This conceptualisation nicely accords with Qutb's construal of *jahiliyya* as a human condition rather than a historical period and his articulation of the concept of a revolutionary vanguard that would pave the way towards the renewal and revival of Muslim civilisation.[77] These striking parallels have led L. Carl Brown to comment insightfully 'that even Islamists most intent on rejecting the "other" in favor of a postulated cultural authenticity often rely on theories and ideologies advanced by outsiders'.[78]

Debating Islam's 'compatibility with democracy': the fault lines of civilisation?

In the last decades of the twentieth century, Islam and 'its compatibility with democracy' or lack thereof (however such a paradigm is constructed) began to be relentlessly discussed in scholarly fora and the popular media. The literature is voluminous and it is not possible to do full justice to the debates that have been vigorously conducted on this topic. Although there is a spectrum of views on the topic, the greatest attention was paid to those who had views at the opposite ends – arguing either that Islam and democracy as monovalent terms are inherently at odds with one another or that Islam and democracy in their inherent multiple inflections were potentially congruent with one another, depending on who the actors were and where and when they exercised their agency. In Muslim-majority societies, these arguments to a large degree may be regarded as building upon the perspectives of Husayn and al-Muti'i on the one side and 'Ali 'Abd al-Raziq on the other (with much grey area in between).

The religious resurgence evident in many parts of the traditional Islamic world in the wake of the Islamic revolution in Iran in 1979 tended to confirm for many in the West that Islam and democracy were destined to part ways forever. The predominant conception of democracy in the West has been (and remains so) is that it is ineluctably predicated on secularism; the inability to secularise is a 'failing' that is routinely ascribed to Muslim-majority societies to explain a fundamental incompatibility between democracy and Islam. Ernest Gellner, for example, regarded Islam as peculiarly resistant to secularisation since in his view the religion provides a rigid and unchanging blueprint for life incapable of adaptation to modern, secular society, and therefore inherently resistant to democratisation.[79] The French-Algerian philosopher Jacques Derrida similarly depicted Islam as 'the other of democracy', for, according to him, democracy is a European notion that belongs to the Graeco-Christian tradition alone.[80] After September 11th, these views have gained more currency in influential circles as prophetic auguries of the inevitable clash between a democratic modern West and an incorrigibly 'medieval' and illiberal Islamic world.

This entrenched view has been challenged by nuanced and theoretically more sophisticated analyses, as evident in the works of Alfred Stepan,[81] and more recently of Nader Hashemi[82] and Ahmet Kuru,[83] for example. These works rightly point out that secularism in the sense of a strict divide between state and religion is not a necessary pre-condition for democracy. Secularism coexists with authoritarian regimes in many parts of the world, as in Uzbekistan and Kazakhstan, while there are Western democracies that claim to be secular but nevertheless have official state religions, as in England (Anglicanism), Denmark (Lutheranism) and elsewhere. Political trends are better explained by sociopolitical and economic variables in culturally specific contexts rather than through ahistorical pronouncements on religious or cultural essences. As Hashemi incisively observes, 'Religious traditions are not born with an inherent democratic or secular conception of politics' and that 'these ideas must be socially constructed'.[84]

Polls and surveys conducted in several Muslim-majority countries have in fact repeatedly affirmed that Muslim populations desire representative and accountable governments – the most basic understanding of democracy – and regard democratic procedures, such as elections, as the appropriate mechanism for establishing such governments. An extensive multiyear Gallup research study conducted between 2001 and 2007 in more than thirty-five nations that have predominantly Muslim or substantial Muslim populations (claiming to have surveyed a sample representing over 90 per cent of the world's total Muslim inhabitants) categorically established that democracy is the preferred system of government among them. Disenchantment with US policy in the Middle East and the campaign to 'promote' democracy under Western military occupation in Iraq, for example, did not dampen the desire of these populations to elect their own representative governments through fair and transparent elections. Interestingly, at the same time, substantial Muslim majorities, male and female, want the Sharia to be at least a source of legislation in their countries, seeing no disjunction between religious beliefs and democratic principles. In a number of Muslim-majority countries, the preference was even stronger. In Jordan, for example, 54 per cent of men and 55 per cent of women want Sharia to be the only source of legislation. Interestingly, from a comparative perspective, a 2006 Gallup poll indicated that 46 per cent of Americans say that they want the Bible to be a source of legislation.[85]

These findings corroborate earlier studies conducted by Robert Inglehart and Pippa Norris which allowed them to conclude that Muslim populations in general tended to be more supportive of democracy than non-Muslim populations worldwide, providing important ballast against the 'clash of civilisations' hypothesis.[86] An important study published by Amaney Jamal and Mark Tessler in 2008 similarly confirmed that in several key Arab countries where they conducted their survey, there was strong evidence of widespread popular support for democracy.[87]

Such facts and figures make political reality very complex indeed and hardly a homogenous global phenomenon. The evacuation of religion from the public sphere as a *sine qua non* for a functioning democracy is a modern myth propagated by certain cultural warriors in the West, often in a polemical vein to set up a contrast to what appears to them the religion-infused societies of the Islamic world. This premise is then seized upon by religio-political reactionaries in a number of Muslim-majority countries in order to undermine democracy as a 'godless' concept, the importation of which would destroy the very fabric of Muslim-majority societies. It would appear that neither position is in tune with the actual aspirations and lived realities of ordinary Muslims throughout the world.[88]

Making the case for democracy in Islamic terms

Democracy stripped down to its bare-bones definition – a system of government that reflects the popular will and holds itself accountable to the people – is therefore not an alien concept within the variegated Islamic milieu. The term 'democracy' itself – rather than its meaning(s) – may be regarded with some scepticism, given its association with what is widely regarded as part of an amoral Western cultural and political onslaught on the non-Western world. More recently, the foolhardy attempt to forcibly impose 'democracy' through the barrel of a gun in Iraq and elsewhere through Western military occupation has unfortunately tainted this term in an even more negative vein.[89] In conscious opposition to hard-line Islamists who have relentlessly propagated the idea that 'democracy' – mired in the cultural and political baggage of the modern West that has historically accompanied it – is conceptually flawed and antithetical to Islamic values, some Muslim scholars have made the opposite case, drawing their arguments from deep within Islamic intellectual thought and history.

In an important work, Khaled Abou El Fadl identifies several features of traditional Islamic political thought and ethics based upon the Qur'an that are conducive to the development of modern participatory forms of government: human dignity, human vicegerency on earth, accountability that is ultimately linked to a fundamental commitment to justice and mercy, an emphasis on consultative decision-making and the rule of law.[90] While God's sovereignty is acknowledged by all Muslim scholars, how that sovereignty is understood to be reflected in the context of law-making and political administration represents the critical fault line between hard-line Islamists and liberal Muslims. In a trenchant critique of the hardliners, Abou El Fadl memorably remarks:

> If we say that the only legitimate source of law is the divine text and that human experience and intellect are irrelevant to the pursuit of the divine will, then divine sovereignty will always stand as an instrument of authoritarianism and an obstacle to democracy. But that authoritarian view denigrates God's sovereignty.[91]

The agency that humans enjoy in interpreting the way of God allows for the assertion of the popular will and 'even promotes it insofar as it contributes to the fulfillment of justice'.[92] Abou El Fadl concludes that from this perspective:

> democracy is an appropriate system for Islam because it both expresses the special worth of human beings – the status of vicegerency – and at the same time deprives the state of any pretense of divinity by locating ultimate authority in the hands of the people rather than the ulema.[93]

Abdulaziz Sachedina has also shown that certain foundational principles within Islam, derived directly from the Qur'an, are conducive to the formation of democratic, pluralist societies. Among such principles are non-coercion in religion (2:256; 10:99), the recognition of righteousness in all sincere believers and of the validity of different ways of life and legal systems and, ultimately, the guarantee of justice for all.[94]

Above all, the principle of *shura* or consultation, endorsed in the Qur'an as the basis for collective decision-making and administration of public affairs (Qur'an 3:158–9; 42:38), is generally understood – by a broad spectrum of scholars ranging from hard-line Islamists to liberal Muslims – to provide the conceptual grounding for consultative governance and collective decision-making. While hard-line Islamists will typically reject any overlap between *shura* and democratic forms of governance, liberal Muslims will usually point to their points of convergence.[95] However this critical concept may be interpreted, history records the continuing endurance of the validity of this principle among Muslims, at least as an ideal to aspire to, even as dynastic rule was instituted very early (a mere thirty years after the death of the Prophet) and became the status quo.

These broad Qur'anic principles that in themselves are not overtly political, however, have been deployed in the public sphere, particularly in the modern period, as having notable political and administrative implications. Whether such principles can provide the impetus for the formation of democratic forms of government today remain a highly debated subject. Most rigorous scholars of Islamic and/or comparative political thought today, whether Muslim or non-Muslim, do not perceive any serious theological or ideational impediments to democratic governments taking hold in Muslim-majority societies. They have instead wondered why despite an overwhelming popular desire for representative governments in such societies and a fundamental proclivity within their religious and political traditions to support such governments, there has remained what is often dubbed as 'a democracy deficit' within them, especially in the Arab world. The more painstakingly researched responses to such a question have focused on structural and cultural factors – for example, the rentier economies in some of the wealthiest Arab nations which allow for oil revenues that are generated to accrue primarily to small elites; in addition to tribal and social organisations that promote a culture of authoritarianism.[96] Outside of the Arab world, there are long-term functional democracies in, for example, Turkey, Bangladesh, Indonesia and Malaysia. More recently installed democratic governments in Pakistan and Palestine further challenge old stereotypes about the links between Islamicate cultures and representative governments. Such facts on the ground clearly establish that when discussing solutions to the democracy deficit in parts of the Muslim world, 'Islam' – invoked as a reified essence in such debates – is clearly not part of the problem.[97]

The Arab Spring

Although the debates centred on Islam's compatibility with democracy continued through the first decade of the twentieth century, the Arab Spring of 2011 has spectacularly transformed the parameters of the conversation. The Arab Spring was literally 'ignited' by a young street vendor in Tunisia named Mohammed Bouazizi who, on 17 December 2010, set his body on fire to protest the confiscation of his wares and harassment by Tunisian police in the town of Sidi Bouzid where he lived. Bouazizi's self-immolation brought to the fore the simmering discontent of the Tunisian population with their strongman ruler Zine El Abidine Ben Ali, under whom they suffered from mass poverty and unemployment, political repression and abuse of human rights. Shortly thereafter on 14 January 2011, faced with a rising tide of social unrest and popular insurrection, Ben Ali fled to Saudi Arabia after twenty-three years in power, setting in motion protest movements and popular uprisings against autocratic governments in other parts of the Middle East. These popular movements have collectively become known as the Arab Spring, spreading from Tunisia to Egypt, Morocco, Jordan, Libya, Bahrain, Syria and even Saudi Arabia. The famous Egyptian uprising concentrated in Tahrir Square led to the ousting of President Hosni Mubarak on 11 February 2011, electrifying the world with the prospect of democracy taking hold in the Middle East. On 30 June 2012, Muhammad Morsi, presidential candidate from the Muslim Brotherhood, won the first democratically held elections in Egypt, riding the crest of a wave of popular support. In other parts of the Arab world, many of these popular movements were eventually contained and co-opted by the current governments in Algeria, Morocco, Bahrain and elsewhere. However, an extended bloody insurrection in Libya eventually led to the fall and death of Mu'ammar Qaddafi while civil war continues to rage in Syria, with Bashshar al-Asad still in power and not easy to dislodge.

The continuing political conflagration in the Middle East, which has exacted a high human toll, has led some to wonder if the Arab Spring is turning into an Arab Winter.[98] The euphoric optimism of 2011 has progressively given way to a more steely sense of the considerable obstacles that still remain on the path to political enfranchisement and support for civil society. In perhaps a sad harbinger of things to come, after just a little over a year after his election, President Morsi and his inept government was removed from office by a military coup led by the then defence minister General 'Abd al-Fattah al-Sisi with considerable popular support.

The picture, however, is not consistently bleak. Tunisia, where it all began, has successfully held free elections and ratified a constitution which enshrines democratic principles. At the same time though, Egypt remains mired in bloodshed and violence, with al-Sisi's military government resorting to brutal tactics to suppress political dissent. As of this writing, al-Sisi has banned the Muslim Brotherhood and embarked upon a killing spree that has been described by Human Rights Watch as 'the most serious incident of mass unlawful killings in modern Egyptian history'.[99] In view of this grim situation, Khaled Abou El Fadl has noted trenchantly:

> What the army did in Egypt is just reaffirm and further aggravate a decades old feud between the secularists who believe that they are the only ones who understand democracy, and the Islamists who believe that secularists only believe in democracy when it serves to exclude and marginalize the Islamists.[100]

This misleading secularist–Islamist dichotomy unnecessarily polarises the Egyptian citizenry, masking as it does deeper issues about the rule of law, political corruption, economic parity and social justice.[101]

Conclusion

History teaches us that 'revolutionaries have eventually learned that without the rule of law and principled adherence to justice, the popular will does not translate into a moral mandate for positive social and political change'.[102] The road to an inclusive and just democracy has proven to be uneven, arduous and perilous in Egypt and elsewhere; the lessons learned along the way may yet lead to the realisation of the original goals of the Arab Spring. As history further teaches us, sociopolitical revolutions do not yield positive results overnight but the commitment to their overarching objectives do in the long haul. Proclamations of an Arab Winter are clearly premature. The death knell that has begun to be sounded in the Middle East for authoritarian and repressive governments, whether secular or religious, is in itself a positive augury and has begun to rewrite the modern political landscape there, a process that may at this juncture in history be regarded as inexorable.

The establishment of a global caliphate (however that may be construed) remains the goal of marginal but vocal elements in the Islamic world today. As this book was going to press, Abu Bakr al-Baghdadi, leader of the so-called 'Islamic State of Iraq and Syria' (ISIS for short; later renamed simply the

'Islamic State'), declared himself to be the 'caliph' of Muslims while he continues a murderous rampage in the Middle East. Not surprisingly, his inaugural
'caliphal' speech at the Great Mosque in Mosul on 4 July 2014 reveals a basic
ignorance of Islamic history and Sunni political theory.[103] Calls for the revival of
the caliphate amount to mere sloganeering on the part of such radical elements
with very little resonance among mainstream Muslim populations. Despite the
potential emotive appeal of such grandiose announcements, the majority of
contemporary Muslims are clearly on record as wanting elected representative
and accountable governments in their countries, as global surveys have consistently and repeatedly established. Elected governments are widely regarded as
being in conformity with the broad Islamic principles of consultation (*shura*)
and consensus (*ijma'*), principles that may be understood to have animated the
earliest caliphate. Muhammad 'Abduh in the nineteenth century eloquently
broached this topic:

> The longing of some people for consultative government and their dislike of
> despotism does not result from imitating the foreigners. It is because consulta-
> tion is a duty of the *Sharia* and despotism is prohibited by the *Sharia*. For the law
> of Islam instructs that the rules of the Qur'an be followed and the sunna of the
> Prophet be adhered to. As for despotism, this contradicts the *Sharia* as it is not
> restricted by law.[104]

The Arab Spring has been one of the most spectacular manifestations in recent
times of this continued desire for democratic, representative governments
among Muslim populations, even among Islamist groups who not too long ago
would have eschewed democratic processes. As Shadi Hamid has pointed out,
contemporary Islamists in a spirit of political realism are increasingly becoming committed 'to many of the foundational aspects of democratic life'.[105]
Ultimately, whether representative and accountable governments are established in the name of *shura* or democracy is a moot point[106] – universal political enfranchisement by whatever name remains the popular desideratum in
Muslim-majority countries and has the aroma of a growing consensus around it.

Notes

1. Quote occurs in article by Michael Hirsh, 'Bernard Lewis Revisited: What if Islam isn't
    an Obstacle to Democracy in the Middle East but the secret to achieving it?' in the
    Washington Monthly (November 2004), 14.
2. Lewis has frequently invoked the mantra of inevitable theocentrism in Islam to advance
    his 'clash of civilisations' thesis and to inveigh against the possibility of democracy
    taking hold in Muslim-majority countries; see, for example, his essay 'Islam and Liberal
    Democracy', *Atlantic Monthly* 271 (1993): 46–56, where he rails that the state in Islamic
    politics was 'God's state, ruling over God's people; the law was God's law; the army
    was God's army; and the enemy, of course, was God's enemy'. Needless to say, ideol-
    ogy, more than history, informs such totalising statements. For a lucid critique of such

views, see, for example, Ali A. Allawi, *The Crisis of Islamic Civilization* (New Haven: Yale University Press, 2010), 159 ff., and the earlier volume by John Esposito and John Voll, *Islam and Democracy* (Oxford: Oxford University Press, 1996).

3. Published by Oxford University Press, 1998.
4. For an insightful critique of these positions and replacing them with a more historically nuanced and sophisticated reading of the sources, see Hayrettin Yucesoy, 'Justification of Political Authority in Medieval Sunni Thought', in Asma Afsaruddin (ed.), *Islam, the State, and Political Authority: Medieval Issues and Modern Concerns* (New York: Palgrave Macmillan, 2011), 9–33. Cf. also Aziz al-Azmeh, 'God's Caravan: Topoi and Schemata in the History of Muslim Political Thought', in Mehrzad Boroujerdi (ed.), *Mirror for the Muslim Prince: Islam and the Theory of Statecraft* (Syracuse: Syracuse University Press, 2013), 326–97.
5. See Asma Afsaruddin 'Theologizing about Democracy: A Critical Appraisal of Mawdudi's Thought', in *Islam, the State, and Political Authority*, 131–54.
6. Yucesoy, 'Justification of Political Authority', 14–15.
7. Cf. Katajun Amirpur, 'A Doctrine in the Making? *Velayet-e faqih* in Post-Revolutionary Iran', in Gudrun Krämer and Sabine Schmidtke (eds), *Speaking for Islam: Religious Authorities in Muslim Societies* (Leiden: Brill, 2006).
8. For a comprehensive discussion of these variegated trends within political Islam, see Mohammed Ayoob, *The Many Faces of Political Islam: Religion and Politics in the Muslim World* (Ann Arbor: University of Michigan Press, 2007), especially 64 ff.
9. For the full report titled 'Most Muslims Want Democracy, Personal Freedoms, and Islam in Political Life', see <http://www.pewglobal.org/files/2012/07/Pew-Global-Attitudes-Project-Arab-Spring-Report-FINAL-Tuesday-July-10-2012.pdf>; last accessed on 30 June 2014.
10. For biographical details, see Charles C. Adams, *Islam and Modernism in Egypt* (New York: Russell and Russell, 1968), 259–68.
11. For a useful discussion of this crisis over the caliphate, along with a synopsis of 'Abd al-Raziq's views, see Hamid Enayat, *Modern Islamic Political Thought* (Kuala Lumpur: Islamic Book Trust, 2001), 78–103; Leonard Binder, 'Ali Abd al Raziq and Islamic Liberalism', *Asian and African Studies* 10 (March 1982): 31–67.
12. For brief discussions of the views of these and other critics, see Souad T. Ali, *A Religion, Not a State: Ali 'Abd al-Raziq's Islamic Justification of Political Secularism* (Salt Lake City: The University of Utah Press, 2009), 103–18.
13. 'Ali 'Abd al-Raziq, *al-Islam wa usul al-hukm* (Beirut: Dar Maktabat al-Hayat), 1966, 11.
14. Ibid. 12.
15. Ibid. 12.
16. Ibid. 13.
17. Ibid. 13.
18. Ibid. 14.
19. Ibid. 15.
20. Ibid. 16. In this somewhat sardonic description of the caliphate, the author wishes to highlight what he clearly understands to be the ahistorical nature of this conventional portrayal of the caliphate and the naivety that he discerns in those who subscribe to the view that the stipulations of the law alone will effectively impose limits on the caliph in the exercise of his authority.
21. Ibid. 17.
22. Ibid. 17.
23. Ibid. 18–21.
24. Ibid. 22–4.

25. Ibid. 113.
26. Ibid. 113–14.
27. Ibid. 114.
28. Ibid. 116–18.
29. Ibid. 118–19.
30. Ibid. 119–21.
31. Ibid. 122.
32. Ibid. 122.
33. Ibid. 123–4.
34. Ibid. 124–5.
35. Ibid. 125.
36. Ibid. 126–7.
37. Ibid. 136–42.
38. Ibid. 144–5.
39. Ibid. 146–50.
40. Ibid. 150–2.
41. The relevant part of the verse reads, 'If God had so willed, he would have made you a single community, but [His plan is] to test you in what He has given you, so hasten to do good!'
42. 'Abd al-Raziq, *Islam wa usul*, 155.
43. Ibid. 191–3. For Abu Bakr's stated revulsion towards this title, see the classic biographical work in Arabic by Ibn Sa'd, *al-Tabaqat al-kubra* (Beirut: Dar al-Sadir, 1957), 3:183–4. For 'Umar's similar revulsion towards the adoption of this title, see ibid. 3:281.
44. 'Abd al-Raziq, *Islam wa usul*, 194–5.
45. Ibid. 198-9.
46. Ibid. 200–1.
47. Muhammad Bakhit al-Muti'i, *Haqiqat al-Islam wa-usul al-hukm* (Cairo: n.publ., n.d.), 4.
48. Ibid. 4–5.
49. Ibid. 12, 19.
50. Ibid. 23–4.
51. Ibid. 24–5.
52. Al-Muti'i, *Haqiqat al-Islam*, 25–6.
53. Ibid. 292 ff.
54. Ibid., 293–5.
55. Al-Muti'i is clearly construing this verb to mean 'rule' in the political sense rather than 'judge', which is the usual sense of the word.
56. Ibid. 296–8.
57. Ibid. 299.
58. Muhammad al-Khidr Husayn, *Naqd kitab al-islam wa-usul al-hukm* (Cairo: Dar al-shuruq, 1989), 329–30.
59. Ibid. 330.
60. Husayn is careful to avoid the word *bid'a* here.
61. Ibid. 330–1.
62. Ibid. 330–1.
63. Ibid. 339–44.
64. Ibid. 341.
65. Ibid. 346.
66. Ibid. 347.
67. The *Kamil* authored by the Basran grammarian al-Mubarrad (d. 898) is a work of Arabic

grammar and linguistics. Husayn is thereby implying that 'Abd al-Raziq is not a deeply trained religious scholar but is merely an *adib* – that is a cultured man of letters knowledgeable about the Arabic language but with no authority to pronounce on religious matters.

68. Husayn, *Naqd*, 351.
69. I am borrowing this term from Rudolph Peters, *Jihad in Classical and Modern Islam* (Princeton, NJ: Markus Wiener, 1996), 28.
70. His thought, however, is enjoying a mild resurgence among contemporary modernist thinkers.
71. Cf. Charles Butterworth, 'Law and the Common Good: To Bring about a Virtuous City or Preserve the Old Order?' in Mehrzad Boroujerdi, (ed.), *Mirror for the Muslim Prince* (Syracuse: Syracuse University Press, 2013), 218–39.
72. See Mawdudi's *Political Theory of Islam* (Lahore:Islamic Publications Ltd., 1976), 20 ff.; and his *First Principles of the Islamic State*, tr. and ed. Khurshid Ahmad (Lahore: Islamic Publications Ltd., 1983), 16; also, in general, see Seyyed Vali Nasr, *Mawdudi and the Making of Islamic Revivalism* (New York: Oxford University Press, 1996).
73. For a discussion of this, see Asma Afsaruddin 'The 'Islamic State': Genealogy, Facts, and Myths', *Journal of Church and State* 48 (2006): 153–73.
74. Muqatil b. Sulayman *Tafsir Muqatil* (Cairo: Mu'assasat al-halabi, 1969), 1:564; 2:343; etc.
75. See Afsaruddin, 'Theologizing about Democracy', 140–1.
76. See William E. Shepard, 'Sayyid Qutb's Doctrine of Jahiliyya', *International Journal of Middle East Studies* 35 (2003): 521–45. For a general concise overview of Qutb's life and thought, see Peter Mandaville, *Global Political Islam* (New York: Routledge, 2007), 76–82.
77. Yousef Choueiri, *Islamic Fundamentalism* (London: Pinter, 1990), 140–55; cf. also John Calvert, *Sayyid Qutb and the Origins of Radical Islamism* (New York: Columbia University Press, 2010), 90–2.
78. L. Carl Brown, *Religion and State: the Muslim Approach to Politics* (New York: Columbia University Press, 2001), 216–17.
79. Ernest Gellner, *Postmodernism, Reason and Religion* (New York: Routledge, 1992), 5–7.
80. Jacques Derrida, *Rogues: Two Essays on Reason*, tr. Michael Naas and Pascale-Anne Brault (Stanford, CA: Stanford University Press, 2005), 28–9. For an extended and illuminating critique of such views, see Anne Norton, *On the Muslim Question* (Princeton: Princeton University Press, 2013), especially 118–40.
81. Alfred Stepan, 'The World's Religious Systems and Democracy: Crafting the "Twin Tolerations"', in his *Arguing Comparative Politics* (New York: Oxford University Press, 2001).
82. Nader Hashemi, *Islam, Secularism, and Liberal Democracy: Towards a Democratic Theory for Muslim Societies* (New York: Oxford University Press, 2009).
83. Ahmet T. Kuru, *Secularism and State Policies toward Religion: The United States, France, and Turkey* (New York: Cambridge University Press, 2009).
84. Hashemi, *Islam*, 2. See further Muhammad Khalid Masud, 'Construction and Deconstruction of Secularism as an Ideology in Contemporary Muslim Thought', *Asian Journal of Social Sciences* 33 (2005): 375–6, where he suggests that the traditional dichotomy in Islamic law between worship (*ibadat*) and social interactions (*mu'amalat*) is conducive to an indigenised notion of secular space.
85. For these detailed findings, see John L. Esposito and Dalia Mogahed, *Who Speaks for Islam? What a Billion Muslims Really Think* (New York: Gallup Press, 2007), 29–63.
86. Robert Inglehart and Pippa Norris, 'The True Clash of Civilizations', *Foreign Policy* 135 (2001): 62–70.

87. Amaney Jamal and Mark Tessler, 'The Democracy Barometers: Attitudes in the Arab World', *The Journal of Democracy* 19 (2008): 97–110. These countries included Morocco, Kuwait, Jordan, Palestine and Algeria.

88. Nader Hashemi points out that such hardened ideological positions elide the fact that in the Anglo-American Western context in particular, liberal democracies emerged in concert with religious politics and that fervent debates about the role of religion in government were part of the process of democratic evolution; *Islam*, 2 ff.

89. See, for example, the article by Maher Osseiran, 'The War on Iraq: A Historical Middle Eastern Perspective', *Global Research*, 30 August 2005, available online at <http://www.globalresearch.ca/the-war-on-iraq-a-historical-middle-east-perspective/884>; last accessed on 3 July 2014.

90. Khaled Abou El Fadl, *Islam and the Challenge of Democracy* (Princeton: Princeton University Press, 2004), 3–46.

91. Ibid. 9.

92. Ibid. 22.

93. Ibid. 36.

94. Abdulaziz Sachedina, *The Islamic Roots of Democratic Pluralism* (Oxford: Oxford University Press, 2001).

95. For a discussion of some of these debates, see Abdelwahab El-Affendi, 'Democracy and Its (Muslim) Critics: An Islamic Alternative to Democracy?' in Muqtedar Khan (ed.), *Islamic Democratic Discourse: Theory, Debates and Philosophical Perspectives* (Lanham, MD: Lexington Books, 2006), 127–256.

96. See, for example, Michael Ross, 'Does Oil Hinder Democracy?' *World Politics* 53 (2001): 325–61; M. Steven Fish, 'Islam and Authoritarianism', *World Politics* 55 (2002): 4–37; Alfred C. Stepan and Graeme B. Robertson, 'An "Arab" More Than a "Muslim" Gap', *The Journal of Democracy* 14 (2003): 30–44; and more recently Steven Fish, *Are Muslims Distinctive: A Look at the Evidence* (Oxford: Oxford University Press, 2011).

97. See further Mohammed Ayoob, 'The Muslim World's Poor Record of Modernization and Democratization: The Interplay of External and Internal Factors', in Shireen T. Hunter and Huma Malik (eds), *Modernization, Democracy and Islam* (Wesport: Praeger; in cooperation with Washington DC: Center for Strategic and International Studies, 2005), 186–204.

98. See, for example, the article by Tom Hayden, 'The Coup in Egypt: An Arab Winter?' *The Nation*, 5 July 2013, available at <http://www.thenation.com/article/175121/coup-egypt-arab-winter#>; last accessed on 16 March 2014.

99. This statement occurs in a report released on 19 August 2013, Human Rights Watch, available at <http://www.hrw.org/news/2013/08/19/egypt-security-forces-used-excessive-lethal-force>; last accessed on 16 March 2014.

100. Khaled Abou El Fadl, 'The Perils of a "People's Coup"', *The New York Times*, 8 July 2013, A21.

101. Some of these issues are raised by Tariq Ramadan in his book *The Arab Awakening: Islam and the New Middle East* (London and New York: Allen Lane, 2012), especially 72–105.

102. See Asma Afsaruddin, 'Egypt and the Problem of Religion', *Religion Dispatches*, 10 September 2013, available at < http://religiondispatches.org/egypt-and-the-problem-of-religion/>; last accessed on 16 March 2014.

103. See my analysis of this speech under the title 'The Pretender-Caliph and Islamic History: The Truth about Abu Bakr', available at <http://www.abc.net.au/religion/articles/2014/07/16/4047157.htm>; last accessed on 26 July 2014.

104. Cited by Aziz Azmeh, *Islams and Modernities* (London: Verso, 2009), 124.

105. Shadi Hamid, *Temptations of Power: Islamists and Illiberal Democracy in a New Middle East* (Oxford: Oxford University Press, 2014), 10.

106. Cf. Fathi Osman, 'Shura and Democracy', in John J. Donohue and John L. Esposito (eds), *Islam in Transition: Muslim Perspectives* (Oxford: Oxford University Press, 2007), 288–95; and Murad Hofmann, 'Democracy or Shuracracy', in ibid. 296–306.

CHAPTER 4

Islam, gender and feminist hermeneutics

Few issues are as sensitive and fraught as those of gender and the status of women vis-à-vis men in the context of contemporary Islam. In the encounter of Muslim-majority societies with European colonialists starting in the nineteenth century, Muslim women became the central trope within a polarising discourse of civilisational conflict that in the twentieth century was formulated as pitting 'the West' against 'the Rest'. As Lila Abu-Lughod tellingly remarked in a recent searing critique of this phenomenon:

> The idea of culture has increasingly become a core component of international politics and common sense. Muslims are presented as a special and threatening culture – the most homogenized and troubling of the Rest. Muslim women, in this new common sense, symbolize how alien this culture is.[1]

In the contemporary Western imaginary nourished by lurid media images of silent, black-robed women and sensational stories of honour killings and stoning as representative of the Arab and Islamic world, Muslim women have become synonymous with oppression and legal and political disenfranchisement (while Muslim men are simultaneously stigmatised as their 'oppressors').[2] Accounts of women heads of state in several Muslim countries and of the enthusiastic participation of female leaders in the Arab spring uprisings[3] have done little to dispel these images, entrenched as they have become in 'culture talk' endemic in influential circles in the West. Such images nurtured by preconceptions are not easily dislodged by facts. When Muslim women in prominent public roles do receive attention, they are often depicted as exceptions to the rule and going against foundational Islamic precepts in seeking self-empowerment. Such perceptions hardly ever match up with those of the women themselves who, more often than not, invoke religious texts and precedents in Islamic history as the impetus for their activism. It is not surprising, therefore, that in most Western laudatory accounts of Malala Yousafzai, the young Pakistani girl who survived an attack on her by the Taliban for publicly advocating for female education in her native country and who subsequently won the Nobel Peace Prize in 2014, her commitment to Islam as a driving force for her campaign is rarely, if ever, mentioned. Many Muslim women today, as in the past, continue to ground their rights specifically in the Qur'an and the Prophet's sunna, even as they have turned a critical eye to the androcentric interpretations of both sources. The chequered story of Muslim women's quest for equality and enfranchisement in various parts of the world today rightly begins in the first century of Islam.

The Qur'an and the 'woman question'

In roughly the third or fourth year of the Islamic era (corresponding to 625–6 CE), a Medinan woman by the name of Umm 'Umara from the first generation of Muslims remarked to the Prophet Muhammad in connection with the Qur'anic revelations he had received up to that point, 'I see that everything relates to men; I do not see the mention of women.' Umm 'Umara was commenting on the fact that Qur'anic verses that had come down so far primarily referred to men and their good deeds and the rewards that they were consequently promised in the hereafter. Were women believers not to be recognised as equal participants in this grand unfolding drama of human agency, fulfilment and salvation?

Clearly God listens to women because subsequently, this particular verse was revealed:

> Those who have surrendered to God among males and females; those who believe among males and females; those who are sincere among males and females; those who are truthful among males and females; those who are patient among males and females; those who fear God among males and females; those who give in charity among males and females; those who fast among males and females; those who remember God often among males and females – God has prepared for them forgiveness and great reward. (Qur'an 33:35)

The Qur'an had settled the question once and for all: women and men have equal moral agency in their quest of the good and righteous life in this world for which they reap identical rewards in the afterlife. Gender had no role to play in the other-worldly, salvific efficacy offered by the Qur'an through its prescription for the well-ordered moral existence on earth. Muslim feminists frequently point to this verse (and others like it) to underscore the gender egalitarianism inherent in the Qur'an.

Unfortunately, women's readings and perspectives on the Qur'an have not been copiously preserved for us through the centuries. When feminine voices can be retrieved from the early, pre-modern extra-Qur'anic sources, they are sometimes heard to argue for justice and equitable treatment for women. We have documented instances of women in our sources occasionally pleading for the proper implementation of Qur'anic and prophetic injunctions that would guarantee their social and economic rights, particularly after the death of the Prophet.[4] Muhammad's youngest widow, 'Aisha, is sometimes heard remonstrating with some male Companions for purveying misogynist reports that they carelessly and mendaciously attributed to him.[5]

Such vignettes provide fascinating glimpses into the Muslim past where an alternatively conceptualised society, in which the gifts and contributions of men and women were deemed equally valuable, was possible. Early biographical works, like that of Ibn Sa'd (d. 845), document that the details of the lives of first generation Muslim women when available, provide instructive examples of women's lives lived to their fullest in service to their community and religion, largely unhampered by later sociopolitical constructions of restrictive, gendered identities.[6] The memory of these inspirational women, however, begins to dim in subsequent centuries. As historians have shown, critical changes that crept into Muslim societies from the outside considerably reshaped their orientations and substantially attenuated the gender egalitarianism of the early period. Persian, Greek and Byzantine notions of social hierarchies and gendered privileges influenced societal and juridical conceptions of women's socio-economic rights over time and led to their eventual circumscription.[7]

These striking societal and cultural transformations leave their broad imprint in the way certain Qur'anic verses that deal with human agency and male–female relations, particularly within the family, were read and interpreted by male scholars through the centuries. Their interpretations provide a valuable window into the progressive 'patriarchalisation' of Muslim societies and the elaborate arguments constructed to support this world-view – all couched in a legitimising religious idiom.

For example, if we look at the verses in the Qur'an that refer to the creation of Adam and his wife before their earthly existence, we are struck by how the Qur'an either: (a) blames Adam exclusively for the Fall; or (b) blames Adam and his wife equally for giving in to the blandishments of Satan. Western readers from a Judeo-Christian background will be struck by the fact that Adam's wife (named Hawwa' [Eve] in the exegetical literature) is not singled out for exclusive blame in the Qur'an, in contrast to the principal biblical creation account contained in the Book of Genesis which makes Eve the sole culprit for the banishment of humans from Paradise. On the balance, Adam in the Qur'an is the one who is morally culpable for failing to heed God's injunctions and succumbing to wrongdoing. He is, however, forgiven by God and both he and his wife are given an equal opportunity to redeem themselves by establishing a righteous and God-fearing community on earth. In its creation accounts (Qur'an 2:30–9; 7:11–27; 15:26–43; 20: 115–24; and 38:71–85), the Qur'an does not assign any kind of ontological moral failing to the woman companion of Adam and thus by extension to womankind in general.[8]

This point has been underscored by Muslim feminists in particular as they argue from within the Islamic tradition for gender egalitarianism. Recuperation of the meanings of the original Qur'anic verses concerning Adam and Eve is highly important in feminist discourses as a corrective to a very different story that emerges from the prolific exegetical literature (tafsir) on this topic. Qur'an commentaries from after the ninth century reveal that the Qur'anic exoneration of Adam's wife proved unpalatable to a number of later Muslim male exegetes and they deliberately imported the biblical creation story into their interpretations to reassign the blame to her. Earlier commentators, including al-Tabari, stayed closer to the Qur'anic text and noted that Adam in the Qur'an bore the brunt of the blame for having caused the 'Fall'. However, later exegetes – roughly after the tenth century –began to show a marked preference for the biblical version, which mandates the wife's subjugation to her husband as a result of her sin, an interpretation that was more in line with the growing patriarchal nature of society. Not surprisingly, the well-known exegete from the late twelfth century Fakhr al-Din al-Razi (d. 1210) embellishes his narrative with the story of woman's creation from the rib of Adam to drive home the point that the female is secondary to the male as a human being, a biblical literary motif that by his time had taken deep root in Muslim exegeses.[9]

Such construals are markedly in contrast to what the Qur'an actually states concerning the creation of humankind. One particularly relevant verse states:

> O humankind! Be careful of your duty to your Lord Who created you from a single soul (*nafs wahida*) and from it created its mate and from them the two has spread abroad a multitude of men and women. (Qur'an 4:1)

Simultaneous creation from the *nafs wahida* negates the possibility of man being granted an ontologically superior status by virtue of having been created first, from whose body is then derived the woman's, as in the biblical account. By leaving unspecified which sexed being was created first, the Qur'an therefore clearly undermines the notion of a hierarchical relationship between man and woman. In spite of this fundamental Qur'anic orientation, the rib story entered the hadith literature and became a favourite of most of the later male exegetes as a way of justifying the woman's ontological, biological, and legally inferior status to that of the man.

Women's moral agency in the Qur'an

Culturally derived attitudes which progressively undermined women's equal status in society in the formative period of Islam and which became enshrined in *fiqh* are belied by several passages in the Qur'an that affirm gender equality in various contexts. For example, a critical verse in the Qur'an (9:71) establishes equal and complementary moral agency for both men and women. The verse states:

> (Male) believers (*al-mu'minun*) and (female) believers (*al-mu'minat*) are the natural partners (*awliya'*) of one another; they command the good and forbid wrong and they perform prayer, give the obligatory alms, and obey God and His messenger. They are those upon whom God has mercy; indeed God is Almighty, Wise.

The obvious intent of the verse is to establish complete parity between men and women as partners in the common venture to promote the good, righteous society on earth and in the fulfilment of their individual and communal obligations towards God.[10] As obvious as this meaning may seem to us, male interpreters from the pre-modern and modern periods have understood this verse in ways that more often than not were consonant with their own culturallyderived views of proper male–female relations and frequently subversive of its egalitarian thrust. A sampling of the perspectives of a number of influential exegetes is now provided below to offer a glimpse into the conceptualisation of such gendered identities in variegated historical circumstances in the pre-modern period, a conceptualisation that persists to this day.

Pre-modern period exegeses of Qur'an 9:71

From the first half of the eighth century during the Umayyad period, the exegete Muqatil b. Sulayman (d. 767) asserts the full and equal partnership of female and male believers in matters of religion (*fi al-din*) and highlights their mutually reinforcing obedience to God in Qur'an 9:71.[11] The celebrated late ninth-century exegete al-Tabari from the 'Abbasid period similarly emphasises that righteous men and women 'who believe in God, His messenger and the verses of His book' are each other's allies (*ansar*) and supporters (*a'wan*). Their fundamental duty to promote what is right and prevent what is wrong consists in inviting people to monotheism and abandon the worship of idols, and to carry out their fundamental religious obligations, such as offering prayers and paying alms.[12]

The eleventh-century exegete al-Wahidi (d. 1076) similarly underscores the complementarity of men and women's religious and familial roles to be indicated in this verse. He quotes from the famous Companion Ibn 'Abbas who stated that believing women and men were allies of one another 'in regard to mercy and affection' (*fi al-rahma wa al-mahabba*). Al-Wahidi understands this statement to mean that they were like 'one hand in supporting [one another]' and, like al-Tabari, stresses that they were particularly called to invite people to worship the one God and to equally observe the fundamental tenets of Islam.[13] Very similar views are expressed by the well-known Andalusian exegete Muhammad b. Ahmad al-Qurtubi (d. 1273), who, on the basis of this verse, characterises the relationship between men and women as one of 'hearts united in mutual affection, love, and empathy'.[14]

Interestingly, al-Qurtubi's predecessor, the famous Fakhr al-Din al-Razi (d. 1210), who is otherwise generally quite prolix in his commentary on individual verses, does not comment at all on the nature of this partnership (*wilaya*) between women and men, as indicated in Qur'an 9:71.[15] The influential Mamluk exegete Ibn Kathir (d. 1373) in the fourteenth century does comment on this special bond existing among believers, men and women, and invokes the hadith in which the Prophet describes the faithful as constituting 'a [single] edifice in which each strengthens the other' in this context.[16] Worthy of note, however, is that Ibn Kathir uses only the masculine noun for believers (*al-mu'minin*) in his commentary, in stark contrast to our earlier commentators who repeated in their exegeses the masculine and the feminine plural nouns occurring in Qur'an 9:71 that refer explicitly to believers of both sexes.

Modern exegeses of Qur'an 9:71

In the nineteenth century, the prominent Egyptian scholar and reformer Muhammad 'Abduh and his student Rashid Rida collaborated together on a Qur'an commentary project, titled *Tafsir al-manar*, which remains influential until today. Since Rida continued with this project after 'Abduh's death in 1905, it is his voice that we hear in the exegesis of the ninth Qur'anic chapter and therefore I am referring to him alone in the discussion below.

It is in the *Tafsir al-manar* that we finally obtain a more detailed explanation of the nature of *wilaya*[17] (partnership) understood to be indicated in the verse, and how that applies to men and women, both equally and differentially. As far as their fundamental relationship is concerned, Rida states, the *wilaya* that exists, according to this verse, between believing women and men has to do 'in general with mutual support, solidarity and affection'. He also invokes hadiths as proof-texts, one in which Muhammad describes the community of Muslims as 'one body' and another (previously quoted by Ibn Kathir) in which the umma constitutes a 'single edifice in which each strengthens the other'. The 'alliance of support' (*wilayat al-nusra*) is specifically constituted so that all may collaborate in defending the truth, justice, the religious community, and the nation.[18]

Where gender does make a difference is in the realm of military defense of the polity. Here, says Rida, women offer their help and efforts in everything short of actual combat. He points to the example of the women Companions during the lifetime of the Prophet who provided water for thirsty combatants, prepared food and tended to the wounded on the battlefield.[19] Aside from this difference, Rida appears to consider men and women to be equally engaged in their efforts to promote what is right and prevent what is wrong.

Analysis and critique of exegeses of Qur'an 9:71

The fairly brief comments on the whole recorded by pre-modern male exegetes on what otherwise strikes us today as a revolutionary verse with potentially striking sociopolitical implications are perhaps telling. They underscore for us that the medieval male imaginary was not capable of extrapolating from this verse a larger scriptural mandate for men and women to work together companionably and on an equal footing in all spheres of life. They restrict the *wilaya* indicated in Qur'an 9:71 to essentially the religious sphere and do not (and perhaps could not) derive a broader empowerment of men and women equally in reforming both themselves and the larger society around them.

Rida in the twentieth century has a more capacious understanding of *wilaya* in connection with both men and women. He, however, places one restriction on the purview of the *wilaya* of women – that it does not extend to fighting on the battlefield, which remains a male preserve. By default, all other activities that constitute the promotion of truth, justice and righteousness are equally available to women and men by virtue of the Qur'anic mandate to serve as 'allies of one another'.

Male guardianship over women?

Whereas Qur'an 9:71 has typically not been the focus of masculine attention, another verse – Qur'an 4:34 – has been, and continues to be, the subject of prolific exegeses. The predicate adjective *qawwamun* that occurs in the verse is deliberately left untranslated below because of its contested meanings, as will be discussed shortly. The later verbal imperative in the verse that can be read either as *wa-dribuhunna* (majority pre-modern and modern reading) or *wa-'adribuhunna* (minority modern feminist reading) is translated to reflect both possible meanings. The verse states:

> Men are *qawwamun* over women because God has preferred some of them over others and because of what they spend of their wealth. Virtuous women are devout (*ganitat*), preserving that which is hidden according to what God has preserved. As for those women whose recalcitrance may be feared, reprimand them, banish them to their beds, and strike/avoid them. And if they obey you, then do not misbehave towards them at all; indeed God is majestic and great.

A sampling of pre-modern and modern exegeses is offered below to establish a range of common interpretations, which have been questioned and revisited by contemporary Muslim feminists.

Pre-modern exegeses of Qur'an 4:34

The Umayyad exegete Muqatil b. Sulayman preserves an early exegetical report on the occasion of revelation for the verse. According to this report, the verse concerns one of the eminent Ansar, Sa'd b. al-Rabi' b. 'Amr, who struck his wife Habiba bint Zayd b. Abi Zuhayr. Habiba and her father came to Muhammad to register a complaint about Sa'd's behaviour and the Prophet said that she was entitled to hit him back in retaliation (*qisas*) for her husband's behaviour. But then Qur'an 4:34 was revealed and the Prophet retracted his opinion and deferred to the divine judgement pronounced in the verse. Muqatil's construal of the implications of this divine judgement is highly revealing of the social mores of his time – the late Umayyad period. He proceeds to explain that *qawwamun* in this verse means that men have been granted authority over women and that men have been granted greater rights over women by virtue of the fact that they pay the bridal gift (*mahr*) to them. Men also exercise their authority in regard to general discipline and power over women. A wife cannot seek financial retribution (*qisas*) against her husband except in the case of loss of life and injury. The rest of the verse refers to virtuous women who are obedient (*qanitat*) to God and **to their husbands** (emphasis added) and who guard their private parts and their wealth in the absence of their husbands. As for those who manifest disobedience (*nushuz*) to their husbands like Sa'd's wife, comments Muqatil editorially, then they should first of all be given a warning, followed by abstention from intercourse with them. If these two measures do not achieve the desired result, then the wife may be struck in a way that does not cause any agony or disfigurement (*ghayr mubarrih ya'ni ghayr sha'in*). Once she has returned to proper wifely obedience, then she should not be burdened with showing affection to her husband 'more than she is capable of'.[20]

Muqatil's exegesis became very influential and has been reproduced in many commentaries after him. Al-Tabari in the late ninth–early tenth century refers to the occasion of revelation listed by Muqatil and provides it with several chains of transmission, thus documenting its widespread dissemination. Interestingly, the couple's names are not given in the versions listed by al-Tabari.[21] It is worthy of note that both Muqatil and al-Tabari clearly understand the verse to refer to the relationship between a husband and wife; therefore, the husband's *qiwama* (verbal noun derived from the same root as *qawwamun* and roughly means 'guardianship') is primarily a functional one, emanating from his position as financial provider for the family, to which a certain moral authority is appended. Only one report cited from the late-eighth-century scholar Ibn al-Mubarak (d. 797) (and attributed to the early Medinan jurist Sufyan al-Thawri, d. 778) does not provide the larger marital context and suggests that the verse be generally understood as referring to 'God's preference for men over women'.[22]

In reference to the Arabic word *qanitat* that occurs in the verse, al-Tabari cites several authorities who understand it to mean women who are obedient to both God and their husbands. The same Ibn al-Mubarak referred to above is cited as voicing the opinion that the word refers solely to 'women who are obedient to their husbands', for which point of view al-Tabari proceeds to express a clear preference.[23] As for the *nushuz* of the women, it consists of their haughtiness towards their husbands, 'rising up from their [husbands'] beds in disobedience', and contradicting their husbands in matters in which they should be obedient. This understanding, al-Tabari notes, is consistent with the etymology of the Arabic word *nushuz*, which has to do with 'elevation'.[24] Other authorities cited by al-Tabari offer similar meanings. One source – the Medinan Successor 'Ata' b. Abi Rabah (d. 733) maintained – significantly – that *nushuz* applied equally to the wife and husband and referred to the desire of each to separate from the other.[25]

Al-Tabari then elaborates upon what he understands to be the distinctive steps recommended by the Qur'an for dealing with a recalcitrant wife. Since this section is fairly long, only a synopsis of the larger points he makes is given here. The first step for the husband is to counsel the wife to remember God and return to the marital bed. According to Mujahid b. Jabr, the husband should plead with the wife to 'Fear God and return to your bed!' When the wife does so, no further action should be taken towards her.[26]

If the wife should fail to heed this counsel, the next step is for the husband to desist from having sexual relations with her and sleep apart from her; this was the view of Ibn 'Abbas, Sa'id b. Jubayr, and many others. A few authorities, such as 'Ikrima, were of the opinion that the husband should also avoid speaking to the wife.[27]

Should these first two steps not suffice, then the husband may lightly beat her (*darabaha ghayr mubarrih*) which leaves no marks on the body (*ghayr mu'aththir*) until she returns to a state of wifely obedience; this was the predominant interpretation attributed to Ibn 'Abbas and others.[28] A more detailed commentary from Ibn 'Abbas warns against striking the wife to the extent of breaking her bones, whether she acquiesces to her husband's entreaties or not. If she is physically hurt, then the husband must pay a compensation (*fidya*) for her injuries.[29] Ibn 'Abbas is also the main source for the view that a 'light beating' amounted to a more or less symbolic tapping with the equivalent of a toothbrush (*al-siwak*).[30] Al-Tabari concludes by asserting that once the wife has returned to obedience, the husband is obligated to fulfil his duties towards her and he may not seek to cause her any kind of physical or emotional harm.[31]

In his brief remarks on this verse, al-Wahidi in the eleventh century indicates to us that certain specific interpretations of Qur'an 4:34 had gained hold and subsequently disseminated as authoritative understandings of key terms in the verse. Thus, he understands the 'preference' that God has shown for 'some of them over others' as a specific reference to the 'superiority, as decreed by God, of men over women, by virtue of their intelligence, their body, knowledge, resolve, martial ability, status as legal witness, and greater rights in inheritance'.[32] What for the earlier exegetes constituted primarily the functional superiority of men over women in a domestic context has now been transformed in al-Wahidi's understanding into both an ontological and functional superiority.

Al-Wahidi further glosses the term *qanitat* as an exclusive reference to women who are 'obedient to their husbands'. Significantly, he does not list the alternate interpretation, more prevalent in the earlier period, that it is a reference to women who are also obedient to God. *Nushuz* is defined by him specifically and solely as the wife's 'disobedience towards [her] husband' and her defiant disagreement with him. Should verbal reprimand followed by abstinence from intercourse with her fail to achieve the desired result, the husband may gently strike her without causing physical harm (*ghayr mubarrih*).[33]

Very similar interpretations are recorded by al-Razi in the twelfth century.[34] He too understands the superiority attributed to men over women in both ontological and functional terms, as in al-Wahidi's commentary, but the list of reasons why men qua men are to be understood as superior to women has grown longer. Thus in addition to the reasons cited by al-Wahidi, al-Razi lists, for example, the man's ability to work harder, to write, his horsemanship and skill in spear-throwing. Furthermore, he reminds that through time the prophets and scholars have all been men, as have been political rulers, prayer leaders, callers to prayer, orators, and many others.[35]

The male's assumed ontological superiority over the female, in addition to the functional one, now becomes pervasive in the exegetical literature, as affirmed by al-Qurtubi in the thirteenth century.[36] Al-Qurtubi indicates on the authority of unnamed sources that by his time it had become customary to believe in the inherent differences in the natures of men and women that are also complementary, so that the nature (tab') of man is assumed to be defined by 'heat and dryness, in which there is force and strength' while the nature of woman is governed by 'moistness and cold, in which there is the essence of tenderness and weakness'.[37] Like a number of his predecessors, al-Qurtubi understands the virtuous qanitat to refer specifically to women who obey their husbands while fulfilling the rights of their husbands over them.[38] Unlike the other exegetes surveyed above, al-Qurtubi references the farewell sermon of Muhammad in which the Prophet cites Qur'an 4:34 and reminds his audience that men and women have specific rights in relation to one another. In this version of the farewell speech, Muhammad refers to 'overt wrongdoing' (fahisha mubayyina) as the reason for banishing women to their beds, followed by non-injurious beating if the first course of action fails to rectify her behaviour. Al-Qurtubi is careful to point out that this does not refer to adultery since that would incur the hadd punishment. According to him, the overall meaning of this part of the farewell speech in regard to the ideal domestic relationship, which serves as commentary on Qur'an 4:34, is that wives are exhorted not to anger their husbands and to concede to their husbands the right to determine, for example, who visits their household while husbands are required to feed and clothe them.[39]

In the commentary of another thirteenth-century exegete al-Baydawi (d. c.1286), men now possess 'perfection of intelligence' (kamal al-'aql) and 'excellence of deliberation' (husn al-tadbir), on account of which, and on account of many other distinctive traits, they enjoy an unqualified guardianship over women. Significantly, however, the virtuous qanitat are glossed as those who are obedient to God while cognisant of the rights that their husbands enjoy over them – a commentary that is in striking contrast to that of most of al-Baydawi's predecessors who showed a marked preference for glossing qanitat as women who owed obedience either exclusively to their husbands or to God and their husbands together.[40]

Ibn Kathir in the fourteenth century leaves no doubt that the guardianship that men are assumed to enjoy over women, according to Qur'an 4:34, is one of unassailable authority over every aspect of their existence and conduct. The words he uses, largely unprecedented in comparison with previous exegeses, in order to describe this aggrandised hierarchical relationship are revealing of the extent to which the marital bond between man and woman has been reconfigured as one of essential domination and subjugation. Thus the man has become the woman's 'head', her 'elder', her 'judge', and 'the one who disciplines her if she should stray'. Ibn Kathir adduces as an authoritative proof-text the solitary report recorded by al-Bukhari in which the Prophet warns that a nation governed by a woman will not prosper. This is a new proof-text that we encounter in Ibn Kathir's commentary in the context of this verse, which is clearly being deployed to warn against the consequences of letting women get 'the upper hand' in any manner or form (not just in the domestic sphere) in relation to men. It is also in his commentary that we see the clearest iteration of the absolute nature of man's superiority over woman by virtue of being male (*fa-'l-rajul afdal min al-mar'a fi nafsihi*).[41]

Not surprisingly, Ibn Kathir glosses the *qanitat* solely as women who are obedient to their husbands, citing Ibn 'Abbas 'and others' as his source. The nature of this unconditional obedience of wives to their husbands is driven home by the purported hadith in which Muhammad declares, 'If I were to command anyone to prostrate himself before another [person], it would be the wife before her husband on account of the rights he enjoys in relation to her.' Again, we had not encountered this hadith previously as a proof-text in the exegetical discussions of Ibn Kathir's predecessors, proving to us once again that male authoritarian attitudes towards women in the later period were progressively projected back to the time of the Prophet in the form of hadiths attributed to him, creating a powerful legitimising source for such changed sensibilities.[42]

Like his predecessors, Ibn Kathir expounds further on the various ways in which a wife can be coaxed back into the desired state of obedience; he similarly emphasises that the last step can only be a gentle and non-pain-inducing beating. Once she has returned to compliance, she cannot be subjected to further discipline or harsh behaviour because that would constitute wrongdoing towards her. Men are explicitly warned against oppressing wives in this manner in the latter part of the verse.[43]

Modern exegeses of Qur'an 4:34
In the *Tafsir al-manar*, Rida very clearly articulates the reasons that establish both the ontological and functional superiority of the man over the woman. He introduces the word *fitri* (ontological) in relation to certain attributes that are unique to men and which establish their privileged status vis-à-vis women. These attributes mainly have to do with the ability of men to protect, lead and defend society and their physical prowess; these essential gendered differences lead to different sets of responsibilities and regulations governing men and women.[44]

The functional superiority of the man is in the context of the family. Rida points out the usual financial responsibilities of the husband – the payment of the *mahr* to the wife, the financial maintenance of the family, and so on – all of which confer upon the husband 'a degree' (*daraja*) above the wife (in reference to Qur'an 2:227). The Sharia shows great honour towards women, continues Rida, but this degree of superiority that men enjoy over women is decreed by virtue of the inborn disposition (*fitra*) of men and the system of financial maintenance within the family that is based upon it.[45]

Rida proceeds to reference the views of Muhammad 'Abduh who had stated that the guardianship (*qiyama*) of the husband over the wife did not imply that the latter was subjugated (*maqhur*) and robbed of her will in general. Rather, the husband acts as a guide and counsellor for the general welfare of the family. The husband and wife are like parts of the same human body – the husband is the head and the wife the body – that seamlessly work together and have complementary demands on one another.[46]

The *qanitat* are women who are obedient to God as well as to their husbands in matters which require their obedience (*bi-'l-ma'ruf*).[47] As for *nushuz*, Rida, like most of his predecessors, understands it as referring to the wife's 'rising up' in disobedience to her husband and denying him his rights over her. As before, he indicates the progressive stages available to the husband to bring his recalcitrant wife into line and takes care to emphasise that the final stage involves only a light beating. Such a situation is understood to be exceptional and represents a last resort for the restoration of domestic harmony.[48] Rida quotes 'Abduh in this context, who had stressed that the normal state of marital relations should be characterised by 'gentleness towards women, refraining from oppressing them, and treating them with respect and dignity'.[49]

In sharp contrast to most of the exegetes discussed so far, the well-known modern scholars of Islam Fazlur Rahman (d. 1988) and Khaled Abou El Fadl have emphasised that the verse has to do only with the functional superiority of men due to their traditional role as breadwinners. If women assume such a role, as they regularly do in the modern world, then they too assume the obligation of *qiwama* or maintenance of the family since it is not *ipso facto* a gendered concept.[50] Others like the Syrian exegete Mohammed Shahrour and the Egyptian scholar Abu Zayd have similarly argued that the Qur'anic notion of *qiwama* is not gender-specific and that the overall message of gender egalitarianism in the Qur'an undermines a privileged status accorded to men qua men.[51]

Modern Islamist interpretations of Qur'an 4:34
The Egyptian Islamist thinker and activist Sayyid Qutb (d. 1966) wrote a Qur'an commentary titled *Fi Zilal al-Qur'an* (In the Shade of the Qur'an), which remains popular in Islamist circles. His emphasis on political and social activism to usher in a utopian 'Islamic state' on earth sets him apart from the modern

Muslim thinkers discussed above. More often than not, Islamists tend to have fairly conservative views about gender roles even as some of them emphasise women's political activism during a 'revolutionary' period as a necessary, albeit temporary, stage that society must pass through in order to achieve its larger permanent objectives. Qutb's exegesis of Qur'an 4:34 is both similar and surprisingly dissimilar in several respects when compared to that of his predecessors, as becomes evident below.

Qutb prefaces his discussion of Qur'an 4:34 with a lengthy disquisition on what he considers to be the nature of the Islamic family. His views on the complementarity of the roles of men and women within the Islamic family are quite romantic and surprisingly quite egalitarian. He begins by reminding his reader that the Qur'an speaks of male and female being created from a single soul (*nafs wahida*). Each is the equal mate of the other by creation and their coupling within marriage is meant to be a mutual source of solace and tranquility. Their equal status is indicated by the fact that men and women earn equal recompense for their good deeds and that women do not lose their independent identity within marriage.[52] Earlier in his *tafsir* work, Qutb had described in great detail the advantages of Islamic marriage for women, since upon entry into it they do not relinquish their name or their legal ability to finalise contracts and hold property independently of their husbands.[53]

So what is intended by the man's 'guardianship'? In addition to marriage being a private, pleasurable union between a man and a woman, Qutb reminds his reader that it is also 'the first organised unit' (*al-mu'assasa al-ula*) of human existence which exerts an inordinate amount of influence upon all other components of society. Within the family, husbands and wives carry out their functions determined by their inborn dispositions (*fitra*) that are mutually reinforcing. Thus, according to their fundamental nature, women become pregnant, deliver their children, nurse them and bring them up. These are, first of all, monumentally important functions, comments Qutb, and secondly, they entail a great deal of risk as well as physical and mental effort and thus hardly to be deemed trivial or easy.[54]

To complement the gentle, nurturing nature of women, men have therefore been endowed with toughness, firmness of resolve and the ability to deliberate upon matters before acting. These attributes had made them hunter-gatherers in the past and continue to allow them to fight to protect their wives and children, to earn a living, and to carry out all the other responsibilities that men traditionally assume. This is why men have been granted guardianship over women but, as Qutb is careful to point out, this guardianship (which he terms *al-qawama*) is exercised particularly within the family. This guardianship of men, he continues, does not in any way 'nullify the independent personhood of the woman within the home or in human society or her civic position'. Men are furthermore obligated to exercise their guardianship with sensitivity and gentleness and out of a desire to protect and support the family, both emotionally and financially.[55]

The virtuous woman who is *qanitat* in Qur'an 4:34 is one who has faith in God and guards her modesty. Her *qunut* therefore consists of being pious and chaste of her own volition, not because she is compelled to do so. Qutb points out significantly that the verse refers to pious women as *qanitat*, which is not to be equated with *muti'at*, which simply means the obedient females.[56] Although Qutb does not explicitly state this, we can understand his comment to imply a criticism of many of his predecessors who had more or less equated obedience to men with obedience to God.

As for *nushuz*, Qutb glosses it in the usual way – as a reference to the act of rising up in defiance and rebellion. In the ideal Muslim society governed by 'the Islamic program', *nushuz* should not prove to be a problem. In the event that it does occur decisive steps, as outlined in Qur'an 4:34, must be taken not to create strife between husband and wife but to ensure the continued welfare of the family and society. The initial reprimand, if unsuccessful, is to be followed by banishment to her bed, and then by a light beating as a last resort. Like all his predecessors, Qutb warns that the husband may not strike his wife out of anger and a desire for vengeance, seeking to cause her anguish and humiliation, but rather in the spirit of a loving father towards his children or a teacher towards his students.[57] It is this kind of positive 'willing acquiescence', not 'coerced obedience', that is intended by these verses; only the former may be considered the proper basis for the founding of 'the organisation of the family' and thus of the whole society.[58]

Analysis and critique of exegeses of Qur'an 4:34
The earliest exegetes in our survey, Muqatil b. Sulayman and al-Tabari, clearly understand Qur'an 4:34 to be applicable exclusively in the domestic context, so that the husband enjoys his preferential status by virtue of his role as economic provider. *Qanitat* is understood by both of them to refer to women who are obedient to God and their husbands. Ibn al-Mubarak (d. 797) emerges as the sole authority in both these early exegetical works who tries to promote a highly patriarchal understanding of this verse – in Muqatil's *tafsir*, he extrapolates a general divine preference for men over women, while in al-Tabari's commentary, he is cited as interpreting *qanitat* as women who are primarily obedient to their husbands. It is telling that al-Tabari expresses his approval of this latter commentary by Ibn al-Mubarak, indicating to us that by the early tenth century, such masculinist interpretations had started to take deep root. Significantly, al-Tabari notes the more egalitarian understanding of a very early authority – the pious abstemious scholar 'Ata' b. Abi Rabah (d. 733) – who notes that *nushuz* applies equally to the husband and wife and was a basic reference to the desire of either party to separate from the other. It is, however, an interpretation that does not find favour with al-Tabari.

Ibn al-Mubarak's perspective clearly proved to be the more enduring one through the vicissitudes of Islamic history. By al-Wahidi's time in the eleventh century, it is evident that male exegetes had made up their minds that a generic male superiority over women is to be assumed on the basis of this verse, rather than a more limited, functional one restricted to the domestic sphere. To this end, al-Wahidi compiles a lengthy list of the superior essential attributes that men enjoy qua men and the weighty sociopolitical roles they play that are denied to women. Significantly, and not at all unexpectedly, al-Wahidi glosses *qanitat* only as women who are obedient to their husbands and *nushuz* as applying only to women. Al-Razi, in the twelfth century, adds even more laudable traits to the list produced by al-Wahidi to underscore the male's intrinsic superiority over the female. It is clear that by this time man's superiority over woman is primarily assumed to be ontological and is taken to be self-evident. This conviction is now projected back to the Prophet's time as we see in the commentary of al-Qurtubi, whose exegesis in the thirteenth century invokes Muhammad's farewell speech as a proof-text. Even though the sermon refers to the reciprocal, potentially equal, rights of wives and husbands, al-Qurtubi puts a hierarchical spin on it and makes wives subordinate to the will of their husbands in adjudicating household matters in particular.

Although his younger contemporary al-Baydawi similarly endorses men's 'guardianship' over women, he notably glosses *qanitat* as a reference to virtuous women who owe their obedience only to God, in sharp contradistinction to most of his predecessors. Al-Baydawi's seems to be a lone, dissenting voice in the late medieval period when an overwhelming majority of male exegetes had convinced themselves that the Arabic root *qnt* in relation to women referred either to obedience on their part to both God and their husbands or exclusively to their husbands, while the same root in relation to men referred to their obedience to God alone.

Rashid Rida in the early twentieth century emphasises not so much a hierarchical relationship between husbands and wives as complementarity in their roles vis-à-vis one another. The functional superiority of the husband within the family resides in his greater physical ability to defend and protect those in his care and to financially provide for his family. The 'degree' of superiority that is accorded to men as a consequence of their familial responsibilities is, however, not interpreted by Rida to indicate a general superiority of men over women.

A generation later, Qutb similarly emphasises the complementarity of the roles of men and women within marriage that reflect their different physical and biological endowments. Outside of the domestic realm, women and men are the exact spiritual equals of one another since the Qur'an promises equal recompense to the faithful for their good deeds regardless of gender. And, surprisingly, it is Qutb with his reputation for radical Islamist views, and not the modernist Rida, who stresses that *qanitat* refers to modest women who place their faith exclusively in God and the word contains no suggestion of obedience to human beings.

More recently, Abou El Fadl, Shahrur, and Abu Zayd have emphasised the general gender egalitarianism of the Qur'an to challenge classical understandings of this verse as promoting a partriarchal familial paradigm and a concurrent inferior social and legal status for women in relation to men. They maintain that when read holistically, the Qur'an cannot be understood to be complicit in such socio-legal constructions of gendered identities.

It is indeed worthy of note that when the pre-modern exegetes referenced above resorted to talking about the ontological superiority of the male over the female, they did not temper their discussion by referring to, for example, Qur'an 33:35, which posits the unequivocal spiritual and moral equality of men and women, or to Qur'an 9:71, which refers to the mutual partnership of men and women and their equal moral agency on the basis of righteousness. In fact the scant attention paid by male exegetes to these otherwise critical verses in comparison with the lavish attention given to Qur'an 4:34 is very revealing of the gendered identities and relationships envisioned by them through time. It is not until the modern period – when we encounter the exegeses of women scholars who focus particularly on cross-referential reading of the Qur'an – that we are exposed to the full potential of Qur'an 33:35, 9:71, and other related verses, to ameliorate the narrow, androcentric readings of particularly their pre-modern male counterparts.

Muslim feminist hermeneutics of the modern and contemporary periods

Beginning in the twentieth century, Muslim feminist scholars started going back to the Qur'anic text itself in order to circumvent what they perceived as the distinctively woman-unfriendly exegeses of specific verses generated by certain male scholars. These feminist scholars hoped thereby to retrieve the original egalitarian élan of the Qur'an itself. Such a feminist hermeneutic enterprise has been richly rewarding. Through their egalitarian lens, these women exegetes offer critiques of traditional methodologies of engaging the Qur'an and offer 'alternative' readings of verses that deal specifically with gendered relations. Their exegeses underscore the polyvalence of the Qur'anic text and the possibilities of extracting multiple meanings from scripture based on specific reading strategies that are fully cognisant of historical contexts and of the frequently diverse semantic spectrum of key terms and concepts. The writings of some of the most prominent of these modern exegetes (women and men) that have proved to be quite influential are selectively discussed below. What their potential for long-term changes may be is also briefly assessed.

Going back to the basics: rereading the Qur'an

A slim volume published by an American Muslim scholar, Amina Wadud, in 1992 by a little-known Malaysian publisher under the title of *Qur'an and Woman* (later reissued by Oxford University Press in 1999) quickly gained the recognition it deserved. Written from the perspective of a female scholar of Islam, it was the first monograph-length treatment of specifically the 'woman question' in Islam's holiest text. [59] Most traditionalist male authors writing on the 'woman question' in the modern period often adopt a didactic tone seeking to instruct Muslim women on how to properly comport themselves.[60] When they invoked the Qur'an to discuss normative gendered behaviour, they frequently reproduced the commentaries of the classical exegetes and added very little that was original to the discussion. Exceptions are to be found among the modernist male thinkers discussed above but their influence was not as extensive as that of the more traditionalist male exegetes. Wadud's work proved to be groundbreaking not only because it was produced by a female scholar but also because it insisted on going back to the actual wording of the original Qur'anic verses, bypassing, as it were, the learned but highly gendered exegeses of the classical male commentators, in order to retrieve a woman-friendly perspective.

In this book Wadud suggests adopting what she calls a 'hermeneutics of *tawhid*', referring to a holistic method of reading the Qur'an that specifically challenged the line-by-line atomistic method of interpretation that was so popular among many medieval exegetes (and remains so till today). If the Qur'anic claim of establishing a 'universal basis for moral guidance' is to be taken seriously, asserts Wadud, then Muslim exegetes must develop a hermeneutical framework that leads to 'a systematic rationale for making correlations [among Qur'anic verses] and [which] sufficiently exemplifies the full impact of Qur'anic coherence'.[61] Universals and particulars must be distinguished from one another; time- and place-bound interpretations must be recognised as such and their limited applicability recognised. Wadud's interpretive venture is thus fundamentally concerned with retrieving an unending 'trajectory of social, political and moral possibilities' that remain consistent with the overall 'Qur'anic ethos of equity, justice and human dignity' in changing historical and sociopolitical circumstances.[62] Wadud, who had studied with Fazlur Rahman at the University of Chicago, was clearly continuing the modernist tradition of emphasising the objectives of the Sharia (*maqasid al-shari'a*) in her hermeneutic project.

Another prominent feminist scholar, Asma Barlas, similarly emphasises the development of a new Qur'anic hermeneutics that would effectively challenge and undermine traditional understandings of key Qur'anic verses related to gender and women's roles in society. Barlas says:

> Even though a Qur'ānic hermeneutics cannot by itself put an end to patriarchal, authoritarian, and undemocratic regimes and practices, it nonetheless remains

crucial for various reasons. First, hermeneutic and existential questions are ineluctably *connected* [emphasis in text]. As the concept of sexual/textual oppression suggests, there is a relationship between what we read texts to be saying and how we think about and treat real women. This insight, though associated with feminists because of their work on reading and representation, is at the core of revelation albeit in the form of the reverse premise: that there is a relationship between reading (sacred texts) and liberation ... Accordingly, if we wish to ensure Muslim women their rights, we not only need to contest readings of the Qur'ān that justify the abuse and degradation of women, we also need to establish the legitimacy of liberatory readings.[63]

This emphasis on a holistic reading of the Qur'anic text is a hallmark of modernist and feminist exegeses so that single verses, especially those that appear to be promoting gender inequity, may be read in conjunction with other verses that are thematically and semantically related, allowing for the emergence of other interpretive possibilities.[64] A classic example of this would be the term *nushuz*, which as we saw in reference to Qur'an 4:34, was understood exclusively as a reference to a woman's arrogant demeanor and behaviour towards her husband. Only a very early source – 'Ata' b. Abi Rabah – is quoted by al-Tabari as understanding *nushuz* to refer to a constellation of negative traits in both men and women.

'Ata' may have been among our very early feminist readers of the Qur'an who preferred to read the text cross-referentially because the Qur'an does in fact refer to *nushuz* on the part of both men and women. The corresponding verse in regard to men is Qur'an 4:128, which states, 'If a woman fears *nushuz* or rejection (*i'rad*) from her husband, there is no blame on them if they reach a settlement, and settlement is better, even though people's souls are miserly.' Al-Tabari understands *nushuz* on the part of the husband to be similar to *nushuz* on the part of the wife – that it is an attitude of haughtiness and pride towards one's spouse and expression of distaste towards her, whether it is on account of her lack of comeliness, advancing years, or other reasons. *I'rad* consists of turning away from her with his face or withholding certain benefits that she is accustomed to receiving from him. In such cases, the couple is exhorted to seek arbitration and reconciliation, which, he comments, is better than separation and/or divorce.[65]

It is highly noteworthy that even though the same term is used in both verses and may be understood to imply the same basic meaning in relation to the husband and wife, none of the male exegetes mentioned above referred to Qur'an 4:128 in connection with Qur'an 4:34. Instead, they showed a clear preference for explaining the term solely as it occurs in the latter verse to sharply demarcate gendered differences, with the earliest commentators delineating these differences within the domestic sphere, progressing to al-Tabari and his successors who proceeded to extrapolate broad ontological differences between the male and the female. The result was a highly patriarchal family with *nushuz* implying primarily wifely disobedience to her husband, who wielded considerable authority over her physical and emotional well-being. Reading the two verses which contain the term *nushuz* together to underscore instead a much more egalitarian and reciprocal concept of marital rights and duties has become the hallmark of feminist exegeses, which seek to question and revise the more predominant androcentric conceptions of marriage and family.[66]

The imperative *wa-dribuhunna* in Qur'an 4:34 provokes similar feminist anxiety – how can the concept of a loving, equal and peaceful union between wife and husband be justified when the man possesses the exclusive right to 'beat' her?[67] It is clear that the verb elicited similar concern on the part of the classical male jurists who under no circumstance condoned violent retribution against a wilful and recalcitrant wife – a light tapping that caused no physical injury was the maximum discipline that was considered permissible by them as a last resort after other non-corporal means of chastisement had been exhausted. The practice of this husbandly 'duty' did not then amount to wife battery as the concept is understood today in reference to physical and injurious brutality perpetrated against the wife by an abusive husband. Such battery, as we saw, is regarded as a criminal, reprehensible activity for which the scholars considered the husband to be legally liable and required to pay compensation to his wife.

At best a symbolic physical chastising, *daraba* in the sense of beating – however light – still remains problematic for Muslim feminist exegetes today. Surely, a number of them ask, an immensely just and infinitely benevolent God would not sanction an act that even hints at physical violence and implies a skewed relationship of power between the husband and wife? The answer for these scholars to such a theodicean question lies in the rich polysemy of the Arabic root *drb*: besides to beat, the root in its various derivative forms can also mean 'to avoid or shun someone'; 'to have sexual relations with a person'; and 'to set an example', among others.[68] Two alternative meanings that have been favoured in feminist exegeses for this imperative are as follows (indicated in bold): (a) as for those women whose *nushuz* may be feared, reprimand them, banish them to their beds and **have intercourse with them**; and (b) as for those women whose *nushuz* may be feared, reprimand them, banish them to their beds and **depart from them/leave them alone**. The second meaning is generated by understanding the imperative as being derived from the fourth verbal form *'adraba* rather than from the first verbal form *daraba*; a slight change in orthography (with the addition of the *hamza* to the initial *alif*) credibly leads to the meaning of 'leave them alone'. This last reinterpretation is quite popular among feminist exegetes, women and men, because it further satisfactorily accords with what is known of Muhammad's conduct towards his wives, whom he is known to have never struck or addressed harshly. The Prophet after all was the living sunna and his behaviour exemplified the essence of the Qur'anic message.[69]

Feminist exegetes will furthermore argue that a fuller sense of the equal, complementary roles that men and women are expected to assume within an Islamic marriage emerges when other Qur'anic verses that are relevant to this discussion are brought in. Prominent among them is Qur'an 2:187 which reads, '[wives] are your garments and you [husbands] are their garments'; 'garments' here are understood to be a metaphor for mutual comfort and joy and the equal rights shared by wives and husbands vis-à-vis one another in the marital relationship. Another equally relevant verse is Qur'an 30:21 which states, 'And among His signs is this, that He has created for you mates from among yourselves, that you may dwell in tranquillity with them; and He has put love and mercy between you'. As Barlas comments memorably, 'the Qur'an does not use sex to construct ontological or sociological hierarchies that discriminate against women'; and that 'the Qur'an recognizes sexual specificity but does not assign it gender symbolism'.[70]

When we import into this discussion the Qur'anic assertion of men and women enjoying equal rights vis-à-vis one another (Qur'an 2:226) and their complementary roles as partners in establishing a good, just society (Qur'an 9:71), for example, the patriarchal conceptions of marriage and family, which spilled over into the socio-economic sphere, are logically rendered untenable within the Islamic milieu, as stressed by Azizah al-Hibri and others.[71] This did not, of course, prevent certain male scholars, particularly jurists, from promoting the patriarchal model of familial and marital relations as worthy of adoption, no doubt because it was in conformity with the prevailing cultural notions and sensibilities of their day.[72] Historicising juridical and exegetical discourses as specific products of their time and milieu that often subverted the fundamental Qur'anic ethos of justice and equality with respect to gender is a major driving force behind feminist hermeneutics and, one should add, its most persuasive and compelling aspect.

Hadiths used as exegetical reports on specific Qur'anic verses
In addition to Qur'anic exegeses, feminist discourses have also been critical of the way certain statements attributed to the Prophet have been deployed by male exegetes to circumscribe women's access to the public sphere and aggrandise the social and legal prerogatives of men over women. Such purported hadiths are used as exegetical reports that frequently transform and subvert the prima facie meanings of certain Qur'anic verses so as to conform to specific gendered perspectives that lead to inequality and discrimination against women. Modernist scholars in general and feminist scholars in particular are concerned with maintaining the primacy of the Qur'an over the hadith literature, especially when certain tendentious hadiths directly contradict either the specific wording of Qur'anic verses or the overall ethos of the Qur'an.

Reports attributed to the Prophet with undeniable misogynist content that are used for exegetical purposes have been severely criticised by feminist scholars. Such a report is cited by Ibn Kathir in his explication of Qur'an 4:34 which intimates that were it not for Islam's strict monotheism, women would have been commanded to prostrate before their husbands. Such a report suggests a highly unequal marital relationship, so much so that the wife is placed in an abjectly servile position vis-à-vis the husband. Even though this purported hadith comes close to violating a fundamental and cardinal tenet within Islam that no one but God may be worshipped by humans and even though to hint at the possibility of any other being even remotely approaching God in this respect is clearly quite egregious in the Islamic context, it is cavalierly deployed by Ibn Kathir to make the larger point that women owe unquestioning obedience to their husbands.

In his critique of this report, Khaled Abou El Fadl first points out that it is one of the solitary reports (*ahadi*) which do not rise to the level of reliability assured by multiple chains of transmission and wide dissemination (*tawatur*).[73] Second, it is also important to analyse the content (*matn*) of the hadith and determine if it is in accordance with or contradictory to Qur'anic injunctions. After taking note of several reports which similarly advocate the 'fatuous adulation of husbands', Abou El Fadl notes that:

> this preeminence given, in these traditions, to the whims and desires of husbands is contrary to Islamic principles that dictate that the merit of a person is defined by his or her piety and good deeds . . .The Qur'anic conception of marriage is not based on servitude but on compassion and cooperation, and the Qur'anic conception of virtue is not conditioned on the pleasure of another human being, but on piety and obedience to God.[74]

Abou El Fadl thus stresses the necessity of analysing the text (*matn*) of the hadith and determining its credibility in accordance with its conformity or lack of conformity with relevant Qur'anic passages. *Matn* analysis, however, is a woefully underdeveloped aspect of the science of hadith criticism, which typically lays emphasis upon scrutiny of the *isnad* or chain of transmission of a report. As a result, hadiths with tendentious content but equipped with chains of transmission deemed irreproachable, according to the detailed criteria developed by the hadith specialists, made their way into authoritative collections. They could then be deployed as proof-texts in critical matters with potentially grave implications. This relative inattention to analysis of hadith texts was deplored by Fazlur Rahman as contributing to legal and moral determinations by jurists and theologians that were at loggerheads with Qur'anic principles.[75]

The report concerning the inability of a nation to prosper if its affairs are governed by a woman, invoked by Ibn Kathir in his exegesis of Qur'an 4:34, has similarly been subjected to extended critique by feminists and modernist scholars. Fatima Mernissi's critique of this report based on both historical reasons and *isnad* analysis has justly become well known. She points out that this hadith is transmitted solely by the Companion Abu Bakra, thus marking it as one of the solitary reports. More problematically, Abu Bakra had once been flogged by 'Umar for giving false testimony in a case involving adultery, which casts serious aspersions on his personal probity and thus his standing as a reliable hadith transmitter. The historical circumstances surrounding the provenance of this report also give rise to suspicion. Abu Bakra happened to have conveniently 'remembered' this so-called hadith around the time of the Battle of the Camel led by 'A'isha, the Prophet's widow. Mernissi notes that a renowned scholar like al-Tabari did not accept the reliability of this report.[76]

It was discussed earlier how the biblical rib story was imported into the exegetical literature to impute secondary status to the female in relation to the male, in direct contravention of the Qur'anic account of the creation of Adam and his wife which makes no such reference and does not specifically grant the male primacy in creation. The Qur'anic version was too starkly egalitarian for a number of our male exegetes in the post-Tabari period, as we noted, which needed to be tempered by the banal inequities of the real world. The importation of such 'hadiths' into the exegetical literature that testified to the secondary status of women and mandated their subjugation to men was in line with the progressive promotion of the patriarchal family as the ideal basic social unit within Islamic society.

Difference between the general and the particular: misreading the Qur'an

A fundamental flaw in traditional Qur'anic hermeneutics has been the inability of many exegetes to distinguish between the general or universal commandments of the Qur'an and the particular, contextualised applications of them. In the discipline of *tafsir*, this division is well recognised in regard to the meaning of verses – *'amm* (general) vs *khass* (particular) – but not necessarily applied in a consistent manner. This has led to what a number of scholars today consider to be misreadings of the Qur'an, especially when it concerns gender (among other issues).[77] This was already evident when we discussed Qur'an 4:34 which prima facie refers to the differentiated roles of men and women within the specific context of the family. However, as our diachronic survey revealed, most post-classical exegetes derived a theory of the general superior status of the male vs the female from this verse and misread what was a functional description of the male's status within the family as a universal one, applicable to all time and place.

Another verse that has been subjected to such a misreading is Qur'an 2:282 which reads, 'Set up two witnesses from your own men, and if there are not two men, then choose a man and two women as witnesses, so that if one makes a mistake, then the other can remind her.' Despite the fact that the context in which this verse is embedded refers to a very specific kind of financial enterprise – a loan transaction – the verse has been invoked by some as a proof-text to establish that a woman's legal testimony in general is worth half that of a man. This disparity is assumed to stem from her tendency to be forgetful and to be not as mentally competent as a man. This position is quite popular among conservative factions today, but, as Muhammad Fadel has shown, this view cannot be attributed uniformly to the medieval *fuqaha'*. Instead, he shows that many medieval jurists had much more complex and sophisticated views on the validity of women's testimony and two of the most prominent pre-modern jurists, Ibn Taymiyya (d. 1328) and his student Ibn Qayyim al-Jawziyya (d. 1350), both of whom incidentally are highly regarded in the same conservative circles today given their Hanbali affiliations, came very close to articulating the equal valid testimony of women compared to men. These two jurists clearly understood that the general cannot be derived from the particular.[78] Because of the restrictive context of Qur'an 2:282, a woman's incompetence in financial transactions in the pre-modern world where such competence would have been rare has no bearing in other matters where she may have competency equal or superior to a man's – in hadith transmission and childbearing matters, for example. In fact, in the field of hadith transmission with its rigorous standards of moral probity and accurate oral transmission, the individual testimony of women narrators about the reliability of hadiths that they related from the Prophet was frequently and freely accepted when they met this high bar. Both the Qur'anic context and the historical practices – the living sunna – of the early community provide irrefutable proof that Qur'an 2:282 was not meant to constitute a generalisable rule about the value of a woman's legal testimony. When this verse is read along with Qur'an 33:35 and 9:71, for example, it is clear that the universal proclamation of women's ontological equality to men and affirmation of their independent moral agency in these two verses trump the particularist understanding of feminine limitations which are attributable to mere historical contingency.

The more rigorous hermeneutics of the Qur'an adopted by feminists and other scholars today point to more interpretive possibilities than were imaginable in the past. In this exegetical process, they are resorting to compelling new readings of scripture that they take great pains to show do not violate the fundamental spirit and intent of the Qur'an – but that in fact represent a greater fidelity to its core message of equality and justice that is not restricted by gender or any other worldly construction of privilege and difference.

Feminist hermeneutics and socio-legal change: a case study

This new feminist hermeneutics is not of mere academic interest; it is being increasingly deployed by scholars and activists in a number of different social and academic contexts. As a case study of this kind of Muslim feminist hermeneutics in action and its potentially transformative consequences in the lives of real women, we will now turn our attention to one of the foremost, if not the foremost of modern women's organisations today to openly challenge traditional male interpretations of the Qur'an and their legal formulations. This organisation is Sisters in Islam, a Malaysian feminist organisation led by the redoubtable feminist activist Zainah Anwar.

Zainah Anwar, born into a prominent family in Johor Bahru in Malaysia, served as a journalist for the well-known Malaysian newspaper the *New Straits Times* and earned a degree in International Law and Diplomacy at the Fletcher School of Diplomacy at Tufts University in 1986. In 1988, she helped found Sisters in Islam along with a group of women lawyers, activists, academics and journalists. This organisation was launched to investigate the problems encountered by Muslim women in Sharia courts in Malaysia and to challenge laws and policies that claim to be founded on Islamic legal principles but are clearly discriminatory towards women. Its members have sponsored public debates and instituted education programmes which tackle controversial topics, such as equal rights for women, issues of dress and modesty, right to hold public office, including judgeships, and the right to guardianship, among others. They have also expanded to deal with larger issues of democracy, human rights and constitutionalism. Not surprisingly, Sisters in Islam has provoked criticism from conservative religious scholars in Malaysia because the women leaders are not traditionally trained scholars. However, some of the more liberal religious clergy have responded positively to overtures from Sisters in Islam and participated in seminars with them.[79]

Anwar has forcefully argued that patriarchal interpretations of Islam are to blame for current social injustices against women, and that a broader conversation about progressive interpretations and the role of Islam in daily life must be initiated.[80] In an article that Zainah Anwar co-authored with Jana S. Rumminger, she identified some key challenges to legal reform in Muslim-majority societies which women's activist groups need to tackle and proactively engage with in order to undermine them. Primary among these challenges are: (1) the popular but inaccurate belief in many mainstream Muslim societies that Muslim family law is God's law and is, therefore, infallible and unchangeable, so that any effort at reform is regarded as un-Islamic and contrary to the well-being of Muslims; and (2) the general belief that men and women do not have equal rights in Islam, so that demands for equal rights to divorce, guardianship and inheritance, for example, are portrayed as going against the Sharia.[81]

Anwar set up the Sisters in Islam in order to address these concerns and offer leadership and guidance to women who were increasingly questioning the non-egalitarian interpretations offered by traditional religious leaders. To this end, Sisters in Islam members strove to educate women in particular about their scripturally mandated rights within Islam and promoted rereadings of religious texts in view of two foundational principles or objectives of the religious law: equality and justice. They have distributed pamphlets among the Malaysian public containing reinterpretations of key Islamic texts emphasising equality and justice irrespective of gender. They also run legal clinics, programmes to raise public awareness of general legal and more specifically gender issues, and carry out research in legislative reform. Anwar has stressed her belief that over time an understanding of Islam and Islamic laws that recognise equality and justice would gain ground in Malaysia and elsewhere.[82]

Sisters in Islam have recently broadened their efforts beyond Malaysian society with the establishment of a new organisation by Zainah Anwar called Musawah, which is an Arabic word meaning 'equality'. As the name indicates, this group's main agenda is to work to ensure that Muslim women are treated equally within the families and communities of Muslim-majority societies. The project was initiated with a global meeting in February 2009 that brought together over 250 Muslim scholars and feminist activists from nearly fifty countries. Musawah focuses on 'knowledge-building,' an enterprise which includes commissioning background research on the roles of *qiwama* and *wilaya* within historical and present-day Muslim legal traditions and attempting to open spaces for scholars and activists to discuss and forge new understandings of *qiwama* and *wilaya*.[83]

As our earlier discussion established, the terms *qiwama* and *wilaya* of Qur'anic provenance have been traditionally understood to refer to men's authority over women and interpreted accordingly by male jurists to mandate women's subjugation and obedience to their husbands. Musawah seeks to undermine the specific legal privileges conferred upon the husband on the basis of classical juridical interpretations of these concepts through the application of 'feminist and rights-based lenses in understanding and searching for equality and justice within Muslim legal traditions'.[84]

Ultimately, as a knowledge-building initiative, Musawah's long-term objective is to create a women's rights- and human rights-based discourse within an Islamic matrix that will create lasting legal and social change in Muslim-majority societies.[85]

Conclusion

It has been suggested that Islamic feminism has the potential to be more radical than secular feminism, since the former calls for comprehensive equal rights in the public sphere as well as the private sphere.[86] In fact, Muslim feminists tend to dissolve the distinctions between the two spheres and argue for full equality within the home and outside. Typically secular feminists in Muslim-majority societies have called for equal rights in the public sphere but have settled for complementarity in the domestic realm, so that the husband continues to be recognised as head of the household and men and women play different and complementary roles within it. Muslim feminists, like Heba Rauf in Egypt, argue instead that the Qur'an mandates full gender equality in all spheres of life and they reject complementarity as a feature of patriarchal societies that is not consonant with the Qur'anic vision.[87]

There is no doubt that Islamic feminism will continue to gain traction in the near future as Muslim women continue to seek a gender-egalitarian hermeneutic for the twenty-first century and beyond. Zainah Anwar speaks for a majority of Muslim women when she remarks:

> For most Muslim women, rejecting religion is not an option. We are believers, and as believers, we want to find liberation, truth and justice from within our own faith. We feel strongly that we have a right to reclaim our religion, to redefine it, to participate and contribute to an understanding of Islam, how it is codified and implemented – in ways that take into consideration the realities and experience of women's lives today.[88]

Muslim women's activism of this kind may bring about some of the most far-reaching transformations in the Islamic legal and cultural domains, indications of which are already becoming quite apparent.

Notes

1. Lila Abu-Lughod, *Do Muslim Women Need Saving?* (Cambridge, MA: Harvard University Press, 2013), 6. See also Saadia Toor, 'Imperialist Feminism Redux', *Dialectical Anthropology* 36 (2012): 147–60.
2. This twin phenomenon is expertly analysed by Katherine Ewing, *Stolen Honor: Stigmatizing Muslim Men in Berlin* (Palo Alto: Stanford University Press, 1992).
3. For accounts of women's participation in the Arab Spring uprisings, see William Cleveland and Martin Bunton, *A History of the Modern Middle East*, 5th ed. (Boulder: Westview Press, 2012), Chapter 26, 'The 2011 Arab Uprisings', 522–40; and Isobel Coleman, 'On the Front Line of Change: Women in the Arab Uprisings', POMED Policy Brief, 26 July 2011; available at <http://pomed.org/wordpress/wp-content/uploads/2011/10/Policy-Brief_Coleman.pdf>; last accessed on 3 August 2014.
4. For one such encounter of a woman chastising the second caliph 'Umar for unilaterally attempting to impose a ceiling on the value of the bride-gift (*mahr*), see al-Shawkani, *Fath al-qadir: al-jami' bayna fannay al-riwaya wa-'l-diraya min 'ilm al-tafsir* (Beirut: Dar al-kutub al-'ilmiyya, 1996), 1:563; Asma Afsaruddin, *The First Muslims: History and Memory* (Oxford: Oneworld, 2008), 40.
5. See, for example, Fatima Mernissi, *The Veil and the Male Elite: A Feminist Interpretation of Women's Rights in Islam*, tr. Mary Jo Lakeland (Reading, MA: Addison-Wesley, 1991), 51 ff.
6. See Asma Afsaruddin, 'Early Women Exemplars and the Construction of Gendered Space: (Re-)Defining Feminine Moral Excellence', in Marilyn Booth (ed.), *Harem Histories: Envisioning Places and Living Spaces* (Durham, NC and London: Duke University Press, 2010), 23–48.
7. Leila Ahmed, *Women and Gender in Islam* (New Haven: Yale University Press, 1992); Louise

Marlow, *Hierarchy and Egalitarianism in Islam* (Cambridge: Cambridge University Press, 2002).

8. Barbara Stowasser, 'The Chapter of Eve', in *Women in the Qur'an, Traditions, and Interpretation* (Oxford: Oxford University Press, 1994), 25–38.
9. Rifaat Hassan, 'Made from Adam's Rib': the Woman's Creation Question, *al-Mushir* (1985): 124–55; Stowasser, *Women in the Qur'an*, 28–37.
10. Azizah al-Hibri, 'A Study of Islamic Herstory?' *Women's Studies International Forum, Special Issue: Women and Islam* 5 (1982): 207–19.
11. Muqatil, *Tafsir*, 2:181.
12. Al-Tabari, *Tafsir*, 6:415.
13. Al-Wahidi, *al-Wasit fi tafsir al-Qur'an*, ed. 'Adil Ahmad 'Abd al-Mawjud (Beirut: Dar al-kutub al-'ilmiyya, 1994), 2:509.
14. Al-Qurtubi, *al-Jami' li-ahkam al-qur'an*, ed. 'Abd al-Razzaq al-Mahdi (Beirut: Dar al-kitab al-'arabi, 2001), 8:186.
15. Al-Razi, *al-Tafsir al-kabir*, 6:101–3.
16. Ibn Kathir, *Tafsir*, 2:353.
17. *Wilaya* is the verbal noun related to *awliya'* (partners/allies), derived from a common verbal root.
18. Rida, *Tafsir*, 10:471.
19. Ibid.
20. Muqatil, *Tafsir*, 1:370–1.
21. Al-Tabari, *Tafsir*, 4:60–1.
22. Ibid. 4:60.
23. Ibid. 4:62.
24. Ibid. 4:64.
25. Ibid.
26. Other authorities are cited for similar interpretations; see the full discussion in ibid. 4:65.
27. See this extensive discussion in ibid., 4:67–9.
28. Ibid. 4:69–71.
29. Ibid. 4:70.
30. Ibid. 4:71.
31. Ibid.
32. Al-Wahidi, *Wasit*, 2:45.
33. Ibid. 2:46–7.
34. Al-Razi, *Tafsir*, 4:70–3.
35. Ibid. 4:70.
36. Al-Qurtubi, *Jami'*, 5:161–7.
37. Ibid. 5:162.
38. Ibid.
39. Ibid. 5:166.
40. Al-Baydawi, *Tafsir al-Baydawi* (Beirut: Dar al-kutub al-'ilmiyya, 1988), 1:213.
41. Ibn Kathir, *Tafsir*, 1:465.
42. Ibid. 1:466.
43. Ibid. 1:466–7.
44. Rida, *Tafsir*, 5:55.
45. Ibid.
46. Ibid. 5:56–7.
47. Ibid., 5:58.
48. Ibid. 5:59–63.

49. Ibid. 5:61.
50. For Rahman, see his *Major Themes of the Qur'an* (Chicago: University of Chicago Press, 2009), 49; for Abou El Fadl, see his *Conference of the Books: The Search for Beauty in Islam* (Lanham, MD: University of America Press, 2001), 273.
51. For these views and the discussion of more modern authors in this vein, see Abdullah Saeed, *Reading the Qur'an in the Twenty-first Century* (London and New York: Routledge, 2014), 118–125.
52. Sayyid Qutb, *Fi Zilal al-Qur'an*, 2: 648–9.
53. Ibid. 2:646.
54. Ibid. 2:650.
55. Ibid. 2:651–2.
56. Ibid. 2:652–3.
57. Ibid. 2:653–4.
58. Ibid. 2:655.
59. Amina Wadud, *Qur'an and Woman: Rereading the Sacred Text from a Woman's Perspective* (New York: Oxford University Press, 1999).
60. One such example is the Urdu publication *Bihishti Zewar* (Heavenly Ornaments) written by the Indian Deobandi scholar Ashraf 'Ali Thanawi (d. 1943). For a partial translation of this work, see Barbara Metcalf, *Perfecting Women: Maulana Ashraf Ali Thanawi's Bihishti Zewar* (Berkeley: University of California Press, 1992).
61. Wadud, *Qur'an and Woman*, xii.
62. Ibid. xii–xiii. See also her subsequent book *Inside the Gender Jihad: Women's Reform in Islam* (Oxford: Oneworld, 2006), which builds on her first book in pushing forward a hermeneutical schema for emphasising gender equality in the Qur'anic context.
63. Asma Barlas, *'Believing Women' in Islam: Unreading Patriarchal Interpretations of the Qur'an* (Austin, TX: University of Texas Press, 2004).
64. For such a holistic reading of the Qur'an, see Sardar, *Reading the Qur'an, passim*; and especially 305–21 for issues related to women and sexuality.
65. Al-Tabari, *Tafsir*, 4:304 ff.
66. See further discussion of *nushuz* by feminist scholars in Mohamed Mahmoud, 'To Beat or Not to Beat: On the Exegetical Dilemmas over Qur'ān, 4:34', *Journal of the American Oriental Society* 126 (2006): 546–9.
67. See this discussion in Ayesha S. Chaudhry, *Domestic Violence and the Islamic Tradition* (Oxford: Oxford University Press, 2014), 1–22.
68. Hadia Mubarak discusses many of the semantic possibilities in her 'Breaking the Interpretive Monopoly: A Re-Examination of Verse 4:34', *Hawwa* 2 (2004), 261–2.
69. This interpretation however does not address the grammatical problem generated by not having the expected Arabic pronoun *'an* before the pronominal suffix *hunna* in *'adribuhunna* to convey the meaning of 'depart **from** them' (*adribu 'anhunna*).
70. Barlas, *Believing Women*, 165.
71. al-Hibri, 'A Study of Islamic Herstory', 218.
72. This development is well illustrated by Behnam Sadeghi in his *The Logic of Law Making in Islam: Women and Prayer in the Legal Tradition* (Cambridge: Cambridge University Press, 2013).
73. Khaled M. Abou El Fadl, *And God Knows the Soldiers: The Authoritative and Authoritarian in Islamic Discourses* (Lanham, MD, University Press of America, 2001), 62–82, where he offers a searing critique of the use of this report that does not meet the highest standards of reliability in order to mandate gender discrimination. As he points out, this hadith does not occur in al-Bukhari's and Muslim's famed *Sahih* collections; it is recorded by al-Tirmidhi, among others, who classified it as a *hasan* report.

74. Ibid. 75–6.

75. Fazlur Rahman, *Islamic Methodology in History* (Islamabad: Islamic Research Institute, 1965), 27–82.

76. Mernissi, *Veil*, 49–61.

77. For an insightful discussion of the interpretive importance and cogency of the principle of *takhsis al-'amm*, especially in connection with the hadith that has the Prophet declare that a community ruled by a woman would never prosper, see Mohammad Fadel, 'Is Historicism a Viable Strategy for Islamic Law Reform? The Case of "Never Shall a Folk Prosper Who Have Appointed a Woman to Rule Them"', *Islamic Law and Society* 18 (2011), 131–76.

78. Mohammad Fadel, 'Two Women, One Man: Knowledge, Power and Gender in Medieval Sunni Legal Thought', *International Journal of Middle East Studies* 29 (1997): 185–204.

79. See, generally, Shelia Nair, 'Challenging the Mullahs: Islam, Politics and Women's Activism, Interview with Zainah Anwar', *International Feminist Journal of Politics* 9 (2007): 240–8; Amy L. Freedman, 'Civil Society, Moderate Islam, and Politics in Indonesia and Malaysia', *Journal of Civil Society* 5 (2009): 107–27; Carol Anne Douglas, 'Malaysian Sisters in Islam Oppose Fundamentalism', *Off Our Backs* 28 (1998):10.

80. 'Sisters in Islam: Protecting Women's Rights in Malaysia', available at <https://tavaana.org/en/content/sisters-islam-protecting-womens-rights-malaysia-0>; last accessed on 7 December 2012.

81. Zainah Anwar and Jana S. Rumminger, 'Justice and Equality in Muslim Family Laws: Challenges, Possibilities, and Strategies for Reform', *Washington and Lee Law Review* 64 (2007): 1529–49; available at <http://law.wlu.edu/deptimages/Law%20Review/64-4Anwar&Rumminger.pdf>; last accessed on 7 December 2012.

82. Interview with Zainah Anwar, available at <http://www.tavaana.org/nu_upload/Zainah_Anwar_En.pdf>; last accessed on 3 December 2012.

83. 'Musawah: For Equality in the Muslim Family', available at <www.musawah.org/sites/default/files/Qiwamah%20Initiative%20Overview%20EN%2026.9.11.pdf>; last accessed on 7 December 2012.

84. Ibid.

85. See further my discussion of the gender activism of Zainah Anwar and other Muslim feminists in Southeast Asia in 'Islamic Feminisms: Gender Egalitarianism and Legal Constraints', in Susan Williams (ed.), *Social Difference and Constitutionalism in Pan Asia* (Cambridge: Cambridge University Press, 2014), 219–352.

86. Margot Badran, *Feminism in Islam: Secular and Religious Convergences* (Oxford: Oneworld, 2009), 250.

87. Ibid. 332.

88. Zainah Anwar, 'When Silence is not Golden, Muslim Women Speak Out', in Abdul Aziz Said et al. (eds), *Contemporary Islam: Dynamic, Not Static* (New York: Routledge, 2006), 108.

CHAPTER 5

War and peacemaking in the Islamic tradition

In the hastily assembled biographies of the Boston marathon bomber Tamerlan Tsarnaev that were published in various newspapers after he was killed on 19 April 2013, it was frequently mentioned that he had publicly declared his intention to carry out jihad subsequent to a trip he had made to Dagestan. This fitted in well with the overall religious profile that emerged of him in the press – he had apparently started to assert a more conscious Muslim identity, had taken to praying and had given up drinking alcohol. Coupled with his Chechen background and apparent interest in radical Islamist narratives, his subsequent murderous actions characterised as jihad seemed almost comprehensible.

The average reader of such news items may thereby be forgiven for thinking that there is a direct causal link between Tsarnaev's declared religiosity and his violent behaviour and contempt for the sanctity of human life. After all, are not religious male Muslims supposed to carry out the military jihad against non-Muslims as an essential requirement of their faith? Such popular perceptions of jihad are quite prevalent among many and are often predicated on the following assumptions:

1. Jihad is relentless, bloody warfare to be waged by Muslims (en masse) against non-Muslims (en masse) until Islam occupies the whole world or till the end of time – whichever occurs first;
2. Muslims can issue the call to such a jihad anytime and anyhow and their only excuse is that stubborn unbelievers will not submit, willingly or unwillingly, at their hands;
3. When Muslims argue that a true military jihad is only defensive and conditional while the internal, non-violent jihad is continuous and unconditional, they are deliberately dissembling about the real nature of jihad and are to be regarded as apologists for their faith.

It is not only anti-Islamic websites that list such perceptions of jihad; popular media and mainstream publications frequently convey approximate versions of the above and contribute to the formation of such views. Militant Islamist websites and print literature reinforce such ideas. More sophisticated and/or more sympathetic sources will often refer to the greater and lesser jihad as indicating the distinction between the spiritual versus the physical jihad, and the greater importance of the former. However, the assertion that Muslims as a collectivity must continue to wage a military jihad against non-Muslims in order to expand Muslim realms while observing humanitarian codes of conduct against civilians is more or less accepted as a given, even by many specialists of Islam. The proof-texts invoked in support of such a position are medieval Islamic legal texts, which frequently did list such a requirement as part of the duties of the Muslim ruler.[1]

And this is where we must start to trace the rise of certain truisms about the nature and purview of the military jihad. Privileging the legal literature above other kinds of literature – particularly the exegetical literature on the Qur'an and ethical treatises – in discussions of jihad almost inevitably leads to the conclusion that it is a military obligation, usually collective, incumbent upon able-bodied Muslim men in the service of state and religion. And because what we usually call Islamic law is assumed to be derived directly from the Qur'an and the hadith, such an obligation is assumed to be mandated by Islam itself.

But if we put on our historical glasses, turn to the Qur'an and plumb the earliest exegetical texts, hadith collections and edifying literary works which stressed ethical and moral concerns above all, a considerably different picture emerges. The earliest connotations of jihad had to do with patient forbearance (*sabr*). Such patient forbearance was to be exercised in the face of harm and represented stoic, non-violent resistance to wrongdoing. After the famous migration to Medina from his birthplace Mecca, the Prophet Muhammad received divine permission to fight in self-defence, according to Qur'an 22:39–40. The Qur'anic term for fighting is *qital*, a term that was introduced as an additional aspect of jihad in the Medinan period. Muslims after all had been physically and verbally attacked for publicly practising their religion and driven out of their homes unjustly; they were allowed to fight back but only to the extent that they had been harmed. These verses state:

> Permission [to fight] is given to those against whom fighting has been initiated (*yuqātalūna*) because they have been wronged, and God is able to help them. These are they who have been wrongfully expelled from their homes merely for saying 'God is our Lord'. If God had not restrained some people by means of others, monasteries, churches, synagogues and mosques in which God's name is mentioned frequently would have been destroyed. Indeed God comes to the aid of those who come to His aid; verily He is powerful and mighty.

It should be noted that the Arabic uses the passive verb (*yuqātalūna*; literally, 'those who are fought against') instead of the active (*yuqātilūna*; literally, 'those who fight') in Qur'an 22:39. However, many English translations inaccurately render the verb as active; for example, those produced by George Sale, A. J. Arberry and Mohammed Marmaduke Pickthall. The passive verb *yuqātalūna* in the verse therefore clearly refers to fighting back only after one has been attacked. Recourse to defensive fighting was established in these verses for

Muslims not for the sake of propagating their religion but for the protection of their lives and property. This military defense may also be undertaken on behalf of non-Muslims who face similar persecution, since non-Muslim houses of worship (particularly monotheistic) are explicitly mentioned in Qur'an 22:39–40 as being worthy of protection.[2]

Another critical verse, Qur'an 2:190, unequivocally forbids Muslims from attacking the enemy first. This verse states, 'Fight in the way of God those who fight you and do not commit aggression for God does not love aggressors.' Accordingly, many exegetes insisted that Muslims could only fight back after they had been attacked – no ifs or buts – and that the counter-attack had to be proportional to the original attack. This is the documented position of the early exegetes Mujahid b. Jabr[3] and Muqatil b. Sulayman[4] who wrote their Qur'an commentaries during the Umayyad period (656–750). These early positions continued to be maintained into the later period. Thus the famous late twelfth-century exegete al-Razi (d. 1210) comments that Qur'an 2:190 is to be read in light of the preceding verse which emphasises *taqwa* (roughly 'God-consciousness') as 'a means of knowing God the Exalted' and as 'a means of obeying God'. God has commanded in this verse, he continues, the severest aspect of *taqwa* and the most difficult for the human self to bear – fighting the enemies of God. But the questions remain: why and how?[5]

In response to why one should fight, al-Razi begins by commenting that the specific occasion of revelation was the year of al-Hudaybiyya (628 CE) and recapitulates the main events associated with this year that provided the impetus for fighting. Al-Hudaybiyya was the name of a place near Mecca where Muhammad concluded a treaty with the pagan Meccans that called for a truce between the two sides for a period of ten years.[6] With regard to how one should fight, al-Razi records three strands of interpretation in reference to Qur'an 2:190. First, citing the well-known Companion Ibn 'Abbas, al-Razi comments that one should only fight those who fight – whether that is construed as those who actually resort to armed combat or display hostile intention by forcibly preventing Muslims from carrying out an essential religious obligation, such as the pilgrimage. Second, one should fight only those who have the ability and the skill to engage in fighting. A third position is that one should fight those capable of fighting, 'except for those who incline to peace' (compare with Qur'an 8:61). Al-Razi expresses a preference for the first viewpoint attributed to Ibn 'Abbas because that is the closest, he stresses, to the obvious meaning of the verse in his view. Al-Razi goes on to add categorically that the divine imperative in Qur'an 2:190 is directed at actual, not potential, combatants, meaning that the verse allows fighting only against those who have actually commenced fighting, and not against those who are able and prepared to fight but have not yet resorted to violence.[7] This represents a rather trenchant critique of the prevailing juridical position in al-Razi's time, which had all but abandoned the categorical Qur'anic principle of non-aggression through legal and hermeneutical legerdemain, as will be referred to again shortly.

The non-aggression position articulated in Qur'an 2:190 is stressed again in another verse, Qur'an 9:13, which states, 'Will you not fight a people who violated their oaths and had intended to expel the Messenger and commenced [hostilities] against you the first time?' Here once again the Qur'an makes clear that the faithful can resort to armed combat only against those people who are guilty of wrongdoing – in this case, people who broke their treaties with Muslims – and who had initiated fighting against them. This requirement is explicitly stated in the verse in Arabic: *wa-hum bada'ukum awwala marratin*. Translated, this means 'they are the ones who began fighting you first'. This is once again an unambiguous articulation within the Qur'an of the impermissibility of commencing attacks against any group of people, even against wrongdoers, under any circumstance. Fighting is allowed not in order to combat the religious beliefs of adversaries, but only on account of their prior acts of aggression, and therefore to specifically defend oneself and others against physical harm.

Some scholars were also of the opinion that the Qur'anic command to fight was only applicable to the first generation of Muslims – that is to say, the Companions – who were contemporaries of Muhammad, since the historical referent in the verses that deal with fighting are the hostile pagan Arabs of Mecca. One verse (Qur'an 2:216) that is often cited in many sources as establishing the obligatory nature of fighting states:

> Fighting has been prescribed for you even though you find it displeasing. Perhaps you dislike something in which there is good for you and perhaps you find pleasing that which causes you harm. But God knows and you do not.

There is no doubt that according to this verse, when war is duly constituted for justified and legitimate reasons, fighting becomes a moral obligation which no adult male believer may shirk without extenuating reason. Among these legitimate reasons are the violation of treaties by the enemy and initiation of hostilities by them, as noted already. However the exegetes differed as to who exactly were intended in the second person plural object pronoun *kum* in the verse which states in Arabic: *kutiba 'alaykum al-qital* ('fighting has been prescribed for you').

According to al-Tabari, the early pious Medinan scholar 'Ata b. Abi Rabah (d. 733) was prominent among those who subscribed to the position that *kum* (plural you) in the verse as direct address referred only to the Muslims who were present with Muhammad. Fighting was therefore prescribed only during the time of the Prophet for his Companions. Al-Tabari quotes 'Ata' b. Abi Rabah, who, when asked whether Qur'an 2:216 made fighting obligatory for people in general, replied that it did not and that 'it was prescribed only for those [who were present] at that time (*hina'idhin*)'.[8]

In the eleventh century, al-Wahidi continues to endorse this early position that fighting as a religiously prescribed duty was temporally limited. He too quotes 'Ata' b. Abi Rabah who had understood Qur'an 2:216 to refer specifically to the Companions of the Prophet because only fighting with the Prophet was an obligatory duty.[9] In the late twelfth century, al-Razi, like al-Tabari and al-Wahidi, also records these early views and documents the divergent opinions that have historically existed among the scholars regarding the interpretation of this verse. In addition to Ata' b. Abi Rabah, al-Razi refers to another well-known Medinan scholar 'Abd Allah Ibn 'Umar (d. 693), son of the second caliph 'Umar b. al-Khattab, who had similarly understood the duty of fighting to have been imposed on the Companions of the Prophet 'at that time only' (*fi dhalika 'l-waqt faqat*); that is to say, solely during the lifetime of the Prophet against the pagan Arabs who had aggressed against the Muslims.[10]

In contrast to Ata' and Ibn 'Umar, al-Razi notes that the Syrian Umayyad scholar Makhul al-Shami (d. c.737) is said to have sworn repeatedly at the Ka'ba that fighting was obligatory in general.[11] It becomes clearly apparent from al-Razi's exegesis that Syrian scholars like Makhul in the context of continuing Umayyad military engagements with the Byzantines allowed for a general injunction to fight to be read into this verse in contradistinction to Hijazi scholars – scholars in Medina and Mecca, for example, outside of the Umayyad orbit, such as 'Ata' b. Abi Rabah and Ibn 'Umar – who derive no such broad mandate from Qur'an 2:216.

Fighting was therefore a complex subject. Both religious and pragmatic imperatives were invoked by Muslim scholars in delineating the reach of the military jihad and to articulate an ethics of initiating armed combat on the basis of the critical verses discussed here. It is abundantly evident that the specific sociopolitical circumstances of our exegetes were frequently decisive in shaping their views, an awareness of which fact allows us to appreciate the highly contingent – and contested – nature of these discourses.

Refraining from fighting and peacemaking

In addition to laying down a specific protocol for conducting a justified war, the Qur'an also establishes an explicit ethic for refraining from fighting and for making peace. In addition to being defensive, fighting in the Qur'an is also limited in nature. The Qur'anic ethics of desisting from fighting and making peace are just as important as the rules it sets down for conducting a justified war. Thus Qur'an 60:7–8 state:

> Perhaps God will place affection between you and those who are your enemies for God is powerful and God is forgiving and merciful. God does not forbid you from being kind and equitable to those who have neither made war on you on

account of your religion nor driven you from your homes; indeed God loves those who are equitable.

Once again, the Qur'an makes very clear that Muslims may fight only those who have clearly aggressed against them and persecuted them for their faith. Non-Muslims who live peacefully with them and evince no hostility are to be treated kindly and equitably, regardless of what they choose to believe.

Another verse, Qur'an 8:61 is the quintessential 'peacemaking' verse that creates a clear moral imperative for Muslims to abandon fighting when the adversary lays down its arms. The verse states, 'And if they should incline to peace, then incline to it [yourself] and place your trust in God; for He is all-hearing and all-knowing.' In his interpretation of this verse, al-Tabari says that God had addressed the Prophet and counselled him to abandon warfare when the adversary inclines to peace either through entry into Islam, payment of the poll tax (*jizya*) or through the establishment of friendly relations. Such reciprocity is mandated for the sake of peace and peacemaking.[12]

As one might imagine, such Qur'anic verses which limited warfare to defensive fighting and commanded peacemaking when the enemy desisted from aggression were not favourable to the process of empire-building. By Umayyad times, the need was soon felt in official and certain legal circles to promote the military jihad as a religiously meritorious activity to allow for the expansion of the Islamic empire after the death of Muhammad during the late seventh and eighth centuries of the Common Era. Certain hawkish scholars starting already in the late seventh century during the Umayyad period framed realpolitik concerns focused on security and territorial expansion in overtly religious idiom and sought to create theological imperatives for fighting on behalf of empire.[13] Thus we observe that later exegetes and jurists began to make frequent exceptions to the injunction against committing aggression contained in Qur'an 2:190 and preferred to understand the verse as mandating primarily non-combatant immunity without placing any restriction on the Muslim army's ability to commence fighting. This progressive watering-down in later exegetical and legal literature of the categorical Qur'anic prohibition against initiating hostilities is revealing of the triumph of political realism over scriptural fidelity.

This trend became quite prominent by the late ninth century during the Abbasid period with its imperial ambitions, as may be detected in the famous exegetical work of the tenth-century scholar al-Tabari, who had close connections with the ruling Abbasid elite.[14] The well-known Abbasid jurist al-Shafi'i (d. 820) was also a member of this 'school' of political realism. It is from this vantage point that al-Shafi'i divided the world into the 'Abode of Islam' (*Dar al-Islam*) versus the 'Abode of War' (*Dar al-Harb*) with an intervening 'Abode of Truce' (*Dar al-Sulh/al-'Ahd*) into which non-Muslim nations could enter by signing treaties of coexistence with the Muslim polity.[15] None of the foundational texts of Islam refer to such a division of the world – but ever the pragmatist, this is how al-Shafi'i made sense of the conflict-ridden world of his time. He was also of the opinion that the caliph should carry out offensive military campaigns against non-Muslim polities as part of his role as defender of Islamic realms. Such offensive military activity was included by him under the rubric of jihad and justified as a necessary moral pre-emptive course of action against a hostile enemy, such as the Byzantines, and for progressively expanding the territorial boundaries of Islamic realms.[16] Ironically, thanks to his efforts, the military jihad thus became inextricably linked to the secular project of empire-building and expansion, although its secular nature was convincingly concealed within a carefully-crafted religio-legal rhetoric.

Some scholars from after the ninth century continued to dispute this co-optation of jihad in the service of realpolitik. These scholars' main area of contention was with the later legal position which viewed lack of adherence to Islam, rather than aggression on the part of the adversary, as the *casus belli* for the military jihad, a position they regarded as unethical and contravening the Qur'anic position on defensive fighting. Among those who registered their opposition to this predominantly statist–legal perspective was the late-twelfth-century exegete al-Razi who was suspicious of extracting politically expedient interpretations from scripture that were contrary to the overt and ordinary meaning of words. As we recall, al-Razi would remark memorably that Qur'an 2:190 is directed at actual, not potential combatants, meaning that the verse allows fighting only against those who have actually commenced fighting. Al-Razi's views reflect the genuinely archaic views of earlier scholars, such as Sufyan al-Thawri (d. 778), Ata' b. Abi Rabah (d. 733), 'Amr b. Dinar (d. 743), and Ibn Shubruma (d. 761), who had unequivocally maintained the defensive nature of the military jihad.[17]

Jihad in ethical and edifying literature

A diachronic comparison of early and late texts that discuss jihad thus affirms the variable trajectory of this term and indicates the moral and legal contestations of its multiple meanings by different groups of people in different historical periods. Jihad, in its fundamental sense, means 'striving', 'struggling', 'effort'. The longer common Arabic phrase *al-jihad fi sabil allah* means 'striving or struggling in the path of God'. As mentioned earlier, a critical aspect of jihad, which is highly stressed in the Qur'an, has not, however, received due attention as such in academic literature produced particularly in the West. This aspect is encapsulated by the Arabic term *sabr*, which can be translated into English as 'patience', 'forbearance', 'steadfastness'. In Qur'anic discourse, *sabr* is a component and a manifestation of the striving of the righteous; quietist and activist resistance to wrongdoing are equally valorised in a number of Qur'anic verses. For example, one Qur'anic verse (16:110) states, 'As for those who after persecution fled their homes and strove actively (*jahadu*) and were patient (*sabaru*) to the last, your Lord will be forgiving and merciful to them on the day when every soul will come pleading for itself.' Another verse (Qur'an 47:31) states, 'We shall put you to the test until We know the active strivers (*al-mujahidin*) and the quietly forbearing (*al-sabirin*) among you.' The Qur'anic coupling of derivatives from *jhd* and *sbr* in several verses is highly significant and invites us to focus on *sabr* as an essential component of the holistic human struggle on earth referred to in Arabic as jihad.

While legal and administrative literature understandably focused on *qital* (fighting) as the most important aspect of jihad, we have to turn to religiously edifying and what today we might call 'self-improvement' literature in order to retrieve this focus on patient forbearance as the most important aspect of jihad in non-juridical and non-statist circles. One of the most celebrated works on ethics and morality from the pre-modern period is the *Ihya' 'ulum al-din* (The Revival of the Religious Sciences) by the famous mystical theologian of the late eleventh century Abu Hamid al-Ghazali (d. 1111). In the thirty-second chapter of the *Ihya'*, titled *Kitab al-sabr wa-'l-shukr* (the Book of Patience Forbearance and Gratitude), al-Ghazali emphasises the internal and spiritual dimensions of jihad that are of greater importance for the individual in his or her daily existence. The external battle between the forces of good and evil that will persist until the last times has been completely internalised by al-Ghazali and transferred to the 'battle-ground' of the human heart. To rephrase this, the external military jihad as envisioned by the jurists, which theoretically has to be waged against the enemies of God until the end of time, has become transmuted into a relentless spiritual struggle in al-Ghazali's discussion of the basic human duty to promote what is good and prevent what is wrong. The military jihad in fact is not even mentioned in the *Ihya'* in connection with the moral and ethical obligations of the pious Muslim, since it is relegated to the realm of the state and statecraft.[18]

Lest one think that only Muslim mystics place such stress on the internal, non-combative jihad, as is sometimes dismissively asserted, it is useful to reference the views of a prominent Hanbali jurist from the 15th century, Ibn Qayyim al-Jawziyya (d. 1350), who was a student of another famous Hanbali jurist Ibn Taymiyya (d. 1328). Ibn Qayyim (like his teacher) is prominent in Salafi circles today as advocating relentless violent jihad – such a view distorts the much more complex and nuanced views that are present in his variegated *oeuvre*. In an ethical treatise whose title can be translated into English as 'The Tools of the Patiently Forbearing and Treasure-trove of the Grateful', Ibn Qayyim mirrors the views of al-Ghazali to a considerable extent by praising those who constantly practice the internal self-purification required of a holistic jihad and who thereby 'strive with regard to God in true striving' (a reference to Qur'an 22:78).[19] Like al-Ghazali, he regards engaging in the greater internal jihad as encapsulated by the term *sabr* (patient forbearance) as the best of all deeds under all circumstances for the individual. In his estimation, the relentless internal human struggle to be patiently enduring of life's vicissitudes is a bloodless yet more exacting battle compared to the lesser, physical jihad.

The internal, greater jihad was not therefore a later post-Qur'anic 'new-fangled' construction subscribed to by 'deviant' Sufis only, as some have maintained polemically.[20] The term 'greater struggle' (*al-jihad al-akbar/al-kabir*) itself may be a later coinage;[21] its semantic and ethical content, however, is firmly grounded in the Qur'anic notion of patient forbearance (*sabr*) as the most enduring and difficult feature of human struggle on earth.

Revisiting the problem of textual abrogation

The hawkish juridical perspective that gained ground from the time of al-Shafi'i onward relies for its validity on the deployment of the hermeneutic principle of abrogation that emerged over time – a principle that, according to a considerable number of scholars, allows for a number of early Qur'anic verses which are markedly irenic and conciliatory in tone to be superseded by later ones which deal with fighting those who had attacked and persecuted Muslims for their faith alone. It is this theory of abrogation that has allowed for an expansionist conception of the military jihad to emerge in deference to realpolitik. Thus Qur'an 9:5 is invoked by a number of exegetes as having abrogated Qur'an 2:190, the no-aggression clause. It is also assumed by some to have abrogated our quintessential peacemaking verse Qur'an 8:61. Qur'an 9:5 states:

> When the sacred months have lapsed, then slay the polytheists (*al-mushrikin*) wherever you may encounter them. Seize them and encircle them and lie in wait for them. But if they repent and perform the prayer and give the zakat, then let them go on their way, for God is forgiving and merciful.

Contemporary polemical literature that discusses Qur'an 9:5 – whether produced by Islamist militants or Western Islamophobes – invariably asserts a mythical scholarly consensus on the abrogating status of the so-called sword verse, whereby numerous Qur'anic verses that call upon Muslims to establish kind and respectful relations with peaceful non-Muslims would be nullified. A survey of some of the most influential Qur'an commentaries of the pre-modern period easily disproves this assertion. Our influential tenth-century commentator al-Tabari himself had forcefully taken issue with certain hawkish exegetes who had stated that Qur'an 9:5 abrogates Qur'an 8:61. One such exegete was the Successor (second generation Muslim) Qatada b. Di'ama (d. 736) who is said to have commented that every pact mentioned in the Qur'an and every truce concluded by Muslims with polytheists through which they entered into peaceful relations with one another were to be understood as having been abrogated by the ninth chapter of the Qur'an, and especially by Qur'an 9:5. Qatada had concluded trenchantly that by the revelation of this chapter God had commanded Muslims to fight the polytheists in every situation until they said, 'There is no god but God.'[22]

Al-Tabari refutes such views by commenting that Qatada's statement on the abrogation of Qur'an 8:61 cannot be supported on the basis of the Qur'an, the sunna or reason. Qur'an 9:5 has to do only with Arab polytheist idolaters whereas Qur'an 8:61 is generally understood to refer to the People of the Book who cannot be fought when they make peace with Muslims. Neither verse invalidates the injunction contained in the other since they concern different sets of people and circumstances and both therefore remain unabrogated (*muhkam*).[23]

Al-Tabari's was not a minority position. After him, al-Zamakhshari (d. 1144), al-Razi (d. 1210), and Ibn Kathir (d. 1373) continued to assert that Qur'an 8:61 remained an unabrogated verse and its commandment to establish peace was normative and valid for all time.[24]

Modern critics of the pro-abrogation position

The pro-abrogation advocates faced trenchant criticism from others in the pre-modern period and their position continues to be criticised by a variety of modern and contemporary Muslim scholars. Modern anti-abrogation scholars have emphasised instead that the Qur'an should be read holistically and that the critical verses contained within it which forbid the initiation of war by Muslims and which uphold the principle of non-coercion in religion (Qur'an 2:256) unambiguously and permanently militate against the conception of an offensive military jihad that may be waged against non-Muslims solely because they are non-Muslims.

In the late nineteenth century, the brilliant scholar and reformer Muhammad 'Abduh rejected the interpretation that the so-called sword verse (Qur'an 9:5) had abrogated the more numerous verses in the Qur'an which call for peaceful relations with non-Muslims. Like al-Tabari before him, 'Abduh argues that the specific historical situation with which the verse is concerned – with its internal reference to the passage of the four sacred months and to the pagan Meccans – restricts its applicability to the time of the Prophet. Other verses in the Qur'an advocating clemency and non-violence cannot be considered to have been abrogated since their applicability is more general. The command contained in Qur'an 9:5 was in response to a specific situation at a specific time in order to achieve a specific objective and has no effect on the injunction contained in, for example, Qur'an 2:109, which states, 'Pardon and forgive until God brings about His command.' The latter is after all a general commandment whose applicability is not restricted to specific historical circumstances and objectives.[25]

'Abduh is therefore highly critical of those who would see the injunction contained in Qur'an 9:5 with its clear reference to Arab polytheists applicable in any way to non-Arab polytheists or to the People of the Book. The latter, he notes, are referred to very differently, as in Qur'an 5:82 which states, 'You will find the closest in affection to those who believe are those who say we are Christians.' There are additionally hadiths that similarly counsel peaceful relations with various groups of people, such as the one that counsels leaving the Ethiopians (as well as Turks) alone as long as they leave the Muslims alone. 'Abduh remarks with regret that if jurists had not read a number of these Qur'anic verses and hadiths 'from behind the veil of their juridical schools', then they would not have so egregiously missed the fundamental point made throughout the Qur'an and in sound hadiths that 'the security to be obtained through fighting the Arab polytheists according to these verses is contingent upon their initiating attacks against Muslims and violating their treaties . . .'[26] 'Abduh goes on to point out that the very next verse – Qur'an 9:6 – offers protection and safe conduct to those among the polytheists who wish to listen to the Qur'an.[27] This verse states, 'If anyone from among the polytheists should ask for refuge from you, grant him such a refuge so that he may hear the word of God, then conduct him to safety; that is because they are a people who do not understand'. The implication is clear – polytheists and non-Muslims in general who do not wish Muslims harm and display no aggression towards them are to be left alone and allowed to continue in their ways of life.

In his 1993 book *al-Jihad fi al-islam*, the prominent Syrian religious scholar Sa'id Ramadan al-Buti (d. 2013) similarly inveighs against the deployment of Qur'an 9:5 as a proof-text by a number of medieval hawkish jurists to justify offensive military campaigns. He is also critical of their invocation of the hadith in which the Prophet is quoted as stating, 'I have been commanded to fight people until they bear witness "There is no god but God" . . .' From the perspective of such hawkish jurists, the so-called sword verse mandated the legitimacy of fighting polytheists and forcibly bringing them into Islam. A majority of jurists and exegetes, however, were opposed to this position, al-Buti says, who maintained that Qur'anic verses which counsel Muslims to invite others to Islam without coercion remain unabrogated and that the above hadith ('I have been commanded to fight . . .') does not contradict the content of these verses. The people referred to in this hadith are specifically pagan idol-worshipers in Arabia; its text therefore has no bearing in the later period. Furthermore, continues al-Buti, the hadith's chain of transmission is characterised as *gharib* (literally 'rare',' 'strange', 'obscure'). While this flaw did not prevent al-Bukhari and Muslim from including this report in their highly regarded hadith collections, other scholars like Ahmad b. Hanbal did not record it in their compilations. The well-known hadith critic from the fifteenth century Ibn Hajar (d. 1449) is known to have provided a list of scholars who discredited the reliability of this hadith. All groups of people, other than the hostile pagan Meccans, were exempt from fighting, according to Qur'anic verses which explicitly forbid coercion in religious matters, such as the well-known verse, 'There is no compulsion in religion', (Qur'an 2:256) and Qur'an 60:8, which states, 'God does not forbid you from being kind to those who do not oppose you in religion . . .' . Al-Buti adds in a footnote that this was the principal view of the Shafi'i and Hanafi schools and the majority of Hanbali jurists. The eponym of the Maliki school of law, Malik b. Anas (d. 795) and his companions, the early Syrian jurist al-Awza'i (d. 774), and a considerable number of other jurists, emphasised that the command to slay the Meccan polytheists in Qur'an 9:5 was predicated on their violent hostility (al-hiraba) and not on account of their unbelief (al-kufr), a position with which al-Buti wholeheartedly agrees.[28]

Like 'Abduh, he also emphasises that if Qur'an 9:5 is understood to command the fighting of polytheists until their death or their acceptance of Islam, then such a command is countermanded by the very next verse which exhorts Muslims to offer refuge and safe conduct to them while they are in their state of polytheism but exhibit no hostility. Al-Buti dismisses as irresponsibly arbitrary the view of those who suggest that Qur'an 9:5 abrogates Qur'an 9:6, which goes against the usual rule of abrogation that a later verse may supersede an earlier verse. He stresses that this understanding of Qur'an 9:5 furthermore contradicts other more numerous verses of the Qur'an which were later revelations, as well as the established praxis of the first generation of Muslims. An example of such a verse is Qur'an 9:13 which states, 'Will you not fight a people who violate their pledges and are intent on expelling the Messenger, while they initiated aggression against you? Do you fear them while God is more worthy of being feared, if you were truly believers?'[29] Al-Buti points out that the verse explicitly mentions the following reasons for engaging polytheists in battle: their reneging on oaths, their breaking of treaties and their initiation of treachery and hostility. Such verses categorically establish once more that the proclamation of war against the polytheists in Qur'an 9:5 is predicated on their hostility, not on their lack of belief. Moreover, many reports describe the Prophet, as well as a number of his Companions, as counselling kindness toward polytheist relatives and non-relatives who displayed no aggressive behaviour. All these proof-texts together provide irrefutable evidence that the only legitimate reason for fighting any group of people is their unrelenting hostility and initiation of aggression (al-hiraba), and not on account of their religious beliefs or lack thereof.[30]

More recently, in 2005, the former Chief Mufti of Egypt, 'Ali Jum'a (Gom'a) composed a short treatise on jihad[31] in which he similarly challenges common misperceptions surrounding this concept and distils for the reader the contested interpretations of the purview of this term. Writing in the charged post-September 11th milieu, he confronts a question that in one form or another may be expected to be posed to Muslims: how would they reply to those who point out that most nations agree that conflicts between them are better adjudicated today through arbitration, rendering wars null and void, whereas 'this Qur'an of yours exhorts you to jihad and to undertake it eagerly?' The answer, says

Jum'a, should focus on Qur'an 8:61, which indicates the eternal wisdom and abiding miracle of the Qur'an in that it foresaw a future world where global non-violence could become a possibility. The combative jihad was necessary for self-defence in a pre-modern, war-ridden world; against such a historical backdrop, the Qur'an (and the sunna) permitted fighting out of necessity while imposing humane and ethical restrictions on waging war. In the modern world governed (at least theoretically) by international treaties and contracts, he maintains that Qur'an 8:61, which is by no means abrogated, is the more appropriate proof-text to be invoked in mandating peaceful relations among nations.[32]

The belligerent perspective, which relies on the principle of abrogation (*naskh*) for its validity, continues to be severely criticised by many modern and contemporary Muslim scholars, including jurists who have parted ways with a number of their pre-modern counterparts. Such modern jurists include Sobhi Mahmassani, Muhammad Hamidullah, Abu Zahra and Wahba al-Zuhayli, among others. These scholars have emphasised that the Qur'an should be read holistically and that the critical verses which forbid the initiation of war by Muslims and which uphold the principle of non-coercion in religion categorically militate against the conception of an offensive jihad that must be waged against non-Muslims qua non-Muslims.[33]

In his influential work *Athar al-harb fi al-fiqh al-islami*, the well-known Syrian scholar of Islamic law and legal theory, Wahba al-Zuhayli has specifically taken issue with the position of certain medieval jurists that Qur'an 9:5 may be deemed to have abrogated about 124 other Qur'anic verses which preach peaceful solutions to conflicts. The pro-*naskh* position cannot be a valid perspective, he maintains, because abrogation would require that there be an intractable opposition between these verses. All the verses on fighting, he says, were revealed to allow Muslims to defend themselves against persecution and attack by their enemies.[34]

As far as legitimate war is concerned in the Islamic context, al-Zuhayli identifies three specific types: (1) War against those who forcibly prevent the preaching of Islam and who foment internal disorder and strife; (2) War in defense of individuals and communities that are persecuted; and (3) War to repel a physical attack against oneself and one's country.[35]

Al-Zuhayli points out that types (2) and (3) are fully compatible with current principles of international law which allow for self-defence against prior aggression and humanitarian intervention in conflict-ridden regions.[36] Type (1), however, has no clear parallel in international law since it is not confined to the boundaries of the modern nation state; it is rather deployed as a moral instrument to ensure religious freedom and contain social instability in general. One may note that such a justified war that may be waged on primarily moral grounds has its parallel in Christian notions of just war and is not based on positive international law.[37]

The three *casus belli* outlined by al-Zuhayli are widely accepted by modern

Muslim jurists. The influential but controversial Egyptian-born scholar based in Qatar, Yusuf al-Qaradawi, similarly states that 'moderate' Muslims (*al-mu'tadilin*) are peaceful towards those who are peaceful towards them, and do not fight except those who fight them, prevent the peaceful propagation of the Islamic message, and persecute believers on account of their faith.[38] This position represents a significant departure from the classical juridical view that the Muslim ruler was obligated to carry out a military foray once a year as expansionist jihad against non-Muslim polities in order to expand the territorial realms of Islam. Modern mainstream scholars reject this position as untenable because first, it violates the Qur'an's prohibition against fighting except in self-defence, and, second, it reflects legal accommodation to a world predicated on non-Muslim hostility to Muslims and in which war was the default situation between nations. In this vein, the American Muslim scholar Sherman Jackson cogently argues:

> While the imperial quest for empire invariably informed the policies of every Muslim state, Muslim juristic writings continued to reflect the logic of the 'state of war' and the assumption that only Muslims would permit Muslims to remain Muslims. They continued to see jihad not only as a means of guaranteeing the security and freedom of the Muslims but as virtually the *only* [emphasis in text] means of doing so.[39]

In a vastly altered world in which mutually binding international treaties exist positing peace rather than war as the default situation, the classical legal rules of war and peace invite revisiting in the context of new historical realities, and as many are now arguing, in a spirit of greater fidelity to Qur'anic principles of war and peacemaking.

Militancy and its contestations

The so-called 'sword verse' (*ayat al-sayf*) was not termed as such before the Mamluk period. A survey of exegetical works by this author led to the conclusion that no commentator before Ibn Kathir (d. 1373) in the fourteenth century used this designation for Qur'an 9:5.[40] Such a development clearly indicates that the specific historical circumstances of this period led to the aggrandised attention given to the verse. Clearly the attacks by the Crusaders and the Mongols during the Mamluk period had created a fraught climate in the Muslim world; Qur'an 9:5 unmoored from its historical context – that is, from the time of the pagan Arabs who had persecuted and attacked Muslims – could be and was redeployed during this time to grant greater moral lustre to the military campaigns waged to rid the Muslim world of its external aggressors.

The verse has similarly been invoked by contemporary militant groups. Needless to say, the militants today favour the pro-abrogation position vis-à-vis

Qur'an 9:5 because it allows them to wield this verse ahistorically and arbitrarily to justify their campaigns of violent vengeance. For example in a tract titled *al-Farida al-gha'iba* (The Missing Duty), attributed to 'Abd al-Salam Faraj, a member of the extremist Egyptian group *al-Jihad wa 'l-takfir* (which assassinated Egyptian president Anwar Sadat), jihad has become rendered into a violent, scorched-earth policy of vengeance, fired by a ruthless zeal for restoring a mythic, divinely sanctioned world order that will empower him and his cohorts – a beleaguered, righteous minority – against the cosmic forces of evil.[41] Faraj's methodology for creating this imperative has become a familiar one – selective and decontextualised quoting of Qur'anic verses and hadith, supporting the abrogating function of Qur'an 9:5 vis-à-vis all other conciliatory verses, and finally, and most importantly, invoking the situation *in extremis* argument, which renders armed combat an individual and immediate obligation, and grants him and his fellow militants considerable licence in the means they adopt in carrying out their violent mission.[42] A particularly dangerous innovation found in *al-Farida al-gha'iba* is the absolution granted to those who would perpetrate terrorism in the name of religion as long as their intent is 'pure' and 'sincere'[43] – that is to say: as long as they adhere to the manifesto of the *Jihad wa 'l-takfir* group. 'Pure' and 'sincere' intent offers blanket legitimation for attacks on civilians, destruction of non-military property and creation of mayhem and terror by whatever means available. A more thorough dismantling of or disregard for the classical legal tradition on war and peace can scarcely be imagined.

Such a viewpoint also justifies so-called 'martyrdom operations' which glorifies suicide bombings. One contemporary militant, an ideologue for al-Qa'ida known as 'Abd al-Qadir b. 'Abd al-'Aziz, has described the love for martyrdom operations as 'a part of the politics of deterrence' and contrasts 'the enthusiasm of the believer for death and the [sic] martyrdom' to 'the fear of the disbeliever of death and his enthusiasm for this life'.[44] The goals of the military jihad, according to 'Abd al-Qadir, are mainly the preservation of the strength of the Muslims and preventing their exposure to destruction through military acts of pre-emption. This is what saves 'martyrdom operations', he states, from being considered acts of self-destruction, which are otherwise forbidden in Qur'an 2:195.[45]

Mainstream authorities like the Syrian scholar Nasir al-Din al-Albani and the Saudi jurist Muhammad b. Salih al-'Uthayman, however, have condemned martyrdom operations as simply a form of suicide and therefore uambiguously forbidden in Islamic law. The most detailed and blistering condemnation of such acts to date has been composed by the Pakistani cleric Muhammad Tahir-ul-Qadri. Qadri particularly takes aim at the argument of some contemporary militants that suicide bombings are justified as long as they are carried out 'with good intention and pious motive'. He marshalls an impressive array of arguments based on the Qur'an and hadith to undermine this and other militant positions. Qadri deploys certain Qur'anic verses as a cogent rejoinder to those who would maintain that protestations of innocence and proclamations of noble motives confer legitimacy on heinous deeds. He points specifically to a group of Qur'anic verses (2:11–12), which, he says, belie the facile, immoral arguments of the militants. These verses state, 'When it is said to them: "Do not spread disorder in the land", they say: "It is we who reform". Beware! (Truly) it is they who spread disorder, but they do not have any sense (of it) at all.' Qadri regards these verses as a reference to modern terrorists who dress up their violent deeds as instances of legitimate jihad and acts of reformation. He remarks trenchantly:

> Terrorism, carnage and mass destruction can never be justified in the name of any intention of enforcing Islamic commands and its judicial system. Nor can these reprehensible activities be any exception to the rule, or be overlooked, or forgiven.[46]

In Islamic law, lawful objectives can be attained only through lawful means. For example, Qadri continues, constructing a mosque is always a pious act, but one cannot do so by robbing a bank. The good is never served by evil means. The famous hadith, 'Actions are judged according to their intentions' is not intended to 'set a wrong thing right', but rather is in reference to 'those actions that are proven pious, permissible and lawful', he reminds. Actions that are unethical, unjust, and unlawful to begin with cannot be rendered their opposite through good intention alone. Qadri's fatwa remains one of the most detailed and cogent refutations to date of justifications for suicide bombing.

A different kind of striving: Jihad as peacemaking

A number of modern and contemporary Muslim thinkers, starting in the twentieth century, have also started to place a renewed, greater emphasis on *sabr* as the most important Qur'anic component of jihad. From their perspective, inculcation and promotion of the attribute of *sabr* is the basis for non-violent resistance to wrongdoing and for personal and eventual social reform. This modern emphasis on non-violent public activism as the best and the most enduring manifestation of jihad has been espoused by a number of thinkers and activists. Three of the best-known contemporary representatives of this school of thought are discussed below: Jawdat Sa'id, Wahiduddin Khan, and Fethullah Gülen, with a focus on some of the key points of their positions.

Jawdat Sa'id

Jawdat Sa'id (b. 1931) is a well-known Syrian writer and thinker known for his pacifist views, which he derives from his reading of the Qur'an, particularly of the story of Adam's two sons. He obtained a degree in

Arabic language from al-Azhar University and eventually settled in Bir Ajam in the Golan Heights, where he lives in the ancestral family house until today.

In the English translation of his work titled *Non-Violence: The Basis of Settling Disputes in Islam*,[47] Sa'id grounds his non-violent understanding of jihad, glossed as the struggle to resist wrongdoing, in his reading of the Qur'anic verses (5:27–30). These verses give an account of the violent altercation between Adam's two sons and state:

> And recite to them the story of Adam's two sons, in truth, when they both offered a sacrifice [to God], and it was accepted from one of them but was not accepted from the other. Said [the latter], 'I will surely kill you.' Said [the former], 'Indeed, God only accepts from those who are righteous [who fear Him]. If you should raise your hand against me to kill me – I shall not raise my hand against you to kill you. Indeed, I fear God, Lord of the worlds. Indeed, I want you to obtain [thereby] my sin and your sin, so you will be among the companions of the Fire. And that is the recompense of wrongdoers'. And his soul permitted him to murder his brother, so he killed him and became among the losers.

Among the relevant ethical and moral imperatives that Sa'id derives from these verses are: (a) that a Muslim should not call for murder, assassination, and/or any provocative acts that may lead to the commission of such crimes; and (b) that a Muslim should not present his opinion to others by force or yield to others out of fear of any such force. These inferences indicate Sa'id's understanding of jihad as an essentially non-violent enterprise undertaken by Muslims for the purpose of bearing witness to the truth and justice of their faith and to propagate it peacefully.[48]

Muslims, continues Sa'id, are primarily entrusted with speaking 'the words of truth under any condition'. In this context, he refers to the hadith in which the Prophet Muhammad affirms that the best jihad is speaking a word of truth to a tyrannical ruler. Our author further suggests that while being a witness to truth in this manner, a Muslim may not resort to violence, even apparently in self-defence. He refers to the hadith in which a prominent Companion, Sa'd b. Ab Waqqas asked the Prophet what he should do if someone were to come into his house and 'stretches his hand to kill me'? The answer was, 'Be like Adam's [first] son'; and then the Prophet recited Qur'an 5:27–30.[49]

But what about the combative or military jihad which the Qur'an clearly permits under certain conditions? Sa'id does not deny that these verses exist but states that their commands are not applicable in the absence of a properly formed Islamic community, which is currently the situation in which Muslims live. A properly formed Islamic community is one in which truth and justice reign, inhabited by Muslims 'who call for the construction of the Islamic society, its reformation or protecting it against the elements of corruption'. They are furthermore 'the kind of people who, out of loyalty to their cause, persevere patiently with the oppression of others when they are subjected to torture and persecution.[50]

Such patient, non-violent activism in the face of oppression and injustice and in the absence of the properly constituted Islamic community is the only form of jihad that can be carried out by Muslims today, asserts Saʻid. Such non-violent activism is in emulation of all the prophets mentioned in the Qurʼan who patiently endured the harm visited upon them by their own people on account of their preaching the truth. One of the examples our author highlights is that of Moses arguing calmly and peacefully before the Pharaoh in defence of the truth that he had been called to preach. In contrast, the Pharaoh resorted to aggression, as tyrannical rulers are apt to do, in order to protect his political dominion. Believers should not resort to violent overthrow of despotic governments, counsels Saʻid – for then they would be following in the footsteps of the Pharaoh by adopting violent methods. Like Moses and all the other prophets, they should attempt instead to bring about a peaceful resolution of conflict through the clear and fearless proclamation of the truth.[51]

Saʻid, however, does not state that fighting is always categorically prohibited; he recognises jihad 'as an ongoing process on condition that a Muslim must know exactly when to resort to armed struggle'.[52] He also emphasises that under specific conditions, the military jihad must only be carried out by individuals who are qualified for such an important task.[53] The improper and excessive recourse to the combative jihad and its cynical manipulation by unscrupulous people have 'caused more harm to Muslims than any other malpractice'.

Muslims are primarily charged today with preaching the message of God and reforming humans, which can never be accomplished by force as stated in the verse 'Let there be no compulsion in religion' (Qurʼan 2:256). Saʻid calls those who advocate unconditional violence in the name of Islam 'preachers of terrorism' whose vicious ideology 'must be quelled with any possible means'. Evil cannot be erased by violence; evil can only be eradicated by the establishment of justice, and justice, he says, is served by the best form of jihad – the proclamation of truth.[54]

Wahiduddin Khan

Wahiduddin Khan, born in 1925, is a contemporary Indian scholar of Islam who is the president of the Islamic Centre in New Delhi, India. For fifteen years he was a member of the *Jamaʻat-i Islami* founded by Mawdudi in 1941 but broke with the latter because of fundamental disagreements concerning the relation between Islam and politics. Khan emphasised, unlike Mawdudi, that peaceful submission to God, rather than political and economic reform, was at the heart of all things Islamic.[55]

In his book *The True Jihad: The Concept of Peace, Tolerance and Non-Violence*[56] written in the aftermath of September 11th, Khan stresses, much like Jawdat

Sa'id, that the main purpose of Islam was the peaceful propagation of the faith (da'wa) and that political and social reform were at best secondary concerns which would inevitably result from the spiritual reformation of Muslims. He begins this short treatise by pointing to Qur'an 22:78 which exhorts the believer to 'strive for the cause of God as it behooves you to strive for it' (wa-jahidu fi 'llah haqqa jihadihi). Jihad in this usage thus points to an earnest struggle for the sake of God, a term which eventually came to be applied to the early battles in Islam as well, since they were part of this overall struggle. Strictly speaking, the term for fighting is qital, and not jihad per se. On the basis of the well-known hadith collection known as the Musnad of Ahmad b. Hanbal, he identifies the mujahid (one who undertakes jihad) as 'one who struggles with himself or herself for the sake of God'. Jihad is therefore essentially a peaceful struggle against one's ego and against wrongdoing in general.[57]

Furthermore, Khan continues, Muslim advocacy of the principle of non-violence today recognises 'that the commands of the shariah change according to altered situations'. In the pre-modern period, war was a way of life; now we are able to imagine and implement peaceful strategies for conflict resolution. Khan scoffs at 'the so-called jihad movements' of the contemporary period for their glorification of violence; in these changed circumstances, 'launching out on a violent course of action is not only unnecessary, he says, but also unIslamic'. A movement, he says derisively, cannot be deemed a jihad 'just because its leaders describe it as such'. A properly constituted jihad must fulfil the essential conditions decreed by Islamic law. The combative jihad, which is essentially qital (glossed as 'armed struggle'), is an activity relating wholly to the state and cannot be placed in the same category as individual acts of worship, such as prayer and fasting. There is no room, he emphasises, for non-state warfare, for war, and it must be defensive war, may be declared only by the ruling government. Non-combatants may not be targeted. On this basis, Khan sternly condemns the perpetrators of the September 11th attacks. He also proscribes the carrying out of suicide bombings, which he declares to be a complete departure from Islamic norms and religiously sanctioned practices. Khan comments, 'According to Islam we can become martyrs, but we cannot court a martyr's death deliberately.'[58]

Muslims are clearly forbidden to initiate wars except in response to a prior act of violent aggression, as in Qur'an 22:39 ('Permission to take up arms is hereby given to those who are attacked because they have been wronged') and in Qur'an 9:13 ('They were the first to attack you'), continues Khan. Commands to fight in the Qur'an are to be understood as 'specific to certain circumstances' and 'were not meant to be valid for all time to come'.[59] God loves non-violence; and He promises in Qur'an 5:16 that 'Those who seek to please God will be guided by Him to "the paths of peace"'. As a consequence of this high valorisation of non-violence, the Qur'an eulogises patience (sabr) as a human virtue, promising reward for it that is beyond measure (Qur'an 39:10). *Sabr* is the equivalent of non-violence as understood in the modern period.[60] Non-violent activism is particularly relevant for Muslims in the contemporary period and is the most important aspect of jihad for them today, asserts Khan.[61]

Fethullah Gülen

Muhammed Fethullah Gülen (b. 1941) is a well-known and somewhat controversial contemporary Turkish Muslim thinker, author and activist. He is the founder of the *hizmet* (altruistic service) movement (otherwise generally known as the Gülen movement), which emphasises peaceful social reform, primarily through education and interfaith dialogue. This philosophy and world-view undergirds a growing network of Gülen schools spread throughout the world. Gülen currently lives in exile in Pennsylvania in the United States.[62]

Gülen grounds his views on jihad and advocacy of peaceful coexistence of different faith and cultural communities in the Qur'an and prophetic sunna. As a practitioner of *tasawwuf* (Sufism), he emphasises the importance of the greater internal jihad without disavowing the necessity of the lesser external jihad in specific situations. Thus in his explication of the distinction between these two forms of struggling in the path of God, Gülen says, 'The internal struggle (the greater jihad) is the effort to attain one's essence; the external struggle (the lesser jihad) is the process of enabling someone else to attain his or her essence'.[63]

The effort to attain one's essence, as Gülen puts it, is therefore a perennial one and the greater jihad is waged daily by the individual to fight against one's carnal self (*nafs*) which, if unchecked, prompts to wrongdoing. The acquisition of knowledge which leads to love for God and one's fellow beings is an important part of this process of self-realisation, he stresses. Gülen's definition of the lesser or external jihad as 'the process of enabling someone else to attain his or her essence'[64] is rather unique and worthy of note.

The lesser jihad, in Gülen's understanding, furthermore has important social and, one may add, global dimensions and it challenges those who would primarily construe it as a military endeavour in defence of Islam. Every human act undertaken with noble intention that redounds to the benefit of society and promotes the common good, leading to a genuine transformation of society, is part of the external jihad. The external jihad must be waged alongside the internal jihad to achieve a desired balance, for Gülen says, 'If one is missing, the balance is destroyed.'[65]

The high estimation in the Qur'an and hadith of *sabr* or patient forbearance as an important component of jihad finds strong reflection in Gülen's writings.[66] Patience is clearly the single most important component of the internal or greater jihad; cultivating it transforms ordinary human beings into God's true friends and worshipers. 'Patience', Gülen affirms, 'is an essential characteristic' of these believers during their journey towards God.[67]

Finally, Gülen warns against the phenomenon of arbitrary violence and aggression against civilians, that is to say terrorism, which has no place in Islam and which militates against its very foundational tenets of reverence for human life and for all of God's creation. In an article that he wrote for the *Turkish Daily News* a few days after the attacks of 11 September 2001 titled 'Real Muslims Cannot Be Terrorists', Gülen lamented the deplorable hijacking of Islam by terrorists who claimed to be Muslims and acting out of religious conviction. He counselled that 'One should seek Islam through its own sources and in its own representatives throughout history; not through the actions of a tiny minority that misrepresent it.'[68]

The antidote to hatemongering and exclusion, Gülen stresses, is the cultivation of the qualities of forgiveness and tolerance enjoined in the Qur'an. He focuses attention on Qur'an 3:134, which describes righteous people as, 'Those who spend benevolently during ease and straitened circumstances, and those who restrain their anger and pardon people; and God loves those who do good to others'. Gülen comments that this verse clearly counsels believers to behave with restraint and civility and forgive their adversaries, even in the face of great provocation, and not to resort to hostile behaviour. The Prophet exemplified such behaviour in his daily interactions with people. The external jihad that the Prophet carried out in his life, Gülen comments, was 'an armed struggle . . . tied to special conditions', and 'was the kind of struggle that is sometimes necessary to carry out in order to protect such values as life, property, religion, children, homeland, and honor'.[69] In his opinion, fighting in the path of God under such highly restricted conditions can never degenerate into the unprincipled and relentlessly hostile acts of terrorism perpetrated by today's extremists.

Conclusion

War and peace are deeply complex and polysemous concepts in Islam as they are in most religious and legal traditions. Our exploration of the historical trajectory of jihad has significant implications for the contemporary period. First, our survey documents the multiple and contested meanings of jihad that are prevalent in the literature particularly outside of the legal sphere and challenges a monolithic, reductive understanding of the term. Second, it establishes the defensive and limited nature of fighting in the Qur'an itself, and that was stressed particularly by exegetes, ethicists and moral theologians. Jihad in the Qur'an is most categorically not holy war,[70] which is aggressive war carried out for the sake of religion. Third, it contextualises the legal positions developed by jurists that legitimised offensive military activity as contingent responses to specific political circumstances, which cannot be deemed to be normatively binding for Muslims for all times and for all places.

Our discussion further notes that modern Muslim jurists are re-emphasising the defensive nature of the military jihad, marking a categorical departure from the classical juridical position which had mandated expansionist military activity as a communal obligation. This modern position represents the recuperation of a genuinely archaic position held by a number of prominent scholars in the pre-modern period, such as Sufyan al-Thawri, 'Ata' b. Abi Rabah, Ibn Shubruma, and others. Following in their footsteps, many modern Muslim jurists are similarly highly critical of the expansionist form of jihad; they tend to undermine it by direct references to relevant Qur'anic verses that explicitly forbid the initiation of attacks by Muslims. If and when attacked first by the adversary, Muslims may defend themselves through a proportional military response, which must cease if and when the other side sues for peace. These scholars also disallow for the most part the classical hermeneutic principle of abrogation (naskh), which is regarded as having been deployed irresponsibly to allow for the endorsement of offensive warfare.

We ended with a discussion of the views of three scholar-activists – Jawdat Sa'id, Wahiduddin Khan, and Fethullah Gülen – who regard violence as an aberration and/or an idea whose time is past and who redefine jihad as primarily peacemaking. From their vantage point, violence may be regarded as a last-resort measure against intractable evil and thus would rarely occur, according to this perspective. This pacifist or near-pacifist strain is genuinely a modern development within Islamic thought and tradition, and is grounded in a retrieval of the Qur'anic emphasis on sabr as the most important and enduring dimension of holistic jihad.

It is noteworthy that younger contemporary Muslim peace scholars and activists today are following in the footsteps of these three trailblazers and others like them. Among them are notably Muhammad Abu-Nimer who directs the Salam Institute in Washington DC and who is also a professor of conflict resolution at American University. Abu-Nimer similarly emphasises the cultivation of the Qur'anic trait of sabr, among other traits, as an antidote to unprincipled violence.[71] Qamarul Huda, formerly of the United States Institute of Peace, and currently at the Hedaya Institute in Abu Dhabi, is also a prominent scholar–practitioner in the field of Islamic peacebuilding and is active in writing on this topic and training fellow activists in many parts of the world.[72] Karim Douglas Crow has long been associated with the non-violence movement; a former professor of Islamic thought at the International Institute of Islamic Thought and Civilization, he passionately advocates for a non-violent approach to conflict resolution based on Qur'anic principles and Muslim praxis in history. Ramin Jahanbegloo, a Canadian scholar of Iranian descent, is greatly influenced by Gandhian principles of non-violence and follows in the footsteps of the Indian Muslims Abdul Ghaffar Khan and Mawlana Abul Kalam Azad in articulating and advocating for non-violence within an Islamic milieu.[73] In Thailand, the academic Chaiwat Satha-Anand (Qader Muheideen) has long been a prominent voice in the field of non-violence and peace studies.[74] There are a number of other such scholar–activists who have embraced non-violence as the best modern articulation of the Islamic imperative to strive in the path of God in order to promote what is good, noble and just on earth and prevent the commission of wrongdoing and combat injustice.

Through a close reading of scripture and the historical contextualisation of later literary productions which chart the storied history of jihad, fundamental Islamic perspectives on peace and war have much to contribute to contemporary global discussions concerning violence and conflict resolution. Such perspectives may also be discovered today to be closely aligned with modern international norms of waging war and making peace. Classical Muslim juridical literature on the topic of international relations and statecraft taken by itself can and has blurred these parallels to a considerable extent, since political realism more than ethics and moral reasoning frequently informed such a genre. Consultation of a broader repertoire of diverse Islamic sources allows one to retrieve multiple perspectives on the permissibility of military activity and allows one to better comprehend the circumstances that allowed for the historical transformation of the Qur'anic defensive jihad into offensive imperial warfare. Such a project of recovery allows Muslims to subscribe to contemporary international norms of defensive, limited war and pursue the preferential option for peace as a moral imperative established by their own tradition. Above all, it allows one to credibly and cogently challenge the views touted in extremist literature produced by both militant Islamist groups and virulent Islamophobes today that military activity masquerading as cosmic holy war is the primary and most authentic meaning of the multivalent Arabic term 'jihad'.

Notes

1. For example, al-Mawardi, *The Ordinances of Government*, tr. Wafaa H. Wahba (Reading, UK: Ithaca Press, 1999), 16.
2. See my discussion of these verses in *Striving in the Path of God: Jihad and Martyrdom in Islamic Thought* (Oxford: Oxford University Press, 2013), 35–43.
3. Mujahid b. Jabr, *Tafsir*, 23.
4. Muqatil, *Tafsir*, 1:167–8.
5. Al-Razi, *Tafsir*, 2:28–8.
6. For a quick overview of this event, see the article 'Al-Hudaybiyya,' *EI²*, 3:539.
7. Al-Razi, *Tafsir*, 2:288.
8. Al-Tabari, *Tafsir*, 2:357.
9. Al-Wahidi, *Wasit*, 1:319.
10. Al-Razi, *Tafsir*, 2:384.
11. Ibid.
12. Al-Tabari, *Tafsir*, 6:278.
13. It is instructive to remember recent American history, especially the rhetoric generated concerning the Iraq war during George W. Bush's presidency, which indicates how powerful such pseudo-theological narratives in service of the state can be.

14.   For more details on al-Tabari's life, see *EI²*, article 'al-Tabari', 10:11–15.

15.   Al-Shafi'i, *Kitab al-umm*, ed. Mahmud Matruji (Beirut: Dar al-kutub al-'ilmiyya, 2002), *passim*.

16.   Al-Shafi'i, *Al-Risala*, ed. 'Abd al-Latif al-Hamim and Mahir Yasin al-Fahl (Beirut: Dar al-kutub al-'ilmiyya, 2005), 337–42.

17.   See further, Afsaruddin, *Striving in the Path of God*, Chapter Ten, for a summary of these contested views through the centuries.

18.   Al-Ghazali, *Ihya 'ulum al-din*, ed. 'Abd Allah al-Khalidi (Beirut: Dar al-arqam, n.d.), 4:84 ff.

19.   Ibn Qayyim al-Jawziyya, *'Uddat al-sabirin wa-dhakirat al-shakirin*, ed. Muhammad 'Ali Qutb (Beirut: Sharikat Dar al-Arqam ibn Abi al-Arqam, n.d.), 25–6.

20.   For example, David Cook, *Understanding Jihad* (Berkeley: University of California, 2005), 166.

21.   The term may however be understood to hark back to Qur'an 25:52, which states in Arabic: *Jahidhum bihi jihadan kabiran* ('Strive against them a mighty striving with it'). The pronominal suffix 'it' is understood by the overwhelming majority of exegetes to refer to the Qur'an; see this discussion in Afsaruddin, *Striving in the Path of God*, 16–18.

22.   Al-Tabari, *Tafsir*, 6:278.

23.   Ibid. 6:278–9.

24.   See further my discussion of this verse and the various exegetical positions in *Striving in the Path of God*, 90–3.

25.   Rida, *Tafsir al-manar*, 10:161–2.

26.   Ibid. 10:162–3.

27.   Ibid. 10:17–5.

28.   Muhammad Sa'id Ramadan al-Buti, *al-Jihad fi 'l-islam* (Damascus: Dar al-fikr, 1993), 52–4; Afsaruddin, *Striving in the Path of God*, 245–52.

29.   See my discussion of the interpretations of Qur'an 9:13 in *Striving in the Path of God*, 58–63.

30.   Ibid. 54–7.

31.   'Ali Jum'a, *al-Jihad fi 'l-islam* (Cairo: Nahdat Misr li 'l-Tiba'a wa al-Nashr, 2005); Afsaruddin, *Striving in the Path of God*, 252–6.

32.   'Ali Jum'a, *Jihad*, 224.

33.   For some of these views, see Sohail Hashmi, 'Saving and Taking Life in War: Three Modern Muslim Views', in Jonathan E. Brockopp (ed.), *Islamic Ethics of Life: Abortion, War, and Euthanasia* (Columbia, SC: University of South Carolina Press, 2003), 129–54.

34.   Al-Zuhayli, *Athar al-harb fi al-fiqh al-islami: dirasa muqarana* (Beirut: Dar al-fikr, 1981), 106–20.

35.   Ibid. 93–4.

36.   Compare with Article 51 and Chapter VII of the UN Charter, which refers to the principle of self-defence and humanitarian intervention, respectively. There is also much debate on 'the responsibility to protect'.

37.   See, for example, Nigel Biggar, *In Defence of War* (Oxford: Oxford University Press, 2013), 310, where he states: 'that military action can sometimes be morally justified in the absence of, and even in spite of, statutory or customary international law.'

38.   Yusuf al-Qaradawi, *Fiqh al-jihad* (Cairo: Maktaba Wahba, 2009), 1:244.

39.   Sherman Jackson, 'Jihad and the Modern World', *Islamic Law and Culture* 1 (2002): 17. Cf. Abdulaziz Sachedina, 'From Defensive to Offensive Warfare: The Use and Abuse of Jihad in the Muslim World', available online at <http://theamericanmuslim.org/tam.php/features/articles/from_defensive_to_offensive_warfarethe_use_and_abuse_of_jihad_in_the_muslim>; last accessed on 1 June 2014.

40.   Ibn Kathir, *Tafsir*, 2:322, where he states in reference to Qur'an 9:5, 'This noble verse is the verse of the sword'.

41. Mark Juergensmeyer considers this belief in a cosmic war between good and evil as symptomatic of militant religio-nationalist groups today; see his *Terror in the Mind of God: The Global Rise of Religious Violence* (Berkeley and Los Angeles: University of California Press, 2003), 3rd edition, 148 ff.

42. Thus Abu Mus'ab al-Suri, a strategist for al-Qaeda, emphasises the *in extremis* argument to justify terrorism; see Brynjar Lia, *The Architect of Global Jihad: The Life of Al-Qaida Strategist Abu Mus'ab al-Suri* (New York: Columbia University Press, 2009), 428.

43. Translated by Johannes J. G. Jansen as *The Neglected Duty: The Creed of Sadat's Assassins and Islamic Resurgence in the Middle East* (London, 1986), 222–5.

44. Ibn 'Abd al-'Aziz, *Fundamental Concepts Regarding Al-Jihad*, (At-Tibyan Publications, Rajab), 1425 (accessed at <www.alqimmah.net>; accessed 31 May 2010), 208.

45. Ibid. 216.

46. Muhammad Tahir-ul-Qadri, *Fatwa on Suicide Bombings & Terrorism*, 2010, available online at <http://www.scribd.com/doc/29876438/Fatwa-on-Terrorism-by-Dr-Muhammad-Tahir-ul-Qadri>; last accessed on 1 June 2010.

47. Translated by Munzer A. Absi and H. Hilwani (Damascus: Dar al-fikr, 2002) from the original Arabic.

48. Ibid. 34.

49. Ibid. 28–9.

50. Ibid. 78.

51. Ibid. 37–40.

52. Ibid. 39.

53. Ibid. 122.

54. Ibid. 77–9.

55. Cf. the article by Irfan A. Omar, 'Islam and the Other: the Ideal Vision of Mawlana Wahiduddin Khan'. *Journal of Ecumenical Studies* 36 (1999): 423–39.

56. Published by Goodword Books, New Delhi, 2002.

57. Khan, *True Jihad*, 13–16.

58. Ibid. 25–39.

59. Ibid. 44–5.

60. Ibid. 42–8.

61. Ibid. 901.

62. For an appraisal of the Gülen movement as it relates to official Turkish secularism, see M. Hakan Yavuz and John L. Esposito, *Turkish Islam and the Secular State: the Gülen Movement* (Syracuse: Syracuse University Press, 2003).

63. M. Fethullah Gülen, *Toward a Global Civilization of Love & Tolerance* (Somerset, NJ: Light Inc., 2004), 171.

64. Ibid. 172.

65. Ibid. 172.

66. M. Fethullah Gülen, *Key Concepts in the Practice of Sufism* (Fairfax, VA: The Fountain, 1999), 100.

67. Ibid. 100.

68. Reprinted in Gülen, *Toward a Global Civilization*, 179–83.

69. Ibid. 178–82.

70. Roland Bainton's definition of holy war in the context of the Crusades is a generally accepted one; he described the Crusades as 'a holy war fought under the auspices of the church or some inspired religious leader, not on behalf of justice conceived in terms of life and property, but on behalf of an ideal, the Christian faith'; see his *Christian Attitudes toward War and Peace* (Nashville: Abingdon, 1986), 14.

71. Muhammad Abu-Nimer, *Non-Violence and Peacebuilding in Islam: Theory and Practice* (Gainesville: University Press of Florida, 2003).

72. He is the editor of *The Crescent and the Dove: Peace and Conflict Resolution in Islam* (Washington DC: United States Institute of Peace, 2010).

73. See Jahanbegloo's book *Introduction to Nonviolence* (New York: Palgrave Macmillan, 2014).

74. He articulates his position in Chaiwat Satha-Anand, 'The Non-Violent Crescent: Eight Theses on Muslim Non-Violent Actions'," in C. Satha-Anand et al. (eds), *Islam and Non-Violence* (Honolulu: University of Hawaii Press, 1993), 7–26.

CHAPTER 6

American Muslims and the expansion of the umma

Pre-modern Muslim jurists hardly ever conceived of the possibility that large numbers of Muslims would live as settled, permanent communities in non-Muslim lands. When they did contemplate it in a hypothetical vein, it was generally to bemoan it and treat it as a temporary legal aberration. To live fully as humans carrying out the will of God Muslims were expected to do so in realms that were guided by the divinely revealed Sharia and governed by a Muslim ruler who was obligated to uphold and implement the interpreted provisions of the sacred law.

Until the modern era, this remained the comfortable and eminently satisfactory way to live as a Muslim. Western colonialism starting in the nineteenth century and the onset of globalisation in the twentieth century have dramatically changed this fundamental assumption of virtuous and self-sufficient Muslim existence. In Chapter One, we have already discussed some of the sociopolitical and cognitive shifts that occurred in Muslim-majority societies and in Muslim self- and communal perceptions as a result of these often cataclysmic changes. In the twentieth century in the postcolonial era, there were substantial immigrations of Muslim populations to Europe and North America who were often escaping from political instability and poverty in their indigenous countries. Muslims living as settled minorities in non-Muslim majority societies have had to come to terms with a situation that for the most part is historically unprecedented and for which there are very few legal pointers.[1]

Such a novel predicament has exposed Muslim citizens of Western nations to formidable challenges since the twentieth century, especially those who choose to remain observant practitioners of their religion while being engaged and productive members of their respective societies. The challenges posed by the forging of possibly competing hybrid and multiple identities have only become further accentuated in the twenty first century. For American Muslims, this has become poignantly true after 11 September 2001. This chapter will focus primarily on the challenges faced by American Muslims in the contemporary period, but with some references to and comparisons with European Muslims as appropriate.

The day that changed everything: American Muslims after September 11th

Until 10 September 2001 American Muslims had every good reason to feel confident and optimistic about their collective future in what remains one of the most affluent and pluralist nations in the world. There was after all tangible and anecdotal evidence of their growing presence and influence in the American public sphere. Surveys consistently showed that the American Muslim community was among the most highly educated and prosperous groups in the country (a characteristic that remains true until the present time). About 59 per cent of American Muslims hold college degrees, far above the American average of 27 per cent. Most of them are white-collar workers or professionals, with a median family income of greater than $50,000 (20 per cent above the national norm). As for their ethnic breakdown, roughly 34 per cent are of South Asian descent, 26 per cent Arab Americans, and 20 per cent native-born African Americans, primarily converts. Thirty-six per cent were born in the US and about 85 per cent are Sunni, mirroring the Sunni–Shi'i proportion in the world at large. A large percentage of American Muslims, up to 88 per cent, are likely to vote and about nine in ten American Muslims support progressive policy positions on health care, school funding, the environment, foreign aid and gun control. However, they tend to be more conservative on social and religious issues, such as abortion and the death penalty.[2]

In pre-2001 America, American Muslims were heartened by perceptible indications of their growing visibility in public and official space. Since the Bill Clinton era, the White House and other federal branches have regularly made a nod in their direction by holding official *iftar* dinners to mark the breaking of the fast at sunset during Ramadan. Mosques continued to dot the landscape of major urban centres in the United States and progressively made inroads into the heartland of smaller towns and more rural communities. Women and men in distinctively Islamic garb might attract curious looks but were considered no more threatening than a teenager with purple hair or a nun in a traditional habit. In the grand mosaic of American society, there was considerable room for diversity and differences that were perceived to be of a non-menacing kind.

A graphic mainstreaming of Muslim identity occurred with the issuance of a stamp by the US postal service in 2001 commemorating the two Eid festivals observed by Muslims every year. The stamp contained Arabic writing and proudly proclaimed Muslim festivals to be part and parcel of the American cultural and religious landscape. The event was much heralded by American Muslims, some of whom had lobbied hard and long to make it a reality. That was in the summer of 2001 – the last summer, as it turned out, when many American Muslims felt they were living the American dream fully and had every right to assume that things would only get better for their progeny.

By the late morning of 11 September 2001 those perceptions had been severely shaken and essentially up-ended – or so it seemed. The smoldering smoke from what had been the Twin Towers of the World Trade Center appeared to end the possibility of normality from that point on for American Muslims. For all American Muslims, in particular above the age of about seven on September 11th, that day will remain indelibly etched in their memory as one that jolted them out of their mostly comfortable and complacent existence into a world that had irreversibly changed for them. Such a changed world has compelled them to engage deeply with harrowing existential questions concerning their hyphenated identity, their loyalty as citizens, and, above all, their faith that had seemingly been besmirched by the actions of a murderous few.

At the writing of this book, more than a dozen years have elapsed since that fateful, grim day and these questions have not evaporated. American Muslims in various walks of life are faced with both daunting challenges and unprecedented opportunities to make their views and presence felt, as they continue to seek to ensconce themselves within the American landscape. The most prominent of these challenges are discussed below, along with a reflection on what the future may look like as Muslims continue to entrench themselves within the mainstream of American society.

Carving out an American Muslim space and identity

Although increased immigration of people from Muslim-majority societies to the United States became noticeable in the twentieth century, Muslims have been part of the American fabric of society for much longer. About 10 per cent of African slaves brought to America in the eighteenth and nineteenth centuries are said to have been of Muslim origin.[3] There were Muslims who served in the military during the American civil war. Already in the nineteenth century we encounter prominent American Muslim converts, such as Muhammad Alexander Russell Webb, who converted to Islam in 1888 and served as the United States Consul to the Philippines.[4] And Muslim holidays figured – albeit modestly – in the public, political consciousness about 200 years before Bill Clinton: Thomas Jefferson is said to have been the first to hold an *iftar* dinner in the White House in honour of the then Tunisian envoy to the United States, Sidi Suleyman Mellimelli.[5] These are little-known historical details that do, however, weave the story of Muslims into the very warp and weft of the fabric of American society.[6]

As already noted, statistics on American Muslims show them to be among the most prosperous and highly educated segments of the US population. American Muslims are furthermore not a homogeneous group. Within the American Muslim population, there is a considerable diversity of ethnic groups represented. If one walks into a mosque in a large urban centre during a congregational prayer, especially on a Friday afternoon or during one of the two major annual festivals (Eid/'Id), one will find a veritable United Nations of members from various backgrounds represented – South Asian, Arab, Malay, Indonesian, African, African American, European, Chinese, and others. A considerable segment of American Muslims is still comprised of first-generation Americans, who remain closely connected to their countries of origin and whose cultural practices often resemble those of their natal societies. Despite these considerable cultural variations and high levels of heterogeneity, the large majority of American Muslims are on the whole socially and economically integrated into American society. Unlike Muslim emigrants to many European nations, many of the Muslim emigrants to the US arrived with advanced university degrees from their countries of origin, possessed fluency in English and evinced a strong desire to adapt to their country of adoption without giving up their religious observances.

Like other ethnic groups who adhere to a minority faith tradition (that is to say other than Protestant Christian), Muslims from various backgrounds strive to carve out a space for themselves within the American mosaic of hybrid identities. Following in the footsteps of other immigrant groups, they have had to grapple (and continue to do so) with some fundamental existential questions: how does being a Muslim – both in the theological/confessional and cultural sense – intersect with being an American in the national, political and cultural sense? How can they uphold and nurture their hyphenated identity without compromising either component of it? Are there specific values that they can embrace equally as Americans and Muslims? Are there specific American cultural practices that they must in good conscience refrain from adopting? Answers to these broad questions entail dealing primarily with issues of citizenship and loyalty and of negotiating the secularism of the larger society in a dialectic with one's personal faith that is subject to often severe public scrutiny.[7] Such questions have achieved a measure of urgency in the post-September 11th milieu. We now proceed to engage two inter-related issues in greater detail and explore their relevance to the formation of a distinctive American Muslim identity in the contemporary period.

Citizenship and negotiating religiosity in a secularised society

There is a vocal and powerful extremist minority within the contemporary United States which insists in a polemical vein that one cannot be both American and Muslim at the same time. This is so, they maintain, because Islam in its fundamental and essential orientation – an orientation perhaps uniquely known to this group – is antithetical to what is broadly conceptualised as 'the American way of life'. The xenophobic bravado of this claim masks the fact that it is a highly unoriginal and banal accusation that has been levelled at practically every immigrant group in the United States that did (does) not come from a Protestant Christian background. American Catholics laboured under a black cloud of suspicion until the election of John F. Kennedy as the president of the nation in 1961. American Jews were the perennial 'Other' in the majoritarian American psyche until roughly the middle of the twentieth century. A repertoire of accusations was hurled against these earlier immigrants calculated to cast doubt on their ability as Catholics and Jews per se to become loyal American citizens: that they owed loyalty to a different sovereign (the Pope) or a different code of law (the Halakhah) by virtue of their religious and ethnic designation; their women dressed differently from 'normal' women; and they were incapable of separating religion from politics on account of the all-encompassing medieval religious/canon law they subscribe to, making them intrinsically anti-democratic and incapable of adapting to modernity. These past accusations should sound depressingly familiar because they have been recycled and redirected at Muslims in the contemporary period.[8]

As history shows us, both minority groups eventually came to be considered part of the American mainstream and the religious differences between them and the still predominant Anglo-Protestant majority are now considered non-threatening. The right to practise the tenets of their faith, however exotic they may appear to outsiders, is fully protected by the United States constitution. This trend in general bodes well for American Muslims in the long run. However American Muslims are also currently burdened by the fact that September 11th has cast an extra, weighty layer of suspicion over them as a collectivity. 'Terrorism' is a label that dogs them persistently in the public sphere and home-grown terrorist acts perpetrated by a handful of Muslim Americans have definitely tarnished their image. But it is overseas acts of militancy carried out in the context of political circumstances – not directly connected to the lives of American Muslims – that have predominantly besmirched their collective standing and credibility as loyal citizens. American Muslims are asked over and over again to condemn terrorist actions committed in the Middle East and South Asia often in the name of Islam. While many of them do – repeatedly – when given a chance, their condemnations do not reach a wider audience and are barely reported in the mainstream media. This creates the false impression that leaders within the American Muslim community (and abroad) have not taken a strong and vocal position against terrorist acts committed in the name of Islam, when in fact they have and plenty of documentation to corroborate this is available for the asking.[9]

Despite the pervasive talk of 'Islamic' or 'Islamist' terrorism, hard statistics provide irrefutable evidence that a violent, extremist minority among Muslims is exactly that – a small minority that represents a sliver of the global Muslim population now numbering over a billion. In his recent book *The Missing Martyrs:*

Why There Are So Few Muslim Terrorists, the sociologist Charles Kurzman documents, for example, that out of the approximately 150,000 people who die daily worldwide, fewer than fifty deaths occur at the hands of Islamist militants, and then mostly in the conflict-ridden areas of Afghanistan, Pakistan and Iraq.[10] However, hard facts do not by themselves readily dissipate impressionistically formed views. Constant and frequently sensationalist media coverage of acts of militancy committed by individuals from Muslim backgrounds contribute further to the hardening of negative stereotypes about Muslims in general. As a consequence, violence and disloyalty to the state are persistently associated with American Muslims. These highly negative perceptions have directly impacted their roles as citizens and their clout as political actors within the variegated American landscape.

A political nadir was reached during the two George W. Bush presidencies (2000–08), when there was a concerted effort by certain vested groups to curtail Muslim participation in American public life. The neo-conservative agenda to militarily reshape the Middle East, starting with the military occupation of Iraq, and increased surveillance of Muslims who were frequently depicted as a fifth column within the United States, has had long-lasting deleterious consequences.[11] In the decade following the September 11th tragedy, surveys conducted by the Pew Foundation and other organisations consistently showed that negative perceptions of Muslims by non-Muslims had grown by significant and alarming percentages. This has adversely affected the ability of a number of American Muslims to find jobs in the public sector, government and intelligence agencies, state and local administrative bodies, among others. A full quarter of American Muslims surveyed by the Pew Research Center in 2007 admitted to having been the victims of discrimination on account of their religion.[12]

The Muslim citizen: negotiating the American political public sphere

The concept of the nation state and secular notions of citizenship are relatively new developments in world history. It is a distinctively modern concept whose origins are usually traced to sixteenth- and seventeenth-century Europe racked by bloody religious wars in whose aftermath the Treaty of Westphalia was signed in 1648. Until the seventeenth century in Europe, as in many other parts of the world, membership in the polity – however that was organised – was based primarily on one's religious affiliation. If one was affiliated with the dominant religious group, one had full rights and privileges. If one was not, one was less than a full 'citizen' and subject to discrimination and worse, persecution and possible annihilation. The modern concept of citizenship within the nation state is usually grounded in an individual's birth and/or continuous residence within it and is extended to all those who qualify for it (at least theoretically) without regard to religious commitments. Religion becomes privatised and is assumed not to shape the person's public identity or political loyalties (or at least not to a great extent, although exceptions to this general rule are plentiful throughout modern European and American history).[13]

As mentioned earlier, pre-modern Muslim political and legal thinkers had not entertained at great length the possibility of long-term legal minority status for Muslims in non-Muslim realms. Medieval Muslim jurists in general discouraged Muslims from settling down in non-Muslim territories because of the constraints they would face on their ability to freely and safely practise the requirements of their faith and to live in dignity – without being subject to enslavement, for example, by foreigners.[14] By the twentieth century, this situation would become dramatically transformed so that we find that up to a third of the world's Muslim population now resides in Europe and North America, including roughly three to six million in the United States and about half a million in Canada.[15] Pre-modern jurisprudence had not anticipated such large-scale immigration of Muslim populations to non-Muslim lands and therefore could not provide adequate answers or a well-developed methodology for dealing with their situation. The fundamental question for Muslim immigrants remains today – how may Muslims continue to be faithful to the precepts of their religion in countries that are not ruled by Islamic law?

Developing a jurisprudence of minorities

Such a question was not comprehensively answered until the 1990s when a specific jurisprudence of Muslim minorities (*fiqh al-aqalliyyat*) emerged in response to this question. The term *fiqh al-aqalliyyat* was coined by a prominent American Iraqi scholar Taha Jabir al-Alwani in 1994, who at that time was the president of the Fiqh Council of North America. Al-Alwani was inspired to formulate this jurisprudence to facilitate interaction between the Muslim minority and the non-Muslim majority and to provide the former with a firm identity and mooring in American society based on *fiqhi* principles. In his book *Nazarat ta'assasiyya fi fiqh al-aqalliyyat* (Foundational considerations with regard to the jurisprudence of minorities), al-Alwani focuses on what he regards as the main questions undergirding the formulation of this specific jurisprudence of minorities. They include: what form of political government does the minority group live under – a democracy, monarchy, and so on? What roles do leaders and various organisations play in the life of the minority? What is the socio-economic, political and cultural standing of the minority? How may one facilitate better cooperation between the majority and the minority populations? In framing these questions and concerns, al-Alwani was drawing on an older strand within Islamic jurisprudence called *fiqh al-nawazil*, which can be translated as 'the jurisprudence of unprecedented or calamitous events'. The *fiqh al-aqalliyyat* was therefore not fashioned out of whole cloth but derived some of its basic principles and orientation from this earlier legal genre.[16]

As an example of this kind of jurisprudential reasoning, we can refer to the response formulated by al-Alwani when frequently queried by many American Muslims about the legality of participating in American politics and forming political alliances with non-Muslims, for which there was little precedent in Islamic history. If anything, traditional *fiqh* could be understood as prohibiting Muslims from associating with non-Muslims who may be understood to harbour malevolent intent towards them; a world-view that had facilitated the juridical division of the world into the abode of Islam (*dar al-islam*) and the abode of war (*dar al-harb*). Al-Alwani issued a non-binding legal opinion (*fatwa*) that Muslims may indeed vote in American elections. He stated:

> It is the duty of American Muslims to participate constructively in the political process, if only to protect their rights, and give support to views and causes they favor. Their participation may also improve the quality of information disseminated about Islam. We call this participation a 'duty' because we do not consider it merely a 'right' that can be abandoned or a 'permission' which can be ignored.[17]

Al-Alwani's answer was motivated by considerations of the common or public good (*al-maslaha al-mursala* or simply *maslaha*), a cardinal principle of *fiqh al-aqalliyyat*. Rather than consider Western nations as part of the *dar al-harb*, in view of changed historical circumstances, they should rather be considered as constituting *Dar al-da'wa* (the Abode of Summoning), where Muslims may safely propagate and practice their faith.[18] In common with other reformist scholars, al-Alwani emphasises the normative authority of the Qur'an over the sunna and asserts that what he calls 'the higher principles' animating juridical thinking can only be derived from the Qur'an. His Qur'an-centred methodology underpinning the *fiqh al-aqalliyyat* accordingly lays stress upon the higher principles of kindness and justice derived especially from Qur'an 60:8–9[19] and 5:8[20] as governing relations between Muslims and non-Muslims.[21] This Qur'an-centred interpretation completely undermines the classical dichotomous view of the world predicated on mutual wariness and hostility between Muslims and non-Muslims – a view derived neither from the Qur'an nor the sunna – and allows instead for a model of coexistence and cooperation to emerge.

Al-Alwani's Middle Eastern partner in shaping the jurisprudence of minorities has been the Egyptian-born Qatari cleric Yusuf al-Qaradawi who, like the former, is an Azhar-trained religious scholar. In his explanation of the justification for this jurisprudence, al-Qaradawi lays great emphasis upon the opportunities to carry out *da'wa* among non-Muslims that legitimises the presence of Muslims in the West. He argues:

Thus there can be no questioning of the permissibility of residing in a non-Muslim country, or in *dar al-kufr*, as it is referred to by the jurists, for if we were to forbid it, as some scholars imagine, we would close the door to the call to Islam and its spread throughout the world. [Had this been done] then the Islam of old would have been restricted to the Arabian Peninsula and not left it. For if we read history and reflect upon it properly we find that the spread of Islam into the lands that we today refer to as the Arabic and Islamic worlds occurred through the influence of individual Muslims, merchants, Sufis and others like them, who migrated from their countries to those lands in Asia and Africa and mixed with the local people, worked together with them and in turn were liked by them for their good morals and sincerity, as was their religion which had implanted these virtues in them. Thus people entered our religion en masse and individually.[22]

It should be noted that al-Qaradawi's views have pre-modern antecedents in the legal rulings of the famous Shafi'i jurist al-Mawardi (d. 1058), who stated that if a Muslim is able to publicly practise his religion in a non-Muslim country, then that country becomes part of the Abode of Islam. Residence in such a country is better than immigrating from it since there is the possibility that others may embrace Islam on account of his presence.[23] Al-Mawardi, one may note, had not necessarily advocated active proselytisation among non-Muslims by Muslim residents in foreign lands, which is often implied by the term *da'wa*, but rather serving as witnesses for Islam through their private comportment and public observance of the requirements of their faith.

The proponents of minority *fiqh* as well as modernist Muslim scholars in general tend to understand *da'wa* in this capacious sense rather than in the narrower sense of proselytisation. In many ways, living as observant practitioners in the West automatically thrusts Muslims into the role of serving as witnesses to their faith. Since they are also frequently called upon, formally and informally, to explain their faith to others, one of their roles as minority citizens is to disseminate information about their religion without intending to convert non-Muslims. Thus the well-known Swiss Muslim scholar and Oxford academic Tariq Ramadan affirms that in the modern world *da'wa*

> must not be confused with either proselytism or efforts to convert: the duty of the Muslim is to spread the Message and to make it known, no more no less. Whether someone accepts Islam or not is not the Muslim's concern for the inclination of every individual heart depends on God's Will. The notion of *da'wa* is based on one principle which is the right of every human being to make a choice based on knowledge and this is why Muslims are asked to spread the knowledge of Islam among Muslims as well as non-Muslims.[24]

Da'wa in the sense of education and public discourse about Islam then simply becomes part and parcel of the free exchange of ideas in the modern public realm, where anyone may freely espouse their cause without giving offence to others or infringing upon others' right to do the same.

Maslaha, identified above as one of the guiding principles of *fiqh al-aqalliyyat* is, of course, a well-known legal hermeneutic that can be invoked to achieve the higher 'objectives of the religious law' (*maqasid al-Shari'a*). These objectives (or 'necessities') are five in number: the protection of life, property, intellect, family [genealogy] and religion (sometimes honour is added as a sixth item).[25] The importance of *maslaha* had already been recognised by Abu Hamid al-Ghazali (d. 1111) in the eleventh century and by other jurists after him, and has become a well-established legal principle employed in particular by modernist and reformist scholars.[26] Al-Alwani has argued for expanding the list of objectives of the Sharia in recognition of the complexities and extra demands of modern existence.[27] Al-Qaradawi has similarly recognised the need for adding to these objectives and accordingly identifies, in addition to the traditional five, the need to protect peace and the rights and freedoms of the individual, to ensure human flourishing, facilitate the removal of oppression, and the promotion of justice, among others. He considers these aggrandised purposes to be natural extensions of the original *maqasid* to which al-Ghazali would very likely have no objection.[28]

Darura or necessity is another juridical principle invoked in a utilitarian manner within the *fiqh al-aqalliyyat* genre. This principle allows Western Muslims to adapt to prevailing local circumstances and convention when no other recourse is available. One such issue concerns the permissibility of the burial of Muslims in non-Muslim cemeteries, a situation that may become unavoidable for Western Muslims in areas where there is not a considerable Muslim presence. When al-Qaradawi was asked concerning this matter, his response was to affirm the permissibility of Muslims being buried in Christian cemeteries in the absence of Muslim cemeteries, while counselling Western Muslims to continue to strive to create cemeteries for Muslims.[29] More controversially, invoking both *maslaha* and *darura*, minority *fiqh* proponents, including al-Alwani and al-Qaradawi, have argued for the permissibility of Muslims serving in non-Muslim armies, as long as they are not attacking other Muslims. They argue that such military service conduces to the protection of Muslim life and property and to good relations between them and the non-Muslim population. It may also be the only way to defend Muslims against external attacks on the non-Muslim polity in which they reside.

This was most dramatically illustrated after September 11th when an American Muslim military chaplain, 'Abd al-Rashid, wrote to al-Alwani seeking his counsel on the moral conundrum presented by serving in the United States army which was clearly preparing for an attack on Afghanistan, a Muslim country. Al-Alwani consulted with al-Qaradawi who in turn consulted with other jurists and a formal, non-binding legal response (*fatwa*) was issued. This was a highly significant legal opinion and therefore considerable parts of it are being reproduced below:

We say: This question presents a very complicated issue and a highly sensitive situation for our Muslim brothers and sisters serving in the American army as well as other armies that face similar situations. All Muslims should be united against all those who terrorize innocents, and those who permit the killing of non-combatants without a justifiable reason. Islam has declared the spilling of blood and the destruction of property as absolute prohibitions until the Day of Judgement . . . It is incumbent upon our military brothers in the American armed forces to make this position and its religious reasoning well known to all their superiors as well as to their peers, and to voice it and not to be silent. Conveying this is part of the true nature of the Islamic teachings that have often been distorted or smeared by the media.

If the terrorist acts that took place in the US were to be evaluated according to the Islamic Law (shari'a) or the rules of Islamic jurisprudence (*fiqh*), the ruling for the crime of *hiraba* (waging war against society) would be applied to the perpetrators thereof . . . Therefore we find it necessary to apprehend the true perpetrators of these crimes, as well as those who aid and abet them through incitement, financing or other support. They must be brought to justice in an impartial court of law and punished appropriately, so that it might act as a deterrent to them and to others like them who easily slay the lives of innocents, destroy properties and terrorize people. Hence, it is a duty on Muslims to participate in this effort with all possible means, in accordance with God's (Most High) saying: 'And help one another in virtue and righteousness but do not help one another in sin and transgression' [Qur'an 5:2].

To sum up, it is acceptable – God willing – for Muslim American military personnel to participate in the fighting in the upcoming battles, against whomever their country decides has perpetrated terrorism against them, keeping in mind to have the proper intention, as explained earlier, so that no doubts will be raised about their loyalty to their country, or to prevent harm from befalling them, as might be expected. This is in accordance with the Islamic jurisprudential rules which state that necessities dictate exceptions, as well as the rule that says that one may endure a small harm to avoid a much greater harm. And God the Most High is Most Knowledgeable and Most Wise.[30]

Other utilitarian principles that anchor this jurisprudence of Muslim minorities are *taysir al-fiqh* (emphasising leniency in jurisprudence) and the recognition of '*urf* or local customs in creating legal responsa. As an example of the first, the European Council for Ifta' and Research, headed by al-Qaradawi, allowed Muslims in northern Europe and North America during the short winter days to combine the early and late afternoon prayers (*zuhr* and '*asr*) and to combine the sunset and late night prayers (*maghrib* and '*isha*) during the long summer days. The Council also allowed Western Muslims to take out interest-bearing mortgages to purchase homes if renting is not an option and if interest-free banks are not present in their area.[31] The *fiqh al-aqalliyyat* literature furthermore tends to dissolve traditional *madhhab* (legal school) boundaries in the search for appropriate solutions for unprecedented circumstances faced by Western Muslims, which may also be considered a part of *taysir al-fiqh*.

The adoption of these tools and principles within the jurisprudence of minorities has led to legal decisions unprecedented in traditional *fiqh* and has thereby exposed its exponents to criticism from more conservative quarters. Such conservative critics have denounced some of these rulings as blameworthy innovations (*bid'a*) that constitute unwarranted departure from traditional juridical reasoning.[32] For many others, however, minority *fiqh* reasoning represents the perennially creative and dynamic nature of the Islamic legal and moral traditions which allows Western Muslims to remain true to the foundational principles of their faith, even as they seek to re-engage and re-interpret them in a bid to make them relevant and applicable in their vastly changed circumstances.

More strategies for rereading the Sharia in the West

Not all scholars find the concept of a jurisprudence of minorities palatable. The late Syrian scholar Sa'id Ramadan al-Buti inveighed against this new *fiqh* as a strategy that would cause divisions among Muslims and undermine the Sharia among Western Muslims. From his perspective, the jurisprudence of minorities would allow Muslims to assimilate harmful and immoral practices current in the West while providing ostensibly Islamic justifications for such unacceptable lifestyles.[33]

Not all reform-minded Western Muslims have embraced the reasoning behind the jurisprudence of minorities either. Oxford scholar and public intellectual Tariq Ramadan has resisted in particular the 'minority' label for Western Muslims which he feels creates a permanent state of disadvantage and even of victimhood among them. Thus while he appreciates how the jurisprudence of minorities has allowed Muslim citizens to participate in Western societies in good conscience and allowed them to reconcile potentially conflicting claims on their loyalties, Ramadan in his acclaimed book *Western Muslims and the Future of Islam* regards this approach as a stopgap one that does not comprehensively address all the issues at stake for them. He comments on the fact that Yusuf al-Qaradawi had titled his book on *fiqh al-aqalliyyat* as (in English translation): *On Law and the Jurisprudence of Muslim Minorities* with the revealing subtitle: *The Life of Muslims in Other Societies*. Ramadan finds the subtitle disturbing because it continues to promote the perception that Muslims are in a diasporic situation when they reside outside of the Islamic heartlands. Not so, he says, Western Muslims, like himself, are fully at home in the West and not temporarily sojourning there. He remarks:

> In his [Qaradawi's] mind, Western societies are 'other societies' because the societies normal for Muslims are Muslim-majority societies. But this is no longer the case, and what were once thought of as some kind of 'diasporas' are so no longer. There is no longer a place of origin from which Muslims are 'exiled' or

'distanced', and 'naturalised', 'converted' Muslims – 'Western Muslims' – are at home, and should not only say so but feel so.[34]

Ramadan comments further:

> Indeed our own sources come to our aid and press us to go beyond three staging posts, which are in the long term to be considered as traps: the dualist approach, minority thinking, and integration thought of only in terms of adaptation . . . To think of our belonging to Islam in the West in terms of Otherness, adaptation to limitations, and authorized compromise (*rukhas*) cannot be enough and gives the impression of structural adjustments that make it possible to survive in a sort of imagined borderland but that do not provide the means really to flourish, participate in, and fully engage in our societies.[35]

A numerically minority status should not lead to a 'minority consciousness' among Western Muslims so 'that they identify themselves only in terms of difference, otherness and even confrontation'.[36] He disparages the ghettoisation of Muslims that occurs as a consequence and the defensive and isolationist mentality that it fosters among them. In contrast, Ramadan's is a confident and nuanced embrace of modernity and life in Western societies, in which Muslim citizens are full and equal participants and who have important contributions to make to these societies when they draw upon the wellsprings of their own rich and complex moral and intellectual traditions. Ramadan underscores the exacting, even Herculean nature of such an intellectual and ethical enterprise that will allow Western Muslims 'to move from integration to contribution, from adaptation to reform and transformation'.[37] Islam's universalism allows Muslims, regardless of where they are, to integrate whatever is positive regardless of its provenance into their own world-view and practices while remaining faithful to the guiding principles of their own heritage.

Ramadan further reminds that pre-modern Islamic civilisation led the world in scholarship and the sciences and contributed much to the Western humanistic traditions and triggered the European Renaissance. This should not be the cause for sustained nostalgia but a spur towards re-establishing 'the connection between religion and science', which can only be effected through a return to the scriptural sources and producing a comprehensive system of ethics and methodologies that do not lead to an artificial bifurcation between faith and reason.[38] A fundamental reconceptualisation of what a holistic education means from the Islamic perspective must occur; at a minimum, such a holistic education must seek to establish 'a virtuous harmony among knowledge, competence, morality, and gift'[39] in the context of modernity; this is an essential requirement for contemporary Muslims. Ramadan is convinced that Western Muslims will lead the way in this regard

> because of the nature and complexity of the challenges they face, and in this their responsibility is doubly essential. By reflecting on their faith, their principles, and

their identity within industrialized, secularized societies, they participate in the reflection the Muslim world must undertake on its relationship with the modern world, its order, and its disorder . . . In my view, the future dialogue between civilizations will not take place at the geopolitical frontiers between 'the West' and 'Islam' but rather, paradoxically within European and American societies. Here again, Western Muslims will bear a heavy responsibility for demanding that the debate be opened and that it be conducted at a serious and deep level that requires listening to and exchanging with their fellow-citizens. They may be able to bring about the avoidance of a break-down and the emergence of a path to fair dialogue and reconciliation.[40]

Ramadan concludes with a heartfelt plea to continue this 'civilisational' dialogue because it is the civilised alternative to prejudice, racism and Islamophobia. It is also the only way forward for all those who emphasise their commonality as humans with shared universal concerns. From this perspective difference instead of causing division leads to mutual inquiry and illumination among fellow travellers in life.[41]

In the United States, many American Muslim thinkers, academics and activists – Fazlur Rahman, Khaled Abou El Fadl, Asma Barlas, Feisal Abdul Rauf, Muqtedar Khan and 'Azizah al-Hibri, to name a few – have similarly argued that the fundamental Islamic world-view is capacious enough to allow for principled accommodation with the requirements of modern, secular societies without having to compromise on the essentials of one's faith. Variegated cultural accretions that have been grafted onto the basic Islamic edifice over time and usually accepted by traditional Muslims as inherently associated with their religion have often been a barrier to creative re-engagement with the Islamic tradition. Recognising these accretions for what they are and excising them in order to resurrect foundational and enduring values that characterise Islam can be (and has already been) an extremely productive exercise. This project of retrieval of core religious and ethical principles to allow for their reinterpretation within the modern American context allows for the harmonisation of the political identity of American Muslims with their religious one.

For those Muslim citizens who need religious and moral justification for public participation in secular and highly permissive American society, a number of reasoned arguments are provided, as we have seen, in the *fiqh al-aqalliyyat* literature and in other genres of writing on the American Muslim predicament by learned authors. The resonance of these arguments among significant cross sections of the American Muslim population is evident, for example, in their increased political participation in the last three national elections since September 11th. Organisations, like the Council on American–Islamic Relations (CAIR) based in Washington DC and the Muslim Public Affairs Council (MPAC), routinely exhort American Muslims to take their electoral and civic duties seriously. In the recent presidential elections of 2012,

CAIR urged prayer leaders (imams) in mosques to urge their congregations to cast their ballot on election day. The Executive Director of CAIR Nihad Awad released a statement declaring that

> voting is the civic duty of every eligible United States citizen and is an important exercise of our constitutional rights. Muslims' votes could be a deciding factor in this year's election. Islamophobes wish to marginalize Muslims and deprive our community of its voice. Voting is a clear message that we will not be pushed aside.[42]

Like Tariq Ramadan and others, we may be reasonably certain that a distinctively Western-inflected Islamic ethos is emerging, which in the American context makes ample room for the exercise of robust democratic values and sociopolitical inclusiveness, values that many liberal Muslims will argue are fully consonant with the objectives of the Sharia. Such an ethos is also the antidote to social and political marginalisation and the gateway to the benefits of full participatory citizenship.

While Muslims are creatively adapting to the demands and necessities of Western secular life, they are also impacting Western societies and their physical landscape in myriad ways through the public observance of the requirements of their faith and creation of institutions that sustain their religious life. Mosques and halal butcher shops now dot large Western cities, and Muslims, especially Muslim women, in distinctive religious attire are fairly commonplace in large American metropolitan centres. There is increasing acknowledgement of Muslim holidays and observances in secular school calendars and accommodation of Muslim daily prayer are frequently made at workplaces and other public venues.

Such developments, however, are not to everyone's liking, as Awad's statement above indicates. While most of America absorbs Muslim citizens in its proverbial melting point, small but powerful factions make a point of vociferously registering their dismay over these demographic developments.

Battling Islamophobia

The Oxford biologist and self-confessed atheist Richard Dawkins portrays Islam as 'analogous to a carnivorous gene complex' in his best-selling book *The God Delusion*.[43] Many people would be hard put to decipher this turgid statement but the animus driving this description is clear and unmistakable. Dawkins has no particular love for any religion centred on the worship of a supreme being but Islam gets singled out by him for what he understands to be its intrinsically violent and irrational core. The virulence of his sentiment is not unexpected. There are a considerable number of very smart and not-so-smart people today in the West who have decided that there is nothing redeemable about Islam and that it is a spent force that has mutated into a hateful, destructive ideology.

Dawkin's totalising characterisation of Islam feeds into a strain of thought today endemic in North America and Western Europe that regards Islam as representing everything that is antithetical to what are understood to be the unique Western values of liberalism and secularism. Islamic exceptionalism – its assumed singular resistance to ideas of democracy and civil society, a presumed exclusive penchant for violence and a fundamental, religiously motivated intolerance for non-Muslims – has become a convenient straw man in the hands of these cultural ideologues deployed to posit the superiority of Western societies over all others.[44] From such a vantage point, one may credibly promote the idea of the almost genetic inability of Muslims to live within such societies. It is no surprise then that Huntington's 'Clash of Civilizations' thesis has enjoyed renewed vigour among these groups pf people and provides, at least to their way of thinking, ideological justification for expression of public revulsion towards Muslims and the codification of such revulsion into law. It is also no surprise that Huntington's dichotomous world-view resonates with hard-line and radical Islamists who similarly imagine a fundamental civilisational divide predicated on irreconcilable values and world-views, providing a rationale for their equally divisive rhetoric and master plans to reshape the world. These cultural supremacists on both sides are far more similar to one another than either would care to admit.

As a conscious rejoinder to Huntington's world-view, Richard Bulliet, a professor of Islamic history at Columbia University, has coined the term 'Islamo-Christian civilisation' to underscore in particular the intellectual and epistemic commonalities which have historically existed between the two world civilisations. Rigorous scholars will note that historical evidence can be cited more in support of Bulliet's position than Hungtington's, when we take into consideration shared modes of social organisation in the pre-modern period, the transmission of classical Hellenic scholarship from the Muslim world to the Latin West and the predominance of Islamic sources in medieval European curricula, as well as similar world-views inflected by Abrahamic monotheism and conceptions of piety in the medieval era.[45] Therefore, it should come as no surprise to us that Westernist and Islamist cultural warriors share a common disdain for history, which they tend to replace with their own idealised image of the past, in which there is no room for the inconvenient 'Other'.

The historical record further shows us that fundamentally dichotomous and adversarial Western attitudes towards the Islamic world mainly came into being in the nineteenth century at the height of the period of Western colonisation. Between the sixteenth and the eighteenth centuries, European scholarly studies of the Muslim East sometimes leaned more towards objectivity and even sympathy. This was due to the rationalist trend that prevailed in Western academic circles at this time and the absence of European overt political involvement in western Asia during this period. Those who were seeking to reform Christianity

in light of this new spirit of rationalism often found in Islam, regarded as com-
bining a balanced regard for the demands of both spiritual and social life, a
kindred system more to their liking. In this spirit, some European scholars of this
period, like Simon Ockley (d. 1718) and Edward Gibbon (d. 1794), could genuinely rise above their own confessional faith to provide fairly impartial accounts
of Islam and its civilisation.[46]

A measure of European receptivity towards Islam persisted through the
eighteenth century and into the early nineteenth century. Some exceptionally
cultivated Europeans in this period harboured a universalist view in which East
and West were assumed to play complementary, rather than antagonistic, roles.
The German poet Goethe (d. 1831) perhaps best symbolised this Enlightenment
receptivity towards Islam and the Muslim intellectual tradition; his *Westösterliche
Diwan* of 1818 is a classic literary example of this kind of receptivity. When
Goethe became exposed to Islam and Muslim thinkers, he added the name
of the Prophet Muhammad as his third source of inspiration after Jesus and
Apollo.[47] Such favourable views were less likely to be encountered in the late
nineteenth century. One notable exception was Thomas Carlyle (d. 1881) who
famously repudiated the widespread idea in Europe that Islam had been spread
by the sword and that Muhammad was 'an imposter'.[48]

As Ziad Elmarsafy has convincingly shown, an element that proved to be
seminal in shaping Enlightenment attitudes towards Islam were translations
of the Qur'an at this time, such as that of George Sale's in 1734. The famous
French writer Voltaire (d. 1778), for example, acquired a copy of Sale's translation, which he read and annotated, after which he seems to have developed a
strong affinity for Muhammad. This attitude was in sharp contrast to the fanati-
cism he had attributed to the Prophet in his play *Mahomet* (although the Pope
is said to have been the actual target of his polemics). Voltaire came to regard
the Bible and the Qur'an as preaching a common morality but thought Islamic
law conformed better to nature than the laws of other religions. He found the
Qur'an's moral message more in line with Enlightenment sensibilities, including
its anti-Trinitarianism.[49] His reading of the Qur'an established for him that the
story of Islam was appealingly one of 'demystified history, free of superstition,'
and above all one of worldly engagement. Elmarsafy summarises Voltaire's
attitude thus: '(A)s children of the Enlightenment, we all have a responsibility
to do right actively rather than wait passively for a deity or an authority figure
to do it for us'.[50] Islamic social ethics provided the desired template for such
worldly activism.

Such a state of affairs began to change drastically when the period of
European conquests and imperialism began in the East in the nineteenth
century. More typical of this era were the sentiments expressed by the French
scholar Ernest Renan (d. 1892) who in a rather (in)famous lecture titled 'Islam
and Science' delivered at the Sorbonne in 1883 pilloried Islam as being opposed

to reason, progress and reform. Continuing a familiar Orientalist theme grounded in the racial theories of the period, Renan attributed earlier Arab advances in the sciences and philosophy to Aryan and non-Muslim (primarily Greco-Sassanian) influences.[51]

In this period, European engagement with the East fostered the following trends: (1) a utilitarian and imperialistic sense of Western superiority, laced with contempt for other civilisations; (2) a romantic exoticism, with its delight in a magical East whose increasing poverty spiced its charm; and (3) the rise of a specialised scholarship whose main concern lay with the study of Semitic languages and texts. This last, the specialised scholarship, led to the founding of a scholarly discipline termed Orientalism in the Western academy. Its practitioners, the Orientalists, tended to portray the East as a place of chaos and quaint practices that could be studied and given order primarily by being filtered through – as was assumed – the rational Western mind.

Because of its historical provenance, Orientalism came to be regarded as a highly politicised and tendentious discipline by the twentieth century, famously and devastatingly criticised by Edward Said (d. 2003), a professor of comparative literature at Columbia University of Palestinian Christian background. In his seminal book appropriately titled *Orientalism* published in 1978, Said lambasted this phenomenon for having engendered what he described as the process of organising knowledge about the East, embedded in a discourse of power, which subjected knowledge to the political concerns of the three great empires of the nineteenth and twentieth centuries, British, French, and American.[52] Whether one fully agrees with Said or not, the impact of his work has wrought a sea change in the way scholarship about the Middle East and Islam is conducted in the Western academy, particularly in the United States. Said's critique (and that of others after him) has allowed for more rigorously analytical and considerably more objective methodologies to emerge which foreground the complexities of Muslim societies and multiple inflections of the Islamic tradition.

However, these modest gains in improving academic approaches to Muslim-majority societies and their histories as well as in public perceptions of Islam and Muslims suffered a sharp setback after 11 September 2001. In the aftermath of this tragedy, the phenomenon known as Islamophobia ('fear of Islam') went into overdrive in the United States.[53] The term Islamophobia itself was not coined in this period; its first appearance may be traced back to the late 1980s. It was first used in print in the American periodical *Insight*, which in reference to the Soviet occupation of Afghanistan in that period stated, 'Islamophobia also accounts for Moscow's reluctance to relinquish its position in Afghanistan, despite the estimated $300 million a month it takes to keep the Kabul regime going'.[54] The term was subsequently made popular by an independent British think tank devoted to race equality called the Runnymede Trust in a report that it issued in 1997 titled *Islamophobia: A Challenge for Us All*. The report defined Islamophobia as 'referring to dread or hatred of Islam – and, therefore, to fear or dislike of all or most Muslims'.[55] This concise statement will serve as a working definition for us.[56]

The Runnymede Report provides a particularly useful checklist of 'closed views of Islam' that are typically distinctive of Islamophobic attitudes. These closed views lead to Islam being seen as:

1. a single monolithic bloc, static and unresponsive to new realities;
2. separate and other –
    a. not having any aims or values in common with other cultures;
    b. not affected by them;
    c. not influencing them;
3. inferior to the West – barbaric, irrational, primitive, sexist;
4. violent, aggressive, threatening, supportive of terrorism, engaged in 'a clash of civilisations';
5. a political ideology, used for political or military advantage.

Furthermore, subscription to these closed views leads to the following results:

6. Criticisms made by Muslims of 'the West' rejected out of hand;
7. Hostility towards Islam used to justify discriminatory practices toward Muslims and exclusion of Muslims from mainstream society; and
8. Anti-Muslim hostility accepted as natural and 'normal'.[57]

These closed views identified by Runnymede Trust that feed into Islamophobia are similarly evident in its various incarnations across the pond from England, as will become evident when we discuss a specific case study below. Although it has deep historical antecedents stretching back to the Middle Ages, Islamophobia as a distinct and palpable modern phenomenon is of a slightly newer vintage in the United States compared to Great Britain where there is an older, well-established Muslim population. As Denise Spellberg recently noted, anti-Islamic polemics were already part of the American political scene during the presidency of Thomas Jefferson but it did not reach the kind of fever-pitch virulence that it has during the presidency of Barack Hussein Obama, himself 'accused' of being a Muslim and therefore not really an American.[58]

September 11th, once again, is the watershed mark for the escalation in anti-Islamic sentiment in the United States. Before September 11th, polls typically showed that most Americans confessed ignorance about Islam and were more or less evenly divided between those who harboured positive views about Muslims and those who had negative perceptions of them. At the beginning of the twenty-first century, about 25 per cent of Americans believed that Islam is inherently violent while 51 per cent disagreed. By 2011, these percentages had dramatically shifted: 40 per cent of Americans were now of the opinion that Islam promotes violence while 42 per cent disagreed. A report from the Gallup Center for Muslim Studies published in 2010 established that as many as four in ten Americans (about 43 per cent) confessed to harbouring at least 'a little' prejudice towards Muslims. This was more than twice as many Americans who said they were prejudiced in any degree towards Christians (18 per cent), Jews (15 per cent) and Buddhists (14 per cent). Muslim attempts to build mosques, especially in the rural South, have often been greeted with dismay and decried as attempts to establish terrorist cells in the heartlands of America, as was the case in Murfeesboro, Tennessee, in 2012. Islam is delegitimised as a religion by Islamophobes and presented instead as a political ideology that is not entitled to protection under the First Amendment. [59]

Islamophobes have proved to be remarkably adept at manipulating the politics and rhetoric of fear to convince those who are less well informed that their views are plausible and to be ignored only at their own peril. As the dust jacket of a popular book about Islamophobia recently asked tongue-in-cheek:

> With the rise of 'stealth jihad', 'creeping Sharia', 'Islamofascism', and 'terror babies' in places like 'The United States of Islamica', 'Eurabia', and 'Londonistan', who wouldn't be scared?'[60]

Highly emotive terms such as those contained in the blurb above are wielded with great effect through well-publicised and well-funded public smear campaigns against Muslims, often through the medium of scurrilous films like *Obsession* and *The Third Jihad*, which warn of an impending takeover of the US by fanatical Muslims intent on destroying the West. The US Navy Seals, until called out on it in 2012, instituted the charming and gallant custom of letting trainees perfect their shooting skills by using the image of an armed Muslim woman in a headscarf for target practice. For good measure – lest the enemy not be clearly identified – the image also included Arabic phrases from the Qur'an in the background.[61]

Key terms reflexively associated in the mind of the public with Islam are sometimes pilloried in public spaces; one may recall the 2012 'Defeat Jihad' advertising campaign carried out in the New York subway system by the American Freedom Defense Initiative, led by Pamela Geller, arguably the *éminence grise* among the current crop of career Islamophobes. The ad read:

> In any war between the civilized man and the savage, support the civilized man. Support Israel. Defeat Jihad.

The reflexive connection made between Islam and savagery is an old, tired trope borrowed, rather ironically, from the lexicon of Nazi anti-Semitism which regularly equated Jews with uncivilised savages. In September 1935, Joseph Goebbels, the Nazi minister for propaganda and public education, warned in a public speech at Nuremberg that if 'Jewish sub-humans' remained unchecked

> it means, in the final consequence, the absolute destruction of all economic, social, state, cultural, and civilizing advances made by western civilization for the

benefit of a rootless and nomadic international clique of conspirators, who have found their representation in Jewry.[62]

The Nazis similarly used various forms of media – film, graphic art, posters – to portray what they depicted as the irredeemably unregenerate nature of Jews, who, if left unchecked in their drive to take over the world, would pollute the German nation. In one such film titled *Der Ewige Jude*, Jews are compared to 'rats that carry contagion, flood the continent, and devour precious resources'.[63] However else one may characterise these Islam-bashers, being capable of original thought is not one of them.[64]

The anatomy of bigotry as evinced by American Islamophobes is usefully dissected through a study of an incident known popularly as 'the Park 51 mosque controversy' that made headlines consistently throughout 2010 and which brought to the fore key issues that continue to dog American Muslims. 'Park 51 mosque' referred not so much to a mosque as to a planned thirteen-storey interfaith community centre that, once built, would contain a Muslim prayer space, in addition to a performing arts centre, a bookstore, a swimming pool, a childcare area, a basketball court and other non-religious facilities. The community centre, which would be open to the general public, was projected to be established at 51 Park Place in Lower Manhattan, formerly the site of a Burlington Coat Factory building. Although many news articles referred to it as the 'Ground Zero Mosque', the projected site was about two blocks away from the World Trade Center. At the centre of the controversy was Feisal Abdul Rauf, prominent imam of a New York mosque, well-known author, and an interfaith practitioner who heads the organisation known as ASMA (American Society for Muslim Advancement) that he founded in 1997.

The first major salvo against the construction of the community centre was fired on 21 December 2009 by the afore-mentioned Pamela Geller in a blog post titled, 'Mosque at Ground Zero: Adding Insult to Agony'. In this post, she called the centre a 'giant victory lap' and characterised the project as representing 'Islamic domination and expansionism', with the location deliberately chosen to give calculated offence. After a hiatus of several months, the matter erupted again in May 2010, when Geller resumed her attack on the Islamic centre. Her attack followed a unanimous resolution passed by the New York Community Board 1 which expressed unqualified support for the Park 51 project. In her new post, Geller asked provocatively, 'What could be more insulting and humiliating than a monster mosque in the shadow of the World Trade Center buildings brought down by Islamic attack?' Until September of that year, she would write around 205 blog posts categorised as 'Mosque at Ground Zero: Takbir!'

Geller's incendiary posts had the desired effect on first the conservative and then the mainstream media. The *Washington Examiner* and the *Investor's Business Daily* ran angry op-ed pieces denouncing plans for the 'Ground Zero Mosque'.

Geller appeared on right-wing commentator Sean Hannity's radio show to further fan the flames. The *New York Post* and Fox News, its television sibling, kept up a steady drumbeat of inflammatory reportage concerning Abdul Rauf and the Park 51 Community Center.

In the ensuing hysterical atmosphere, anti-Islamic sentiment peaked. The Islamic Center of Northeast Florida was firebombed. Conservative radio talk show host Michael Berry remarked on air: 'I hope the mosque isn't built, and if it is, I hope it's blown up' (for which he later apologised). On 6 June 2010, Geller and her organisation, Stop Islamization of America, held a rally to protest the Park 51 Center, at which between 350 and 1,000 protesters turned up, according to various news estimates. Geller herself placed the figure as high as 10,000 and continued to inveigh against 'Islamic supremacists [who] want to build a monster mosque . . . on the cherished site of land they think they conquered'. Tea Party doyenne Sarah Palin memorably asked Muslims to 'refudiate' the Islamic centre on 18 July 2010.

Three days later, a pastor by the name of Terry Jones at the Dove World Outreach Center, a Florida church, announced plans to 'host an "International Burn a Qur'an Day" on the ninth anniversary of the September 11 attacks this year'. The National Republican Trust Political Action Committee created an advertisement intended to run on television stations which began with a Muslim call to prayer followed by graphic images of terrorism. The narrator of the advertisement then announced that mosque supporters celebrate the September 11th attacks. The major networks refused to air the advertisement because of its sweeping indictment of Islam and its inflammatory content. Media Matters for America reported, however, that sensationalist Fox News coverage of the Park 51 Community Center project remained relentless through August 2010 and a majority of its guests voiced strident opposition to its construction. Right-wing columnist Jeffrey Kuhner vilified Abdul Rauf as 'an unrepentant militant Muslim' in an essay published in *The Washington Times* on 5 August 2010. A few days later, the Associated Press reported incidents of hate crimes directed against Muslims, commenting that '[f]oes of proposed mosques have deployed dogs to intimidate Muslims holding prayer services and spray painted "Not Welcome" on a construction sign, then later ripped it apart'. Undeterred by the rising tide of violence against American Muslims, *The Washington Times* published an editorial on 19 August in which it stated that 'The Ground Zero Mosque is not healing a rift but deepening a wound. If the mosque is constructed, the terrorists win.'

Even President Obama was not spared. Right-wing media lambasted him for his 13 August statement that he 'believe[s] that Muslims have the same right to practice their religion as everyone else in this country' and are entitled to build a mosque in lower Manhattan. This elicited caustic responses from right-wing *Washington Times* columnist Frank Gaffney, another Islamophobic luminary, who remarked that Obama 'stands with shariah', while Geller said Obama 'has, in effect, sided with the Islamic jihadists'. On 29 August, vandals set fire to the proposed site of a new Islamic centre in Murfreesboro, Tennessee, causing significant damage to a construction vehicle.

As 11 September drew near, President Obama, Secretary of State Hillary Clinton and the Secretary of Defence Robert Gates, urged pastor Jones not to follow through with the Qur'an-burning episode. Jones agreed to 'suspend' his plans to burn the Qur'an and agreed instead to fly to New York and meet with Abdul Rauf, from whom he said he had received a promise to move the Park 51 Center. When Abdul Rauf denied making such a promise, Jones then declared that he would go ahead with the burning. Copycat threats to burn the Qur'an ensued. Randall Terry, the anti-abortion activist and host of a daily TV show 'Randall Terry: The Voice of Resistance', planned to organise a protest at the White House, where they would tear out pages from a Qur'an and ask: 'President Obama, do you support the Sharia law, the Qur'an, and Islamic violence; or do you stand with religious freedom, American liberty, your professed Christianity, and peaceful protest?'

On 11 March 2011 Terry Jones finally publicly burned a copy of the Qur'an for 'crimes against humanity', setting off violent protests in Afghanistan. He has burned other copies since then and continues to keep company with a select group of like-minded people who have made a career out of denigrating all Muslims as dangerous terrorists.

Every instance of closed views identified by the Runnymede Trust as defining and nourishing Islamophobia was on full display during the Park 51 crisis. The overblown inflammatory rhetoric of hate and fearmongering invariably depicted Islam as a monolithic diabolical belief system whose adherents are predictably violent and intolerant fanatics. Muslims are the complete 'Other', 'monsters' devoid of any redeeming characteristics. Hatred of such monsters becomes normalised in these contexts because it is linked to a natural desire to defend oneself against those who are ontologically evil and intend you harm. Over a billion inhabitants of this world are tarred by the actions of a few among them and there is no acknowledgement of the immense internal diversity of cultures, political beliefs and intellectual traditions within the global Muslim population. Muslim leaders and intellectuals may voice criticism of specific US foreign policies that adversely affect their lives, which does not imply wholesale denunciation of the United States and its values. As worldwide polls and surveys have repeatedly affirmed, a large majority of Muslims globally have genuine admiration for the United States and all its achievements. They tend to maintain a careful distinction between American governments (and what they do) and the American citizenry (which can be just as critical of their government's specific actions overseas). But such nuance and refinement would be detrimental to the cause of Islamophobes; as the Runnymede Trust report stated, 'it is easy in these circumstances to argue from the particular to the general – any episode in which an individual Muslim is judged to have behaved badly is used as an illustrative example to condemn all Muslims without exception'.[65]

Coping with terrorism and its afflictions
There is no denying that there is a small but powerful minority of violent extremists among Muslims who articulate visceral hatred not just for non-Muslim Westerners but also for those they perceive as 'dissident' or 'sell-out' Muslims, wherever they may be located. 'Militant Islam' remains a lethal problem not just for non-Muslims but primarily for mainstream Muslims who are disproportionately the target of militants. From within their own world-view, militant Muslims offer detailed rationales for their violent agendas. Their discourses reveal that they see themselves as victims of persistent injustices committed by those they describe as exploitative and profiteering Westerners, starting especially with the period of European colonisation beginning in the nineteenth century, followed by the dismemberment of Palestine and the creation of Israel, and culminating in the recent American military incursions into the Middle East that have resulted in massive losses of lives. Sometimes the historical memory of the militants stretches back to the Crusades, whose gruesome legacy provides a formidable pedigree for their list of historical grievances against the West. Like American neo-conservatives and many right-wing evangelical Christians, they too like to promote the idea of irreconcilable differences between the West and the Islamic world – with a concomitant urgent need for the former to be civilised by the latter. Such a conflictual view is useful for promoting a violent militarist agenda for reforming the world, as they see it. A black-and-white Manichaean vision of the world makes simplistic reflexive solutions to crises arising from genuine historical injustices justifiable.

There is therefore a serious ideological rift between these hardliners and the vast majority of Muslims, who range from traditional to liberal in their perspectives on a broad spectrum of moral and political issues. As some have stated, it is the internal fault lines within the variegated Islamic world across which these ideological clashes occur that are of greater concern than the assumed unbridgeable divide between the West and the rest.[66] In the campaign to win valuable Muslim allies against terrorism launched during the first presidential term of George W. Bush, this internal clash did gain the attention of certain government officials who set out to exploit its potential benefits with single-minded determination. Unfortunately, in the hands of these ill-trained State Department policymakers and ideologues, the bid to ostensibly support mainstream Muslims against the militants became a sharply divisive, ideological bludgeon. Hand-picked on the basis of criteria devised by these government 'experts', a small coterie of 'moderate Muslims' was coaxed into being who would, under official patronage, stage the true Islam, the 'Islam' that could be counted on to say all the 'right' things on cue and would be the faithful ally of the US Government in its bid to tame what was regarded as an unruly part of the world. The results, not surprisingly, were counter-productive and only accentuated an uneasy relationship with the large majority of American Muslims.

Looking for 'moderate' Muslims – attempts to co-opt 'Islam'

Not too long after September 11th, the hunt for 'moderate' Muslims began on the part of the Bush Government and certain well-funded conservative think tanks situated in Washington DC. Who exactly is a 'moderate' Muslim? A very clear answer was given by neo-conservative Cheryl Bernard in a publication sponsored by the National Security Research Division of the Rand Corporation in 2003: a moderate Muslim is one who is receptive to a 'Western vision of civilization, political order, and society'.[67] According to this self-serving definition, most Muslims were written out as 'unacceptable' as far as the neo-conservative power elite in Washington DC was concerned. Bernard's document was not only critical – understandably – of militants and fundamentalists, it took more extensive aim at traditionalist Muslims who are broadly depicted as adhering to 'orthodox norms and values and conservative behaviour' and whose fundamental religious beliefs and practices are considered a threat to world security. How? Because, Bernard avers, following traditional Islam leads to a condition that is 'causally linked with backwardness and underdevelopment, which in turn are the breeding ground for social and political problems of all sorts'.[68]

The crude polemics of this document was not atypical of the time – Cheryl Bernard, married to Zalmay Khalilzad who served as the US ambassador to Afghanistan and Iraq under George W. Bush, was parlaying the neo-imperialist ideology predominant in Washington DC at the time to refashion the Middle East and South Asia in its own image. Shortly thereafter, the Muslim World Outreach programme was launched by the National Security Council, with an initial allocation of $1.3 billion and the stated objective of 'transforming Islam from within'.[69] The programme's main objective was to identify individuals and organisations in the Muslim world who would serve as allies of the US in this enterprise. For this project to be successful, 'moderate' Muslims had to be found and, if need be, created *ex nihilo* with the infusion of plentiful cash.

It was in this general ambience that the careers of a number of a cadre of professional 'moderate' Muslims were launched, who could be trusted to say the right kind of things about Islam and Muslims in pungent sound bites delivered to the media. None of these 'moderates' had any kind of scholarly training in Islamic studies nor any kind of standing within the American Muslim community (or elsewhere). Some of them were even lapsed Muslims and could be counted on to make predictably derogatory and totalising remarks about Islam and Muslims.[70]

In this ugly ideological atmosphere, it became increasingly hard for bonafide academics and intellectuals, Muslim and non-Muslim, to make their views heard in the public arena and offer thoughtful and nuanced assessments of volatile political and ethical issues, which might include reasoned critiques of specific US government policies. Those who did so were often maligned by certain watchdog groups, like Campus Watch, and punished in subtle and not-so-subtle ways. Those Muslim scholars who also identified themselves as people of faith were often excoriated for their informed views on highly charged issues like Sharia, which did not accord with the 'moderate' positions endorsed by the neo-conservatives. Khaled Abou El-Fadl, for example – a brilliant scholar of Islamic law and ethics and a prolific author who teaches at the University of California at Los Angeles – has been vilified by Daniel Pipes, the founder of Campus Watch, as 'a stealth Islamist'.

Another prominent victim of such neo-conservative vigilantism has been Tariq Ramadan, who now teaches as a chaired professor of Contemporary Islam at the prestigious St Antony's College at the University of Oxford in the United Kingdom. In 2004, when Ramadan was given a chaired, tenured position at the University of Notre Dame in the United States and granted a visa to teach there, the right-wing fringe within the United States geared itself into action and had his visa revoked. Ramadan is a prominent European intellectual who happens to be an observant Muslim and inhabits both identities with seamless confidence and little dissonance. He may be regarded as personifying a home-grown European-inflected Islam that has its roots in the Middle East but is fully naturalised in the West. It is precisely because he is Muslim and perfectly at home in the modern secular West that he represents such a threat to the nativists – whether in Europe or in the US. Ramadan's confident blending of these identities affirms that one can be modern in many different ways, not least of all in a religious way, which strikes at the very heart of the exclusivist grand narrative of a ferociously secular 'liberalism', especially as practised in Europe.[71] After Barack Obama's election to the presidency in 2008, the State Department lifted the ban on Ramadan's entry to the United States. Ramadan has now become a regular presence on the public lecture circuit in the US; the much-anticipated doomsday scenario that, according to the fearmongers, was supposed to have ensued on his arrival in the US has yet to materialise.

When life hands you a lemon, make a lemonade – the way forward

The preceding discussion may convey the impression that much is dark and gloomy on the American Muslim front and looking for a silver lining, much less the proverbial rainbow with a pot of gold at the end, may turn out to be a fool's errand. But, as everyone knows, bad news tends to dominate the print and broadcast media and goes viral on social media, burying the good news that is not fit to print because it will not meet the low bar of sensationalism. The silver lining is not hard to find – recent events on the aggregate have clearly demonstrated that virulent anti-Islamic sentiment remains confined to a rabid minority fringe and that its contagion is being contained by better education and communication by concerned Americans of goodwill. The attempt to demonise Muslims qua Muslims is failing, as was the case with wholescale demonisation of Catholics, Jews and African Americans in the past.

Starting with the aftermath of September 11th, American Muslims have received overwhelming support and comfort from many of their compatriots. One of the most strongly worded statements of support came from a group of US and Canadian scholars who denounced the terror attacks and also distanced themselves from the campaign of fear and vilification that had been instigated by some against Muslims as a collectivity. One critical segment of the statement affirmed that:

> Statements of hate or racial slurs are not a part of the American way, and we join President Bush and others calling on all Americans to respect the rights of Muslim Americans. Further, we urge people of good faith everywhere to reach out to Muslim neighbors . . . American Muslims are good neighbors, devoted to their families and to following God's commands to do good works. There are now some eight million Muslims in the United States, and mosques are to be found in most every major city. The overwhelming majority are peace-loving human beings who share the shock and despair of all Americans. They know that terrorist acts in the name of Islam are a perversion of their most sacred beliefs, and the actions of a few should not characterize the whole.[72]

Following the tragedy, prominent American Muslim organisations such as the Council on American–Islamic Relations, the Islamic Society of North America (ISNA), the American Society for Muslim Advancement, and others, have concentrated on outreach and on building enduring liaisons with other faith-based and community activist groups. These efforts have begun to pay rich dividends. Interfaith events are now in fact more common than ever and are being carried out by low-profile but highly effective religious practitioners. Over time, interfaith liaisons and community outreach have proved to be the most effective way to counter religious bigotry and promote the public good.

For example in Omaha, Nebraska, deep in America's heartland, a tri-faith initiative is currently building an interfaith campus, due for completion in 2015, consisting of a synagogue, a mosque and a church on a thirty-seven-acre tract of land. The initiative has already launched a Tri-Faith Shared Holidays programme through which members of the three Abrahamic faiths learn about and share in each others holidays – Eid, Pesach (Passover), Christmas and other celebrations. As for the Park 51 Community Center, although the controversy loudly orchestrated by the right-wing fringe over its building would suggest that the opposition to it is deep-seated and widely shared, the project in fact enjoys the wholehearted support of the September 11th Families for Peaceful Tomorrows, an association of families who lost loved ones during the fateful attacks. Thanks to such people and the persistence of the project's developer, Sharif El-Gamal, there is a happy postscript to the 'Ground Zero Mosque' brouhaha. On 21 September 2011, Park 51 was opened to the public as 4,000 square feet of renovated space in the Burlington Coat Factory building without much fanfare. Visitors were able to view a special exhibit titled 'NY Children' which displayed 160 portraits of immigrant children living in New York. A carpeted prayer room is located in the lower level. El-Gamal expects to complete the new building within several years, which will be, as it is now, open to all visitors, and focused on building interfaith relations.

Other recent indices of progress can be documented. In July 2013, Sadia Saifuddin was elected as the first Muslim to serve as student representative to the University of California Board of Regents, despite a vicious campaign that was whipped up against her, painting her as a young militant on account of her visible personal faith (she wears a headscarf) and social activism. Anti-Sharia legislation has been defeated in Florida, Missouri and Oklahoma, and the fight continues in other states. In 2011, the American Bar Association (ABA) passed a resolution opposing various anti-Sharia measures saying:

> Initiatives that target an entire religion or stigmatize an entire religious community, such as those explicitly aimed at 'Sharia law', are inconsistent with some of the core principles and ideals of American jurisprudence.[73]

As for Pamela Geller, she was recently barred from entering the United Kingdom by the British Home Office on account of having established anti-Muslim hate groups in the US. Her subway campaign against jihad resulted in a counter-campaign led by Ahmed Rehab, the executive director of the Council on American–Islamic Relations in Chicago, called MyJihad, which documents what the word means to ordinary American Muslims. A volunteer for one of the MyJihad advertisements that ran on Chicago buses referred to his struggle to lose weight, another (an Iraqi refugee) described the effort to start a new life in America as a single mother, while some children referred to their jihad against bullies. The point about the polyvalence of the term jihad was being made effectively, graphically, rationally and, above all, peacefully.[74]

And Pastor Jones? Today he is a lonely man abandoned by most of his parishioners for his extremism. A *New York Times* feature on Jones in 2011 reported that in front of his church, signs that declare 'Islam is of the Devil' have been edited by outsiders to say 'Love All Men'.[75] The list could go on.

An apt way then to describe the years after September 11th is that they have been challenging, frustrating and inspirational – all at the same time. It is a decade that brought many raw emotions and prejudices to the fore, forcing Americans to deal with them in the public sphere where they could not be ignored. In an editorial I wrote in 2011 to commemorate the tenth anniversary of the September 11th attacks, I stated: 'For every act that has threatened to bring us back to the precipice of polarization and hatred, there has however been another that showed us a much more humane and enlightened way forward'.[76] Ultimately the glorious American tradition of giving refuge to all those who seek freedom, particularly freedom from fear and political persecution and, above all, justice within its borders is still vibrant and strong. Although justice in particular takes a beating from time to time, especially at the hands of those who would let bigotry and suspicion get the better of them, the generosity of spirit and fairness which characterise the national American ethos frequently prevail and remain the basis for optimism for the future. Barring a major catastrophe, Muslim citizens will continue to become better-integrated and more visible within American society, claiming their rightful place at the American public table and continuing to contribute to the public good.

Notes

1. See a brief discussion of this by Dina Taha in her article 'Muslim Minorities in the West: Between Fiqh of Minorities and Integration', *Electronic Journal of Islamic and Middle Eastern Law* 1 (2013): 3–4; available at <www.ejimel.uzh.ch.> last accessed on 20 July 2014.
2. These are composite statistics derived from major surveys conducted by the Pew Research Center, available in the published report *Muslim Americans: Middle Class and Mostly Mainstream* (Washington DC: Pew Research Center, 2007), and Zogby International between 2001 and 2011. See the op-ed piece by John Zogby summarising these findings titled 'American Muslims have Mainstream Values', *Forbes*, 26 August 2010; available at <http://www.forbes.com/2010/08/26/muslims-polls-mosque-opinions-columnists-john-zogby.html>; last accessed on 3 March 2014.
3. A. D. Austin, *African Muslims in Antebellum America: A Sourcebook* (New York: Garland Publishing Co.), 1984.
4. For an account of his life, see Umar F. Abdullah, *A Muslim in Victorian America: The Life of Alexander Russell Webb* (Oxford: Oxford University Press, 2006).
5. Denise Spellberg, *Thomas Jefferson's Qur'an: Islam and the Founders* (New York: Alfred A. Knopf, 2013), 218–22.
6. For a detailed history of Islam and Muslims in America, see Kambiz GhaneaBassiri, *A History of Islam in America: From the New World to the New World Order* (Cambridge: Cambridge University Press, 2010). For a rich array of issues concerning American Muslims, see the recently published Yvonne Y. Haddad and Jane I. Smith (eds), *The Oxford Handbook of American Muslims* (Oxford: Oxford University Press, 2014).
7. A book that deals with a number of these issues in an engaging manner is Zarina Grewal, *Islam is a Foreign Country: American Muslims and the Global Crisis of Authority* (New York: New York University Press, 2013).
8. See the helpful essay by John T. McGreevy and R. Scott Appleby titled 'Catholics, Muslims and the Mosque Controversy', *New York Review of Books*, 27 August 2010, which foregrounds the historical similarities in the accusations hurled at Catholics decades earlier and at Muslims in the contemporary period; available at <http://www.nybooks.com/blogs/nyrblog/2010/aug/27/catholics-muslims-mosque-controversy/>; last accessed on

3 March 2014. Cf. further José Casanova, 'Catholic and Muslim Politics in Comparative Perspective', *Taiwan Journal of Democracy* 1 (2005): 89–108.

9. At a minimum, one may check the website created by Charles Kurzman, professor of Sociology at the University of North Carolina, which lists many of these public statements made by Muslim leaders from a variety of backgrounds at <http://kurzman.unc.edu/islamic-statements-against-terrorism/>

10. Charles Kurzman, *The Missing Martyrs: Why There are so Few Muslim Terrorists* (Oxford: Oxford University Press, 2011), 14 ff.

11. For a detailed accounting of the curtailment of the civil liberties of American Muslims after September 11th and the legal pushback against it, see David Cole, *Enemy Aliens: Double Standards and Constitutional Freedoms in the War on Terrorism* (New York and London: The New Press, 2003).

12. See the report *Muslim Americans: Middle Class and Mostly Mainstream*, Pew Research Center, 22 May 2007, 4. The Council on American–Islamic Relations (CAIR) has also over the years assiduously documented the escalation of Islamophobic sentiments in the US, which includes resistance to recognising Muslim religious holidays and practices in the public sphere and accommodation of them in the workplace; hostile reactions to women's hijab and other Islamic attire; physical violence and verbal abuse directed against Muslims, etc.

13. Because of their primarily religious designation, Muslims in the modern United States are assumed by some to be incapable of overcoming what are assumed to be their obscurantist religious sensibilities and becoming model secular citizens. Most ironically then, because Muslims, like Catholics and Jews before them, are not members of the dominant ethnic-religious group (Anglo-Protestant) in the modern American nation state, they are assumed to be less politically loyal or incapable of loyalty altogether – a paradoxical throwback to the pre-modern conception of membership in the polity, both in the Muslim and non-Muslim worlds, along religious lines.

14. As Khaled Abou El Fadl points out, there was actually a diversity of views on this topic among jurists until about the twelfth century, when typically the tendency became to forbid Muslims from taking up long-term residence in non-Muslim territories because of the dangers such a situation posed to their selves and religious beliefs; see his 'Islamic Law and Muslim Minorities: The Juristic Discourse on Muslim Minorities from the Second/Eighth to the Eleventh/Seventeenth Centuries', *Islamic Law and Society* 141 (1994): 141–87.

15. Yvonne Yazbeck Haddad and Jane I. Smith (eds), *Muslim Minorities in the West: Visible and Invisible* (Walnut Creek, CA: Atamira Press, 2002), 6.

16. Tauseef Ahmad Parray, 'The Legal Methodology of "Fiqh al-Aqalliyyat" and Its Critics: An Analytical Study', *Journal of Muslim Minority Affairs* 32/1 (2012): 88–107; Taha, 'Muslim Minorities', 8–10.

17. Citation given in Dilwar Hussain, 'Muslim Political Participation in Britain and the "Europeanisation" of Fiqh', *Welt des Islams*, 44 (2004): 386.

18. Taha Jabir al-Alwani, *Fi Fiqh al-aqalliyyat al-muslima* (Cairo: Nahdat Misr, 2000), 49–50.

19. Qur'an 60:8–9 state, 'God does not forbid you to be kind and just to those who have neither made war on your religion nor driven you out of your homes. God loves those who are just. But He forbids you from befriending those who have fought against you on account of your religion and evicted you from your homes or aided others in evicting you. Those who befriend them are wrongdoers'.

20. The verse states, 'Believers, fulfil your duties to God and bear true witness. Let not the hatred of others toward you cause you to deviate from justice. Behave justly; that is nearer to true piety. And be conscious of God; God is aware of all your actions'.

21. Taha Jabir al-Alwani, *Towards a Fiqh for Minorities: Some Basic Reflections* (London and Washington DC: IIIT, 2003), 18–27.

22. Yusuf al-Qaradawi, *Fi fiqh al-aqalliyyat al-muslima – hayat al-muslimin wasat al-mujtama'at al-ukhra* (Cairo: Dar al-Shuruq, 2001), 33–4; translation given by Andrew March, 'Sources of Moral Obligation to Non-Muslims in the *Fiqh al-Aqalliyyat* (Jurisprudence of Muslim Minorities) Discourse', *Islamic Law and Society* 16 (2009): 34–94.

23. March, 'Sources of Moral Obligation', 70.

24. Tariq Ramadan, *To be a European Muslim* (Leicester: Islamic Foundation, 2000), 134. See further idem, *Western Muslims and the Future of Islam* (Oxford: Oxford University Press, 2004), 77, where Ramadan states that by entering into 'the world of testimony', Western Muslims are able to discharge their fundamental obligation 'to contribute wherever they can to promoting goodness and justice and through the human fraternity'.

25. For a detailed discussion of the *maqasid al-shari'a*, see Jasser Auda, *Maqasid Al-Shariah as Philosophy of Islamic Law: A Systems Approach* (Herndon, VA: International Institute of Islamic Thought, 2008).

26. The term *maslaha* has become an important *ratio legis* (underlying principle) in Islamic law, invoked to justify emendation or abrogation of existing legal rulings and/or promulgation of new ones. After al-Ghazali, the fourteenth-century jurist Abu Ishaq Ibrahim al-Shatibi (d. 1388) became one of the best-known proponents of this principle which he elucidates in his *al-Muwafaqat fi usul al-shari'a* ('The [Points of] Agreement regarding the Principles of the Religious Law'), ed. Khalid 'Abd al-Fattah Shibl (Beirut: Mu'assasat al-Risala, 1999). For an accessible discussion in English, see M. H. Kamali, 'Have We Neglected the *Shari'ah* Law Doctrine of Maslahah?' *Islamic Studies* 27 (1988): 287–304.

27. Al-Alwani, *Fi fiqh al-aqalliyyat*, 27–8; see also H. A. Hellyer, *Muslims of Europe: The 'Other' Europeans* (Edinburgh: Edinburgh University Press, 2009), 81–94.

28. Yusuf al-Qaradawi, *al-Siyasa al-shar'iyya fi daw nusus al-shari'a wa maqasidiha* (Beirut: Mu'assasat al-risala, 2000), 84.

29. Al-Qaradawi, *Fi fiqh al-aqalliyyat*, 83.

30. Translation taken from Basheer M. Nafi, 'Fatwa and War: On the Allegiance of the American Muslim Soldiers in the Aftermath of September 11', *Islamic Law and Society* 11 (2004): 80–2.

31. For a detailed study of this, see Alexandre Caeiro, 'The Social Construction of Shari'a: Bank Interest, Home Purchase and Islamic Norms in the West', *Die Welt des Islams* 44 (2004): 35–75.

32. For further discussion of some of these views, see Muhammad Al Atawneh, *Wahhabi Islam Facing the Challenges of Modernity: Dar al-Ifta in the Modern Saudi State* (Leiden and Boston: Brill, 2010). Neo-Salafis typically invoke the principle of *al-wala' wa al-bara'* ('association and disassociation'), which in their understanding prevents Muslims from befriending non-Muslims and interacting with them beyond necessity.

33. Taha, *Muslim Minorities*, 7.

34. Ramadan, *Western Muslims*, 53.

35. Ibid. 53.

36. Ibid. 107.

37. Ibid. 55.

38. Ibid. 56–61.

39. Ibid. 138.

40. Ibid. 226.

41. Ibid. 224–7.

42. According to a CAIR Action Alert #683, issued on 25 October 2012.

43. (New York: Houghton Mifflin Harcourt, 2006), quote at 232.

44. Some of these points are stressed by Francis Fukuyama in his 'Has History Started Again?' *Policy* 18 (2002): 3–7 in which he invokes the rabid term 'Islamofascism'. The title of this article is meant to be a reference to his earlier influential book *The End of History and the Last Man* (New York: The Free Press, 1992) in which Western liberal democracy and market capitalism are assumed to represent the apogee of human accomplishments.

45. Richard Bulliet, *The Case for an Islamo-Christian Civilization* (New York: Columbia University Press, 2006), especially 24–46.

46. For example, Ockley expressed the following favorable assessment of Islam and the Prophet Muhammad in his influential *History of the Saracen Empires* (London, 1870), 54: 'The intellectual image of the Deity has never been degraded by any visible idol; the honors of the Prophet have never transgressed the measure of human virtues; and his living precepts have restrained the gratitude of his disciples within the bounds of reason and religion'. Such views influenced Edward Gibbon and his depiction of Islam in his *The Rise and Fall of the Roman Empire*.

47. See, for example, W. P. Friederich, 'Goethe', *The Georgia Review* 3 (1949): 147.

48. Thomas Carlyle, *On Heroes, Hero Worship and the Heroic in History* (London: Ginn & Co., 1901), 54.

49. Ziad Elmarsafy, *The Enlightenment Qur'an: The Politics of Translation and the Construction of Islam* (Oxford: Oneworld, 2009), 81–120.

50. Ibid. 120.

51. Albert Hourani, *Arabic Thought in the Liberal Age: 1798-1939* (Cambridge: Cambridge University Press, 1983), 120–1. An account of al-Afghani's spirited response to Renan's accusations is given in ibid. 121 ff. For a discussion of how these Orientalist views laid the foundation for today's Islamophobia, see Kate Zebiri's 'The Redeployment of Orientalist Themes in Contemporary Islamophobia', *Studies in Contemporary Islam* 10 (2008): 4–44.

52. Edward Said, *Orientalism* (New York: Vintage Books, 1979).

53. For some of the tragic consequences of Islamophobia affecting the lives of many American Muslims up to 2005, see Juan Cole, 'Islamophobia as a Social Problem: 2006 Presidential Address', *Middle East Studies Association Bulletin* 41 (2007): 3–7.

54. *Insight*, 4 February 1991, 37.

55. *Islamophobia, A Challenge to Us All*, Report of the Runnymede Trust Commission on British Muslims and Islamophobia, The Runnymede Trust, 1997, 1; available at <http://www.runnymedetrust.org/publications/17/32.html>; last accessed on 5 August 2013.

56. Hamid Dabashi suggests that such anti-Islamic sentiments represent not so much of a 'phobia', which 'is a deeply rooted fear of uncertain or repressed origins' but rather 'a deliberately and consciously manufactured loathing systematically cultivated by right-wing extremists . . .' It represents 'the transmutation of an entire people into a metaphor . . . categorically hanging on those interchangeable terms "Muslims" and "terrorists"'. See his *Being a Muslim in the World* (New York: Palgrave Macmillan, 2013), 99.

57. *Islamophobia, A Challenge To Us All*, 5.

58. Spellberg, *Thomas Jefferson's Qur'an*, 9, 200–5, 212–13, 271–2.

59. A number of recent monographs provide expert analyses of Islamophobia and its various manifestations; cf. *Islamophobia: The Challenge of Pluralism in the Twenty-First Century*, eds John Esposito and Ibrahim Kalin, (Oxford: Oxford University Press, 2011); Carl Ernst, *Islamophobia in America: The Anatomy of Intolerance* (New York: Palgrave, 2013), and others.

60. From the dust jacket of the book by Nathan Lean, *The Islamophobia Industry: How the Right Manufactures Fear of Muslims* (London: Pluto Press, 2012).

61. See the article by Kate Wiltrout, 'SEAL training range won't show woman as target', pub-

lished in *The Virginian-Pilot*, 30 June 2012. For a list of prominent Islamophobic incidents in the United States and Europe through 2010, see <http://theamericanmuslim.org/tam.php/features/articles/islamophobia_incidents/0013129>; last accessed on 29 July 2014.

62. Transcript of speech available at <http://www.ushmm.org/wlc/en/media_fi.php?MediaId=192>; last accessed on 29 July 2014.

63. See the article, 'Defining the Enemy', the *Holocaust Encyclopedia*, published by the United States Holocaust Memorial Museum, available at <http://www.ushmm.org/wlc/en/article.php?ModuleId=10007819>; last accessed on 5 June 2013.

64. For an incisive dissection of Islamophobic rhetoric which often simply recycles accusations hurled earlier at Jews in Europe and America, see Norton, *On the Muslim Question*, especially Introduction, 1–14. She notes: 'The Muslim question, like the Jewish question before it, is connected to fears for national and international security;' ibid. 6.

65. *Islamophobia, A Challenge to Us All*, 5.

66. See, for example, Joanna Breidenback and Pál Nyíri, *Seeing Culture Everywhere: From Genocide to Consumer Habits* (Seattle, WA: University of Washington Press, 2009), especially 30–83.

67. Cheryl Bernard, *Civil and Democratic Islam: Partners, Resources, Strategies* (Pittsburgh: Rand Corporation, 2003), 4.

68. Ibid. 32–4.

69. David Kaplan, 'Hearts Minds and Dollars: In an Unseen Front in the War on Terrorism, America is Spending Million . . .. To Change the Very Face of Islam', *US News and World Report*, 25 April 2005; available at <http://www.globalissues.org/article/584/hearts-minds-and-dollars>; last accessed on 27 July 2014. For a penetrating critique of this neo-conservative project, see Saba Mahmood, 'Secularism, Hermeneutics, and Empire: The Politics of Islamic Reformation', *Public Culture* 18 (2006): 323–47.

70. Prominent among these 'luminaries' were/are personalities such as Irshad Manji, Wafa Sultan, Zuhdi Jasser, and others, who have carved out a niche for themselves as professional 'moderate Muslims'. For an analysis of the modus operandi of Manji and her fellow 'experts', see Tarek El-Ariss, 'The Making of an Expert', *Muslim World* 97 (2007): 93–110.

71. One has only to be exposed to Paul Berman's demonisation of Tariq Ramadan to get a sense of the paranoid insecurity the latter can induce among certain Westernist ideologues; see Berman's *The Flight of the Intellectuals* (Brooklyn, NY: Melville House Publishing, 2010). For an incisive review of the book, see Marc Lynch, 'Veiled Truths: the Rise of Political Islam in the West', *Foreign Affairs*, July/August 2010 issue. Lynch observes astutely, 'Ramadan's primary adversaries are not liberals in the West but rather literalistic Salafists whose ideas are ascendant in Muslim communities from Egypt and the Persian Gulf to western Europe'. This is a point lost on Berman and his ilk.

72. 'US and Canadian Scholars of Islam Issue Statement Condemning Attacks', Al-Hewar Center: The Center for Arab Culture and Dialogue'; available at <http://www.alhewar.org/SEPTEMBER%2011/us_and_canadian_scholars.htm>; last accessed on 27 July 2014.

73. Available at <http://www.americanbar.org/content/dam/aba/directories/policy/2011_am_113a.authcheckdam.pdf>; last accessed on 29 July 2014.

74. See article 'Using Billboards to Stake Claim Over "Jihad"', *The New York Times*, 7 March 2013, A15.

75. Lizette Alvarez, 'Koran-Burning Pastor Unrepentant in Face of Furor', *The New York Times*, 3 April 2011, A4.

76. 'A Brave New World after 9/11 Attacks', *Common Ground News Service*, 16 August 2011; available at <http://www.commongroundnews.org/article.php?id=30212&lan=en&sp=0>; last accessed on 27 July 2014.

CHAPTER 7

Religious dialogue and interfaith relations

Can Muslims accept non-Muslims on equal terms? Do their sacred texts allow for the possibility of salvation through religious paths other than Islam? Can non-Muslims be coerced into accepting Islam? What about the traditional division of the world into the Abode of Islam and the Abode of War, which suggests enduring conflict between Muslims and non-Muslims?

In the context of modern, pluralistic societies, these questions are often posed to cast doubt on the ability of Muslims to either integrate within non-Muslim 'liberal' societies or to refashion Muslim-majority societies as open, multifaith ones in the twenty-first century where non-Muslims can safely coexist with Muslims. Though these questions are modern and appear to be new, Muslims through the centuries have in fact grappled with them in some form or another and have come up with varying responses. In the current century, as Muslims increasingly intermingle with non-Muslims, issues of coexistence and peaceful interactions at many levels of life are assuming paramount importance.

In this chapter I discuss the scriptural and ethical imperatives that are being foregrounded in the contemporary period from within the Islamic tradition to create a moral mandate for engaging the 'Other' in kind and respectful ways. Such engagement is not for the purpose of proselytisation but for conducting mutually illuminating, civil and non-coercive conversations that allow people to learn from one other. In the multifaith civil societies that are emerging globally and that many Muslims inhabit today, this is a mode of being and interacting with one's fellow human beings that is increasingly emerging as the predominant and preferred one. Such a mode entails venturing into relatively uncharted territory for which there remains the need to develop an authoritative, morally compelling roadmap(s).

Establishing a moral imperative to talk to the 'Other': the hermeneutics of dialogic engagement

For Muslims who routinely engage in interfaith dialogue, the imperative to undertake such activity comes from the Qur'an itself. The Qur'an after all is fundamentally concerned with the relations of Muslims with, especially, other Abrahamic communities, to which Islam is organically and historically related. There are a number of verses in the Qur'an which specifically deal with the mechanics of inter-Abrahamic dialogue and the fostering of peaceful relations with the People of the Book. One particular verse also goes beyond addressing only the Abrahamic communities and counsels respect for the religious sensibilities of all, including idol-worshippers. Three of these verses will be discussed here in view of frequent references to them in the context of creating a scriptural mandate for Muslims to engage in respectful interfaith dialogue. These verses are: Qur'an 29:46; 3:64; and 6:107–8. A sampling of exegeses of these verses in different historical periods convey to us a sense of how Muslim scholars have understood the meanings of these verses through variegated circumstances and establish their significance for interfaith relations today. This diachronic survey, once again, underscores the malleability of these interpretations, tied as they are to specific sociohistorical milieux. Re-engagement with these verses by modern Muslims similarly reflects their contemporary concerns to a considerable extent, which derive their legitimacy, however, through a conscious linkage with past interpretive traditions.

We deal first with Qur'an 29:46 and 3:64, which are concerned specifically with Muslim relations with Abrahamic scriptuaries. Qur'an 6:107–8, which outline a general protocol for interfaith relations that potentially extend to all religious traditions, are discussed later in the chapter.

Exegeses of Qur'an 29:46

Qur'an 29:46 is often cited in the context of interfaith relations as the quintessential verse establishing a distinctive protocol of dialogue with Jews and Christians. The verse states:

> Do not dispute with the People of the Book save with what is better; except for those who do wrong among them, and say [to them]: 'We believe in that which was revealed to us and revealed to you, and our God and your God is one, and we submit to Him.'

The earliest extant commentary on this verse is that of the very early Umayyad exegete Mujahid b. Jabr (d. 722). In his brief but significant exegesis, Mujahid understands the first part of the verse as counselling Muslims 'to speak what is good when they [namely the People of the Book] utter what is wrong'. 'Those who do wrong among them' is glossed as those among the People of the Book who speak falsehood concerning God: for instance, in ascribing partners to Him, or those who cause harm to the Prophet Muhammad. According to a variant exegesis attributed to the pious, anti-Umayyad Kufan scholar from the second generation of Muslims, Sa'id b. Jubayr (d. 714), 'those who do wrong among them' refers to a specific contingent from among the People of the Book who have not signed a treaty with the Muslims and consequently engage in hostilities against them.[1] In these two strands of interpretation preserved in this very early commentary, we note the tension between those who would ascribe wrongdoing to the People of the Book for doctrinal reasons as opposed to those who would do so for behavioural reasons – primarily on the basis of hostile conduct on their part. These two different interpretive strands have different consequences for defining Muslim relations with non-Muslims.

In the late ninth century, Muhammad b. Jarir al-Tabari (d. 923) focuses briefly on the phrase 'save with what is better' in the verse and remarks that it means that Muslims should invite the People of the Book 'to God by means of His verses and by drawing attention to His proofs'. 'Those who do wrong' among the People of the Book are those among them who ascribe partners to God, including Christians who maintain that Jesus was the son of God, and refuse to submit to Muslim authority.[2] Al-Tabari therefore links doctrinal aberration from the Muslim perspective with behavioural culpability – one presupposes the other. It is also not without significance that he does not dwell on the common ground delineated by the Qur'an in this verse when it stresses that faithful Jews and Christians worship and submit to the one and same God as faithful Muslims. We would therefore be justified in concluding that by minimising this commonality, al-Tabari is more concerned with stressing the doctrinal divisions between Muslims and the two other Abrahamic communities, a tendency that is perhaps not surprising in his milieu.[3]

Some of the later post-Tabari exegetes, however, offer more nuanced and less confessional approaches to this verse. For example, al-Zamakhshari (d. 1144) glosses 'what is better' in this verse as 'what is offered of gentleness in response to roughness; of equanimity to anger; and of forbearance in the face of harshness or violence'. He offers a non-confessional understanding of 'those who do wrong among the People of the Book' (in comparison with al-Tabari), commenting that they are those who are 'excessively hostile and obstinate, refusing to accept good counsel, and with whom gentleness and compassion are of no avail'. It is highly noteworthy that in al-Zamakhshari's understanding, those who do wrong among the Scripturaries are so considered not on account of theological error on their part, but on account of their bad manners and hostile attitude.[4] Thus al-Zamakhshari upholds the early position documented by Mujahid b. Jabr that only those contingents among the People of the Book who are hostile and aggressive towards Muslims are to be considered wrongdoers.

It is in the commentary of the brilliant theologian Fakhr al-Din al-Razi (d. 1210) that we begin to discern the fuller potential of this verse in the context of interfaith dialogue. Al-Razi understands this verse to counsel Muslims in general to deal gently with the People of the Book because of the religious tenets they have in common with the latter. He reminds that Jews and Christians after all have also placed their faith in the one God, believe in the revelation of books, in the sending of messengers and in the final resurrection. Each of these articles of belief is designated 'a goodness' (*husn*) by al-Razi. Where the People of the Book have gone awry, he continues, is in their failure to acknowledge the mission of the Prophet Muhammad, despite the fact that their scriptures contain references to him. Their partisan attachment to their prophets to the exclusion of others invites criticism. However, in acknowledgment of the aggregate goodness of the People of the Book, Muslims should debate with them with what is better/best. Al-Razi leaves undefined here the precise nature of 'what is better/best'. But since he next proceeds to say that Muslims should not treat the opinions of Jews and Christians lightly nor ascribe error to their ancestors, as they might in the case of polytheists, then we may assume that 'what is better/best' is a reference to the adoption of such conciliatory and respectful modes of conversation across religious lines.[5]

In al-Razi's commentary, therefore, we have the articulation of a thoughtful, reasoned protocol of dialectics between Muslims and the People of the Book, which, while stressing commonalities, also candidly acknowledges the differences between them. Acknowledgement of these differences is not meant to generate disrespect for these Abrahamic interlocutors nor the imputation of fundamental theological error to them. Although al-Razi does not state this explicitly, his line of reasoning implies that the common ground that may be retrieved between Muslims and the People of the Book on the basis of Qur'an 29:46 is broader than the points of contention between them; it is this common ground which serves as a more fruitful point of departure for interfaith encounters.

The fourteenth-century exegete Ibn Kathir (d. 1373) from the Mamluk era points to the existence of two distinctive schools of thought in regard to this verse. One school led by a second generation Muslim, Qatada b. Di'ama (d. 736), known in general for his rather pugnacious views, asserted that this verse was abrogated by the *jizya* verse' (Qur'an 9:29) and therefore there could no longer be dialogue with the People of the Book. They were left with three choices: acceptance of Islam, payment of the *jizya* (the poll tax) or fighting. The other school maintained that this verse was unabrogated and remained in force for those who wished to gain insight into the religion of the People of the Book and debate with them with what is better so that there might be greater benefit in it. This group of people pointed to another Qur'anic verse (16:125), which exhorts Muslims to 'Invite to the path of your Lord with wisdom and good counsel', as a supporting proof-text.[6]

Rules of interfaith engagement may similarly be derived from Qur'an 20:44, continues Ibn Kathir, in which God counsels Moses and Aaron when they were being dispatched to the Pharaoh 'to say to him words of gentleness so that he may reflect or be fearful [of God]'. For this school of thought, gentle and reflective speech in the course of such interreligious dialectics with one's interlocutor, even with those who have no faith like the Pharaoh, represents 'that which is better' mentioned in this verse. As for those who do wrong, continues Ibn Kathir, they constitute a faction from among the People of the Book who have veered away from the truth and deny clear proofs out of obstinacy and arrogance and resort to fighting to uphold what was forbidden them. The lack of theological language in defining this wayward contingent from among the People of the Book persuasively suggests that it is their roughness of behaviour and hostile attitude towards Muslims that is the object of denunciation, rather than their religious beliefs as such.[7] We therefore find in Ibn Kathir's exegesis further corroboration of the continuity of the early school of thought attested to by Mujahid which attributed wrongdoing to specific groups from among Jews and Christians primarily on the basis of their belligerent and abusive behaviour and not on the basis of their religion and/or doctrinal positions.

Exegeses of Qur'an 3:64

This verse has received considerable attention in recent times, the reasons for which will be explained below. Like Qur'an 29:46, it is also concerned primarily with Muslim relations with Jews and Christians. The verse states:

> Say, O People of the Book, let us come to a common word (*kalimat sawa'*) between us and you that we will not worship but the one God nor ascribe any partner to Him or that any of us should take others as lords besides the one God. If they should turn their backs, say: 'Bear witness that we submit to God (*muslimun*).'

In his brief commentary on this verse, the early Umayyad exegete Muqatil b. Sulayman (d. 767) glosses the phrase *kalimat sawa'* as 'a just word' agreed upon sincerely by Muslims and the People of the Book that they will worship the one God alone and not ascribe partners to Him. If they should turn away at that, it means that they have disavowed monotheism; Muslims are instructed in any case to assert that they have submitted to God. Muqatil then goes on to assert (ominously) that Qur'an 6:107 should be regarded as abrogated by Qur'an 9:5.[8]

Al-Tabari notes that some earlier exegetes believed that the People of the Book mentioned in this verse was an exclusive reference to the Jews of Medina while others thought that it referred specifically to the Christian delegation consisting of about sixty men from Najran who met with Muhammad in 631 CE. As an aside, it should be mentioned that according to our sources, the Christians of Najran were received kindly by the Prophet and allowed to pray in the mosque at Medina over the protests of some. The Christians also concluded a pact with Muhammad, according to which they were granted full protection of their churches and their possessions in return for the payment of a tribute.[9]

Al-Tabari's own understanding is that the verse refers to both Jews and Christians who are summoned by the Qur'an to 'a word of justice between us and you'. The 'word of justice' indicates the common belief in the unity of God and 'repudiating all other beings as objects of worship except Him'. The phrase 'that any of us should take others as lords besides the one God' is understood to mean that one should not obey any human in matters which contravene God's commandments nor exalt one another by prostrating before another as one prostrates before God. If they should fail to affirm that, the believers (*al-mu'minun*) should assert that they are Muslims; that is, that they have surrendered to God.[10]

Al-Zamakhshari in the twelfth century similarly points to the different interpretations of the People of the Book, variously understood to be a reference to the Christians from Najran, the Jews of Medina, or to both communities. The Arabic word '*sawa*' refers to what is '[deemed] upright by us and you, regarding which the Qur'an, the Torah and the Gospel do not differ'. The 'word' or 'statement' is elaborated upon by the verse itself, explains al-Zamakhshari: 'that we worship none but God and not ascribe partners to Him and that none of us should take others as lords besides the one God'. If the People of the Book disregard this summons, he continues, then Muslims are free to assert that only they have truly submitted to God.[11]

Considerable agreement can therefore be noted among pre-modern exegetes until the twelfth century regarding the meaning of '*kalimat sawa*' as a 'just/ equitable statement' that underscores the shared monotheism of Jews, Christians and Muslims. The verse is further understood to contain an exhortation to the People of the Book to affirm this basic monotheism which characterises them and to assert, alongside Muslims, that they will continue to believe in the absolute unity of God by refusing to ascribe any partners to Him.

In comparison with this standard commentary on Qur'an 3:64, al-Razi in the late twelfth century offers us a somewhat refreshingly new reading of this important verse. In summary, he understands this verse to be concerned specifically with the Christians of Najran, like a number of exegetes before him. Al-Razi comments that the revelation of this verse occurred after the Prophet had engaged in a vigorous debate with these Christians and had apparently frightened them to a certain extent with the fervor of his arguments and his call for 'mutual imprecation' (*al-mubahala*).[12] Al-Razi comments that it is as if God was saying to Muhammad in this verse, 'Give up this manner of speaking and adopt another which the sound intellect and upright disposition recognises as speech founded upon fairness and justice (*al-insaf*)'. Accordingly, the Prophet abandoned disputation with the Christians of Najran and instead, as the verse exhorted him, summoned them to arrive at a common word or statement based upon fairness between them with no preference shown towards anyone at the expense of the other. The statement is, as given in the verse 'that we worship none but God and we do not ascribe partners to Him'.[13]

The conciliatory nature of this verse directed towards the Christians of Najran is indicated by the Arabic appellation *ahl al-kitab* (People of the Book) for them, says al-Razi. He says that this is so because it is the best of names and the most perfect of titles, for it indicates that the Christians of Najran were 'worthy [*ahlan*] of the Book of God'. Its equivalents are the titles conferred upon those who have memorised the Qur'an, such as in the address, 'O the bearer of the Book of God' (*ya hamil kitab allah*) and upon the exegete of the Qur'an, 'O commentator upon the Speech of God' (*ya mufassir kalam allah*). Such sobriquets coined in conjunction with 'the Book [of God]' (*al-kitab/kitab allah*) are intended to honour those who are so addressed and to cultivate their goodwill, and to persuade people to abandon the path of disputation and obstinacy and embark instead on a quest for fairness and just relationships.[14]

The phrase *kalimat sawa'* is further understood by al-Razi to refer to 'a word which embodies fairness or equality between us', so that no one is accorded any preference. He explains the Arabic word *sawa'* as occurs in the verse as specifically referring to 'justice and fairness' (*al-'adl wa-'l-insaf*). Fairness (*al-insaf*) furthermore implies equality, says al-Razi, because it implies equal sharing (*nisf*) and thus avoiding oppressing oneself and others, which involves getting more than your equal share. *Kalima* in this context refers therefore to a word that is just, upright and egalitarian. The word held in common between Muslims and Christians is a reference to that 'we will worship no one but God nor ascribe any partner to Him and not take each other as lords other than God.' Al-Razi then goes on to document what he describes as the erroneous beliefs of Christians, particularly their trinitarian conception of God and their tendency to exalt and obey their priests uncritically, which, according to him, seriously undermines their adherence to the 'common word'. Despite this critique of specific Christian tenets and practices, al-Razi's commentary is remarkable nevertheless for its emphasis on establishing common ground between Muslims and Christians on the basis of Qur'an 3:64 and for its insistence that such common ground is best established by approaching one another with civility, good will, respect and forsaking the desire to vanquish the other through harsh or clever arguments.[15]

After him, Ibn Kathir[16] and the nineteenth-century reformer Muhammd 'Abduh[17] replicated much of what is stated by al-Razi in their own commentaries on this verse, indicating that al-Razi's views emphasising respectful and kindly interfaith dialogue between Muslims and the People of the Book were widely accepted and continued to resonate in diverse locales, even during the fraught Mamluk period and the period of Christian European colonisation through the early twentieth century.

Analysis of Qur'an 29:46 and 3:64

The Qur'anic verses discussed above are highly relevant to relations between Muslims and non-Muslims today. From a contemporary vantage point, a number of the pre-modern exegetes surveyed appear not to do full justice to the wide-ranging implications of these verses for interfaith dialogue and a few even tend to undermine their irenic potential. Thus in his commentary on Qur'an 29:46 which is often privileged today as promoting, even mandating, courteous and respectful interfaith encounters, al-Tabari in his more religiously divisive world reads into it an unequal relationship between Muslims and the People of the Book and as implying the hardening of theological boundaries between them. In different periods, other exegetes, like al-Zamakhshari and al-Razi, however, would discern in this verse a more irenic and universal injunction to cultivate gentler and more cordial relations between religious communities. This attitude is amplified in al-Razi's insightful commentary where he notes that in its usage of the term *ahl al-kitab*, the Qur'an displays affection and approval for righteous Jews and Christians who intend Muslims no harm.

Not all exegetes, we noted, were inclined to uphold the imperative contained in these verses for Muslims to maintain courteous and even cordial relations with righteous and peaceful Jews and Christians. Qatada b. Di'ama specifically asserted that Qur'an 29:46 had been abrogated by Qur'an 9:29, the so-called *jizya* verse, which through his particularist lens sets restrictions on establishing amicable relations between Muslims and the People of the Book. 'Abduh's (or his student Rashid Rida's) exegesis on this verse is not available to us since the *Tafsir al-Manar* does not cover the later chapters of the Qur'an. This position of the pro-abrogation school of thought is, however, forcefully criticised elsewhere in the *Manar* by Muhammad 'Abduh, who described it as self-serving and rather arbitrary, for it ignores other verses in the same Qur'anic chapter (*al-Tawba*, Chapter Nine) – therefore also to be regarded as late revelations – which counsel Muslims to take no punitive action against those who refuse to accept Islam.[18]

In this context we may do well to ask: what does the Qur'an intend by encouraging dialogue, particularly among the Abrahamic faiths? Dialogue for its own sake is a laudable activity – it promotes goodwill, trust and conviviality, always a better alternative to mutual distrust and hostility. Respect should be extended to non-Abrahamic communities as well, as clearly asserted in Qur'an 6:107-8 and other verses (see further below). This in turn elicits respect for Muslims. Dialogue leading to mutual understanding and knowledge (*al-ta'aruf*) is even better, as indicated in the famous verse, Qur'an 49:13. One of the exegetes in our survey noted this beneficial consequence of interfaith encounters. Ibn Kathir, as we recall, in his interpretation of Qur'an 29:46 highlighted the insight to be gained by Muslims in respectfully engaging the People of the Book in conversation and attempting thereby to find common ground among fellow monotheists. This is a perspective that is gaining ground among Muslim interfaith practitioners today, as we will see further below.

Dialogic conversations today: the hermeneutics of interfaith relations

In a number of academic and popular venues today, a new hermeneutics of interfaith relations that draws upon past exegeses of the Qur'an, often to put a new interpretive spin on them, is becoming quite evident. According to this modern hermeneutic trend, a number of verses in the Qur'an that have a bearing on interfaith relations are being read with fresh eyes today in the context of our own sociohistorical circumstances, while yet attempting to remain faithful to their actual wording and semantic landscape. A case in point is provided by the reinterpretation of the Qur'anic phrase *kalimat sawa'* in Qur'an 3:64 offered in what has now become widely known as 'the Common Word' statement issued by 138 Muslim scholars and religious leaders in 2007. The 138 Muslim scholars and leaders who represented the original signatories were deliberately selected to represent all major schools of law and theology within Islam: Sunni, Shi'i, including Ja'fari (Imami or Twelver Shi'i), Zaydi and Isma'ili, as well as Ibadi (the later peaceful incarnation of the seventh century dissident faction, the Khawarij).[19] The Common Word statement was addressed to Christian religious leaders and communities representing various denominations (with the exclusion initially of the evangelical Protestants) in 2007 and has received considerable attention in religious circles worldwide for drawing attention to the common theological ground between Muslims and Christians. Among the first Christian leaders to respond enthusiastically and in great detail to this overture was the Reverend Dr Rowan Williams, Archbishop of Canterbury at the time. The Archbishop, in a follow-up official statement released on 14 July 2008, described *A Common Word Between Us and You* as 'a powerful call to dialogue and collaboration between Christians and Muslims', and stated that he and his coreligionists

> are committed to reflecting and working together, with you and all our human neighbours, with a view both to practical action and service and to a long term dedication to all that will lead to a true common good for human beings before God.[20]

The Common Word statement followed an earlier communiqué issued by Muslim leaders in 2006 titled 'An Open Letter to the Pope', which was generated in response to Pope Benedict's controversial Regensburg Speech in the same year. The 2006 letter provided a response to the Pope's unfortunate and rather inscrutable allegation that Islam was inherently irrational because of its emphasis on submission to a transcendent God, as opposed to Christianity whose Trinitarian and immanentist doctrine was assumed to exclusively predispose humans to rationality. In that speech, the Pontiff had also intimated that Islam had spread through violence, which would further corroborate the irrationality at its core and foreclose the possibility of having a genuine dialogue with Muslims.[21]

The Common Word statement challenged these rather insular and polemical perspectives. Instead of focusing on doctrinal and assumed intellectual differences, the statement stressed the two commandments of the love of God and love of neighbour as providing the basis for meaningful theological engagement to emerge between Christians and Muslims. This common ground does not elide essential theological differences that do exist between the two faith communities but rather accepts these differences as part of a broader ethic of respectful dialogue and peaceful coexistence.

The title *A Common Word between You and Us* given to the statement reflects within it a contemporary translation of the Arabic phrase *kalimat sawa'* in Qur'an 3:64, some of whose pre-modern and modern interpretations were discussed above. The phrase in turn was further amplified by the Muslim signatories to refer to 'love of God and love of neighbour' as the commandment held in common with Christians. The introductory paragraph to the Common Word statement reads as follows:

> Muslims and Christians together make up well over half of the world's popula-
> tion. Without peace and justice between these two religious communities, there
> can be no meaningful peace in the world. The future of the world depends on
> peace between Muslims and Christians.
>
> The basis for this peace and understanding already exists. It is part of the
> very foundational principles of both faiths: love of the One God, and love of the
> neighbour. These principles are found over and over again in the sacred texts
> of Islam and Christianity. The Unity of God, the necessity of love for Him, and
> the necessity of love of the neighbour is thus the common ground between Islam
> and Christianity.[22]

As we recall, all the exegetes surveyed earlier with regard to the phrase *kalimat sawa'* are in agreement that it is primarily and broadly a reference to 'a word of justice', a locution which in itself is open to interpretation. Justice is variously interpreted as 'sincerity' by Muqatil; as 'upright' and an assertion of the oneness of God by al-Tabari and al-Zamakhshari; as 'fair' and 'equitable' by al-Razi, Ibn Kathir and Muhammad 'Abduh. With interpretive creativity, the signatories to the Common Word statement may be regarded as having distilled these various significations of justice into the pithy commandment 'Love God and your neigh-bour'. What after all could be more upright, sincere, just and common than this commandment which resonates immediately with Abrahamic communities, and reaching even further, with all religious and ethical people? Such interpre-tive discernment in the context of dialogue is born of deep reflection on the whys and wherefores of interfaith encounters and existential necessity.

Aref Nayed, a prominent Libyan scholar of Islam, and an influential phi-lanthropist, was one of the original signatories to the Common Word state-ment. Nayed emphasised the importance of such rereadings of sacred texts by knowledgeable scholars who can authoritatively pronounce against hateful and divisive speech and promote instead what he described as a 'proper and whole-some creedal discourse'. Nayed commented:

> In an era of hateful, vengeful, and destructive discourses, every human commu-
> nity, religious or otherwise, is called upon, for the sake of God, and for the sake of

our common humanity, to develop, articulate, and clearly proclaim alternative discourses, discourses that are loving, forgiving, and constructive . . . The deeper the creedal roots of a discourse, the more potency and efficacy it has in the arena of action.[23]

In the wake of its proclamation in 2007, the Common Word statement has led to three high-level meetings between Muslim and Christian religious leaders, academics and interfaith activists. The first was held at the Yale Divinity School in July 2008, where Muslim and primarily Protestant theologians discussed at length the two themes of the Common Word statement. A highly significant letter, which articulated a very favourable response to the statement following this meeting, was signed by three hundred prominent Protestant theologians and scholars and subsequently published in *The New York Times*.[24] The second meeting was hosted by the University of Cambridge in October 2008 which culminated in a meeting with the then Archbishop of Canterbury in London. The third high-level meeting took place at the Vatican in Rome on 4–6 November 2008 between sixty Muslim and Catholic scholars and religious leaders, which was constituted as the first Seminar of the Catholic–Muslim Forum that continues till today. Since 2008, several follow-up meetings have taken place at Georgetown University in Washington DC, as well as spin-off meetings at Oxford University, Heythrop College in London and, most recently, at Mater Dei University in Dublin, Ireland (2013).

The Common Word statement may therefore be regarded as a seminal interfaith document of our time that has galvanised a new era of Muslim–Christian relations founded on commonalities rooted in the scriptures of the two communities. The various follow-up and spin-off meetings, which have resulted in the issuance of joint communiqués and several publications, have kept the momentum going.[25] Other interfaith initiatives have also been born in the aftermath of September 11th that are directly or indirectly the result of the Common Word project, while yet others are independent initiatives.

One such example of an independent Christian–Muslim dialogue is the Building Bridges seminar, hosted until 2012 by the office of the Archbishop of Canterbury. Starting in 2013, the dialogue continues under the aegis of Georgetown University. This initiative was launched in Doha, Qatar, in 2002 by the then Archbishop of Canterbury Lord Carey and continued with great enthusiasm by his successor, the Reverend Dr Rowan Williams, from 2003–12. The seminar convenes an annual gathering of Muslim and Christian scholars to discuss broad-ranging themes, such as prayer, human dignity, revelation, death and resurrection, tradition and modernity, peace and reconciliation, on the basis of scripture. Publications resulting from these meetings represent another visible and enduring legacy of these dialogues. The Building Bridges seminar has published over a dozen volumes which contain the original papers of the participants as well as transcripts of the actual conversations that took place during small, intensive sessions. Such conversations are expected to lead above all to better understanding among the interlocutors of each other's beliefs and world-view and often to genuine friendship and camaraderie.[26] A number of the participants are religious leaders who return to their parishes and congregations and spread their newly acquired insights and empathy among them. The published volumes have been adopted as textbooks in some academic programmes and continue to engender discussions on the relevant themes at various fora.

In addition to Christians, Muslim organisations have reached out to Jewish interlocutors to similarly engage in interfaith dialogue with them on broader issues of ethics and the common good. At the forefront of such initiatives in the United States is the annual 'Weekend of Twinning' programme that was inaugurated by the Foundation for Ethnic Understanding (FFEU), in partnership with the Islamic Society of North America (ISNA), America's largest national Muslim organisation in 2007. The purpose of the Weekend of Twinning is to strengthen Muslim–Jewish relations worldwide by providing opportunities for mosques, synagogues and other Muslim and Jewish institutions to form partnerships in order to promote better communication, cooperation and reconciliation between Muslims and Jews. Twinning events have led to Jews and Muslims working together to feed the hungry and homeless under the 'Feeding the Hungry' programme, a hallmark of the initiative. In 2011, thousands of people from over 250 synagogues, mosques and Muslim and Jewish groups took part in the Weekend of Twinning in sixteen countries around the world. On 20 November 2012 in the aftermath of Hurricane Sandy, Jews and Muslims on Long Island brought blankets, warm coats and non-perishable food items to a homeless shelter serving the victims. Similar Weekend of Twinning events have been held in Chicago, Morristown in New Jersey, St Louis, Los Angeles, and as far away as Baku, Azerbaijan. As ISNA's website states, such socially engaged acts of charity give 'expression to the shared moral imperative in Islam and Judaism to help those most in need'.[27]

In the Middle East, the Royal Institute for Interfaith Studies (RIIFS) based in Amman, Jordan, promotes interfaith dialogue among the three Abrahamic religions. Overseen by Prince El Hassan bin Talal, the Institute hosts conferences and symposia on interfaith topics and publishes the well-regarded *Bulletin of the Royal Institute for Inter-Faith Studies* annually which 'provides a venue for interdisciplinary academic inquiry into all fields of the humanities and social sciences that bear on cultural or civilisational interaction'.[28] Its quarterly Arabic publication *al-Nashra* 'provides a forum for the discussion of interfaith issues, particularly as they relate to Arab and Islamic societies'.[29]

The current King Abdullah of Jordan has also been very active in the realm of interreligious dialogue, and has served as a key advocate for the Common Word statement. His namesake King Abdullah of Saudi Arabia has similarly been quite proactive in fostering interfaith and intercultural dialogue within

Saudi Arabia and overseas. In 2013, a major dialogic initiative was launched under the aegis of the governments of Saudi Arabia, Austria and Spain leading to the establishment of the KAICIID Dialogue Centre (King Abdullah Bin Abdulaziz International Centre for Interreligious and Intercultural Dialogue) in Vienna. The Centre is an independent international organisation whose purpose is 'to enable, empower and encourage dialogue among followers of different religions and cultures around the world'.[30] Its Board of Directors include representatives of the major world religions: Judaism, Christianity, Islam, Hinduism and Buddhism. In its short period of existence, the Centre has already sponsored a number of high-profile conferences and workshops to facilitate dialogue among these world religions and on thematic issues such as media ethics, conflict and peacemaking, among others. Recently, KAICIID has teamed up with UNESCO (United Nations Educational Scientific and Cultural Organisation) to further dialogue among different cultures and religions. Given its trajectory of activities, KAICIID promises to become a major international actor in the field of intercultural and interfaith dialogue.

Such interreligious encounters – whether at the institutional or communal level – often take place below the radar, as far as the general public is concerned. Such initiatives are usually not covered by the media and other popular outlets since they are not deemed to be newsworthy unless they are embroiled in a major conflict or scandal. In terms of the goodwill and religio-communal solidarity that such initiatives have engendered and continue to do so, there is no empirical measure for gauging their effectiveness and strength. In the United States in particular, the enduring, tangible benefit of such dialogic encounters has often been foregrounded in times of crisis when interfaith groups have banded together and challenged rank bigotry directed at religious groups, particularly Muslims, in the aftermath of September 11th.[31]

Revisiting pre-modern legal and theological concepts: the hermeneutics of interfaith dialogue in the twenty-first century

The twenty-first century arguably presents unique opportunities for reimagining historical relations between different religions and cultures, particularly for Muslims as they occupy the centre stage of the global arena and play a pivotal role in defining such relations. Scriptural hermeneutics remains a vital dimension of this process of reconceptualisation of interreligious and cultural dynamics in our own time. Reinterpretations of key Qur'anic verses as indicated earlier are essential as the first step towards imagining a different world based on peaceful coexistence rather than one based on conflict and strife, as was the default situation in the pre-modern world. We have already indicated how the Common Word initiative and the Building Bridges seminars have launched a productive and ongoing conversation between Christian and Muslim scholars and practitioners regarding some of the key issues that both unite and divide these communities. The long-term success of these ventures replicated elsewhere on a smaller scale at the grassroots community level depend, of course, on the continuing commitment and goodwill of the people involved on both sides.

Those who are far less sanguine about – and even openly hostile to – the idea of interfaith dialogue between Muslims on the one hand and Jews and Christians on the other often point to what appears to them as irreconcilable differences between these groups that cannot be bridged by what they might derisively describe as 'simply making nice' with one another. They base their criticism on specific aspects drawn from the classical Islamic legal tradition dealing with religious minorities that in their understanding represent insurmountable stumbling blocks to genuine interfaith dialogue. Such sceptics will often comment that their reservation is primarily based on the conventional juridical status that was assigned to non-Muslim minorities as *ahl al-dhimma* (literally: people of protection) in the pre-modern period and which signalled their second-class status in Muslim societies.

Historically, this legal, protected status was traditionally granted to Jews and Christians by the Muslim polity in recognition of their adherence to monotheism. This is not a Qur'anic designation and reflects the deliberation of Muslim jurists who wished to make a legal distinction between those who worshipped multiple deities as opposed to those who worshipped only one. In juridical and administrative usage, the term *ahl al-dhimma* overlapped with the Qur'anic *ahl al-kitab* (People of the Book), and was often shortened to *dhimmi*. Over time, this status was extended to Zoroastrians, Hindus and Buddhists as well, in recognition of the fact that these religious practitioners also had sacred scriptures and signalled their willingness to coexist peacefully by paying a tribute to Muslim rulers. Most historians would argue that by medieval standards and at its best, the *dhimma* arrangement allowed non-Muslims to live a humane and tolerated existence under Muslim rule, with guarantees of protection for their lives and property and the right to practice their religion.[32]

In modern nation states with Muslim-majority populations, the *dhimma* system has fallen into disuse and non-Muslim minorities are promised equal citizenship in the constitutions of most of these countries, a promise that has been unevenly realised. In specific political circumstances, local Christian populations from time to time have faced the suspicion of being sympathetic to a Christian West and working in its interest on the basis of their religious affiliation (a situation not unlike what American and European Muslims are facing in the contemporary period). Despite specific legal guarantees of equal rights, non-Muslim minorities often face real discrimination in the job market and in other spheres of life (once again not unlike the situation in regard to American and European Muslims today).[33] Religious bigotry can be whipped up by right-wing political and religious groups for their benefit, often during times of economic and political crises, leaving non-Muslim minorities vulnerable to mob violence.

There is no doubt that the pre-modern system of *dhimma* protection is no longer valid and applicable today, given our modern understanding of citizenship and notions of political belonging.[34] While the *dhimma* system was purely a juridical construct and can be set aside as an historical artifact, one may remonstrate that the payment of the *jizya* connected to the status of a *dhimmi* is mentioned in the Qur'an (9:29) and therefore to be regarded as normatively binding. Past historical praxis, however, allows us to ameliorate the absolute nature of this view. Historically speaking, *jizya* has been a much more malleable concept than is generally assumed and was applied (or not) at the discretion of the ruler. This malleability was already evident during the time of Muhammad and continued into the early period of Islam. For example, the Prophet exempted Christian Abyssinians from the payment of any taxes in recognition of the refuge they had provided to early Muslims fleeing from the persecution of the pagan Meccans. On account of their palpable goodwill toward Muslims, they were automatically considered to be part of the abode of treaty/peace. The Nubians of North Africa, despite being non-Muslims, were also exempted from the *jizya* and not considered *dhimmis* (protected people). Instead they entered into a trade agreement (*baqt*) with Muslims according to the terms of which they mutually traded goods. There are also instances when non-Muslims requested to pay the *zakat*, the poor tax enjoined on Muslims, in lieu of the *jizya* and the request was granted. Thus, 'Umar ibn al-Khattab exempted the Christian tribe Banu Taghlib from the *jizya* when the latter protested its imposition on them and allowed them to pay *zakat* instead; the Christians of Tanukh were treated similarly by him. The Jarajima tribe agreed to serve in the military in lieu of paying the *jizya*.[35] These historical instances clearly underscore the contingent nature of the so-called poll tax and its imposition. Modernist Muslims are particularly heartened by these concrete historical examples, which they invoke to bolster their argument that in an era of an international commonwealth of nations subscribing to shared values of human rights and peaceful coexistence, these examples of Muslim and non-Muslim interaction yield a much more pertinent and appropriate model for international relations today.

It bears emphasis that the Qur'an prescribes worldly relations between Muslims and non-Muslims, based on what people do, not on what they believe. From the Qur'anic perspective, humans do not adjudicate between humans on the basis of their religious affiliation and doctrinal beliefs – that is a purely divine prerogative. The Qur'an makes it very clear that theological differences between religious communities can only be resolved in the next world by God alone and therefore should not be the subject of human debate and conflict on earth (Qur'an 39:3; 5:48; 26:113; 2:113; 3:55; 22:17; 22:69, and others). Humans may judge one another only on the basis of how they treat one another.

This is a point that liberal Muslims often stress to make the case for freedom of belief as scripturally guaranteed. Thus Asghar Ali Engineer, an ardent advocate of religious pluralism, has argued on the basis of the Qur'an that 'it is not for human beings to decide for themselves who is right or wrong [since it] will lead to disturbances and breach of peace'.[36] Engineer's pluralism is particularly evident when he discusses Qur'an 5:48–9, which states:

> We have sent the Scripture in truth, confirming the scripture that came before it, and guarding it in safety, so judge between them by what God has revealed and follow not their vain desires, diverging from the Truth that has come to you. To each among you have we prescribed a law and a way. If God had so willed, He would have made you a single community, but (His plan is) to test you in what He has given you; so hasten to do good. To God is your return all together, and He will [then] inform you concerning that over which you used to differ.

Engineer interprets this critical verse to mean that God has purposefully created different religions and different groups of people so that He may test us to see if we can live in harmony and peace and to spur humans to do good works.[37]

Similar views in an irenic and pluralist vein are expressed by other liberal Muslim thinkers, such as Abdulaziz Sachedina, Khaled Abou El Fadl, Nurcolish Majid, Fathi Osman and Mohamed Talbi. Talbi, a modernist Muslim thinker from Tunisia, has in fact been insistent that pluralism is an integral feature of the Qur'an and the Islamic tradition as a whole and that dialogue (*hiwar*) based on mutual respect (*ihtiram mutabadal*) is the practice of pluralism and therefore required by Islam.[38] Fathi Osman, an American-Egyptian scholar who until his death in 2010 was a prominent leader of the American Muslim community, similarly stressed that the Qur'an fosters an ethic of pluralism by mandating respect for differences in beliefs and practices which are part of the divine design. He states:

> God's grace lies not in the abolition of difference in beliefs and views, nor in changing human nature which He himself has created, but in showing human beings how to handle their differences intellectually and morally and behaviorally.[39]

As our previous discussion in Chapter Five has already revealed, the *jizya* was imposed in Qur'an 9:29 on a group from 'among those who were given the Book' (*min alladhina utu 'l-kitab*) who 'do not believe in God nor in the Last Day and do not forbid what God and His messenger have forbidden and do not follow the religion of truth'. The Arabic partitive *min* indicates a group 'from among' the People of the Book that is clearly guilty of some moral and legal infraction, the nature of which is not explicitly made known to us in the verse. The People of the Book are therefore not being criticised here as a collectivity, even though many Muslim exegetes of the Qur'an imputed such a meaning to the verse. The understanding that only an erring faction from among the

People of the Book is indicted in Qur'an 9:29 is further corroborated by looking elsewhere in the Qur'an where righteous members of the People of the Book are promised their heavenly reward on a par with righteous Muslims. For example, Qur'an 2:62 states unambiguously:

> Surely those who believe, and those who are Jews, and the Christians, and the Sabians, whoever believes in God and the Last Day and does good, they shall have their reward from their Lord, and they will not fear nor shall they grieve.

This statement is repeated practically verbatim in Qur'an 5:69. These two verses therefore clearly promise salvation to monotheists who have faith in the one God and are righteous in their deeds. This general Qur'anic perspective is not undermined by Qur'an 9:29, but actually bolstered by it: righteous and peaceful scriptuaries, like the Banu Taghlib, may win exemption from the poll tax (although everyone, including Muslims, is required to pay some kind of a tax), but should they fail to live up to their own high moral standards and resort to wrongdoing, then they are subject to sanctions, including the imposition of the *jizya* on them. *Jizya*, it should be noted, was a compensation paid by adult, able-bodied, and free male scriptuaries to the Muslim ruler who was expected in return to defend them militarily in the case of external attacks on the polity. It was not paid by non-Muslim males when they chose to serve in the army.[40] Should the Muslim ruler fail to defend non-Muslims who have paid the *jizya*, the former was required to return the amount to the affected community.[41] Since non-Muslims serve in the standing armies of modern Muslim-majority nations, this archaic tax does not apply to them.

The Prophet's selective application of the *jizya* and 'Umar's flexibility in its imposition, as mentioned above, provide valuable historical instances of the basic Qur'anic perspective that relations with non-Muslims (or, more broadly construed, with all humans) are governed not on the basis of religious affiliation but on the goodwill, peaceableness and the actions of the people involved. Muslims have often failed to live up to this basic Qur'anic precept and have violated it repeatedly. This makes it all the more necessary for them to return to their foundational scripture in order to retrieve what Fazlur Rahman described as 'normative Islam' that stands as a corrective to the political realism and opportunism manifested at many points in historical Islam.

The problems of abrogation and supersessionism

We had occasion to mention in Chapter Five that the exegetical tool of *naskh*, usually translated as 'abrogation', has remained a highly contested tool of hermeneutics and has resurfaced in the modern period as a particularly thorny issue. Throughout the pre-modern period, there was no unanimity among scholars about the status and number of abrogating and abrogated verses, and such unanimity remains just as elusive as ever in our own time. The validity of this interpretive technique is also increasingly being debated by contemporary Muslim scholars. The proponents of *naskh* will usually point to Qur'an 2:106 as their proof-text, which states: 'Such of Our revelations as we abrogate (*nansakh*) or cause to be forgotten (*nunsiha*), we bring one better or the like thereof; do you not know that God is able to do all things?' The verse, however, explicitly refers to God as the abrogating agent and makes no reference to humans making these determinations on their own. In spite of this, *naskh* became deployed fairly frequently by exegetes and jurists to justify particularist interpretations of key Qur'anic verses, usually, but not consistently, on the basis of chronology, so that later verses could be understood to nullify the applicability of earlier verses on the same or closely related subject.

It is not hard to discern why this hermeneutic tool was developed and used to great effect shortly after the death of the Prophet. If we start clustering the verses that are deemed to be abrogated by a significant number of exegetes, a certain pattern begins to emerge. First of all, almost all the verses are Meccan to early Medinan, according to traditional chronology. Second, all the abrogating verses tend to promote a narrower, privileged definition of being Muslim at the expense of 'others.' Third, without the mediation of the 'abrogated verses' the abrogating verses may be understood to set up antagonistic, binary relationships – primarily between Muslims and non-Muslims. In contrast to this approach, relevant Medinan verses, when read cross-referentially with related verses of earlier revelation, may instead be understood to provide necessary 'specification' (*takhsis*) rather than abrogation of Meccan verses, which tend to be broader and more universal in their import. This in fact has been the understanding of a significant number of scholars who have found the deployment of the principle of *naskh* to represent an unwarranted exercise of human exegetical privilege.

The problems associated with wielding *naskh* to derive hawkish views of the military jihad were clearly evident in Chapter Five. We observed there that Makhul al-Shami, Qatada and other authorities from the second generation of Muslims, who were aggressive in their positions on this topic, relentlessly invoked the hermeneutic of *naskh* to derive an understanding of the military jihad consonant with their views on military expansionism. As we noted there, the Qur'anic text read as a coherent whole – not 'truncated' by *naskh* – readily and clearly indicates that *qital*, the military component of jihad, can be resorted to only in the case of prior aggression by an implacably hostile enemy who is not open to reconciliation. The *casus belli* is therefore the specific act of hostility on the part of the enemy combatants, not their religious affiliation. Specific Medinan verses therefore provide valuable specifications for the more general Meccan commandments to strive in the path of God; fighting (*qital*) is identified as a necessary aspect of this striving under specific conditions. As we had occasion to discuss earlier, such an understanding of the limited military aspect of jihad proved to be an inconvenient impediment to a number of pro-Umayyad scholars who wished to bolster the Umayyad dynasty and concoct a theological mandate for empire-building, as it did to a number of scholars affiliated with subsequent dynasties.

We see a similar process underway in criminalising matters that have to do with doctrinal preference where the Qur'an stipulates no worldly punishment whatsoever (such as for apostasy). Once again, 'abrogation' of relevant Meccan verses allowed for harsher, more restrictive, and non-egalitarian measures to emerge, so that one could make a case for declaring the world of Islam to be on a perennial collision course with the non-Muslim one and to assert that doctrinal variation was susceptible to punitive, this-worldly sanctions. Such views were perhaps more understandably congenial in the pre-modern world where one had good reason to be suspicious of the outsider and those who were 'different'. Law is after all an extension of culture; that legal specialists would incorporate these medieval cultural views into their conceptions of what constituted the well-ordered society should not come as a surprise to us.

It is therefore equally not surprising that modern sensibilities which value egalitarianism and freedom of conscience should find this historical, pragmatic development within the Islamic tradition to be in need of revisitation. And that is precisely what is happening in modernist, liberal Muslim circles. It is possible to articulate this growing predilection in the following way: if in the past Muslims had to 'cut down the Qur'an to their size', so to speak, through the process of abrogation to adjust to the prevalent norms of their time and place which often represented a subversion of foundational Qur'anic principles, then the time has come for contemporary Muslims to 'rise to the level of the Qur'an', by setting aside the principle of abrogation and revealing in full the Qur'an's empowering message of inclusiveness, egalitarianism and justice. The results, particularly for interfaith relations, would be dramatically transforming.

Among the strongest critics of the phenomenon of *naskh* in the modern period have been the Egyptian scholars Rashid Rida (d. 1935) and Muhammad al-Ghazali (d. 1996), and the Indian reformer Sayyid Ahmad Khan (d. 1898). Khan in particular understood *naskh* in Qur'an 2:106 to refer to the abrogation of previous scriptures, not of verses in the Qur'an. The Shi'i scholar Abu al-Qasim al-Khu'i (d. 1992) rejected the concept of *naskh* altogether.[42] In contrast, those whom we can refer to as 'hard-line Islamists' and some 'conservative traditionalists' continue to invoke *naskh* to maintain special legal privileges for the Muslim over the non-Muslim and to ascribe a divinely ordained superior moral status for Muslims on the basis of certain positive characteristics assumed to be possessed by them alone.

Moderation and righteousness: characteristics only of Muslims?

Among these positive characteristics assumed to be the exclusive prerogative of Muslims by many is moderation/temperateness, an attribute which in turn has significant implications for personal and communal salvation in the Islamic milieu. The *locus classicus* for traditional Muslim self-perception as a moderate community which avoids the excesses of other religious communities is Qur'an 2:143. Over time, the notion of 'a moderate community' (*umma wasat*) became conflated with 'the best community' recognised by God for its singular attributes of justice and temperate behaviour. A number of exegetes (but not all) therefore went on to suggest that such a community alone was destined for salvation, and all others were in manifest error, and worse, destined for hellfire.[43]

Such exegetical conclusions would be hard to sustain on the basis of the Qur'an alone. The Qur'an after all speaks highly of righteous Jews and Christians who are true to their own Scriptures and who conjoin good deeds to faith in tandem with righteous Muslims. These passages are frequently cited by irenic Muslims in particular who wish to point to a Qur'anic ethos of inclusivism and recognition of moral probity, regardless of who practises it (primarily within an Abrahamic context). As mentioned above, these verses include Qur'an 2:62 and 5:69; both of which affirm that all those who believe in one God and do good deeds, including Jews, Christians and Sabians, will earn their reward in the next world. Not surprisingly, a number of exegetes have asserted that Qur'an 2:62 has been abrogated by the chronologically later verse Qur'an 3:85, which states: 'And whoever desires other than Islam as religion – never will it be accepted from him, and he, in the Hereafter, will be among the losers.' As might be expected, exclusivist exegetes understand 'al-Islam' in the verse to be a specific reference to the religion of Islam, which would indeed exclude adherents of other religions from the possibility of salvation. Inclusivist exegetes, particularly in the modern period, note that al-Islam, as can be corroborated by other Qur'anic passages, is better understood in this context to broadly mean 'submission' to the one God, which would be a characteristic of all faithful monotheists. There is therefore no contradiction between Qur'an 2:62 and 3:85. The exclusivist interpretation was favoured by a majority of pre-modern exegetes while the inclusivist interpretation was hinted at by a few early exegetes and is amplified upon by liberal and reform-minded Muslims today.[44]

Interestingly, the pro-abrogation exegetes do not address the issue of the revelation of the fifth chapter of the Qur'an, which is understood by a number of scholars to have occurred even later than the revelation of the ninth chapter. According to the rationale developed by the pro-abrogation camp, Qur'an 5:69, whose wording is practically identical to Qur'an 2:62, should therefore trump

Qur'an 3:85, which is later than Qur'an 2:62 but earlier than Qur'an 5:69. However, this has not been the case for the pro-abrogation exegetes, confirming the assumption that *naskh* was generally wielded as a hermeneutic tool by the pro-abrogation scholars frequently to promote narrow, exclusivist and self-serving objectives which undermined what more irenic exegetes in the modern period in particular understand to be the Qur'an's overall message of justice, egalitarianism and inclusiveness, if not pluralism.

One of the hardest things for many religious people of a certain bent to acknowledge is that goodness and righteousness may exist in people who are not one of them. Today, we call this proclivity 'exclusivism' but for a long time many religious people behaved and thought this way as a normal and accept-able part of being faithful to their religious tradition. It was a comfortable, reassuring world-view according to which you were guaranteed salvation in the next world by a Supreme Being who favoured only your religion. Life was so much more self-assured and wending one's way through this world so much simpler when one could subscribe to such a belief. In a world in which com-munities were much more self-contained than ours today and in the absence of rapid transportation, broadcast media, and now the Internet and social media, such comfortable and complacent assumptions were understandable and not likely to be challenged very much, if at all, by the presence of the 'Other'.

But Islam's milieu was pluralist to begin with – in addition to Meccan poly-theists, Muslims were in contact with Jews and Christians from their earliest history. Muhammad's prophetic mission was conducted against the backdrop of his frequent encounters with members of these faith communities. The Qur'an therefore concerns itself with the relations of Muslims with these communities as well. In Chapter Five, we discussed Muslim relations with pagan Arabs in the context of jihad; for the next few pages we will concern ourselves with mainly the People of the Book.

If one listened primarily to conservative traditionalists and hard-line Islamists today, we would have no doubt that Islam came into this world to supersede Judaism and Christianity and to eventually overtake the world through active proselytisation and military expansion of Islam's territorial realms (however that may be defined in the modern period today). Other religious traditions may be tolerated but they cannot be recognised as salvifically efficacious and producing righteous believers as Islam. Since such beliefs are strongly affirmed by these largely exclusivist groups and their views are often broadcast in many different public fora, one may be forgiven for thinking that such views are fundamental to Islam and therefore must be mandated by the Qur'an. This is where the dis-sonance begins.

In addition to Qur'an 2:62 and 5:69 cited above, other verses in the Qur'an, based on their explicit wording, grant fulsome recognition to righteous Jews and

Christians as constituting moderate and upright communities equivalent to the moderate Muslim community. The Qur'anic definition of righteous Muslims as constituting a 'middle' or 'moderate nation/community' (*umma wasat*) in Qur'an 2:143 has its clear parallel in Qur'an 5:66 in which righteous Jews and Christians are similarly described as constituting a 'balanced' or 'moderate community' (*umma muqtasida*). There is also a significant cluster of verses (Qur'an 3:113–15) which praise righteous Jews and Christians who recite their scriptures especially deep into the night, bow down in adoration of God, place their faith in Him and remember their accountability to Him on the Day of Judgement, uphold what is good and noble and prevent wrongdoing. Such righteous believers constitute an 'upright community' (*umma qa'ima*). In these verses, the Qur'an thus clearly indicates that it is subscription to a common standard of righteousness and moral, ethical conduct that determines the salvific nature of a religious community – not the denominational label it chooses to wear.[45]

However, this is not how many Muslim exegetes have understood these verses through time. A diachronic survey of key exegetical works from the pre-modern and modern periods reveals that a number of influential exegetes resorted to certain reading strategies by the third century of Islam (ninth century of the Common Era) that allowed them to undermine the ecumenical potential of these verses, chief among which was the invocation of the principle of supersessionism. As Muhammad 'Abduh noted in the nineteenth century, many pre-modern Muslim commentators for various sociohistorical reasons were unwilling to recognise genuine righteousness in those belonging to other religious traditions, and progressively crafted a more exclusivist theology.[46] Fraught relations with the Byzantines during the Umayyad period and continuing through the Abbasid period, the growing influence of *dhimmi* populations in the urban areas of the Islamic world from the ninth century onwards; the onset of the Crusades, followed by the Spanish Reconquista and the Mongol attacks from the twelfth century onwards clearly left their mark on how Muslims envisioned their relations with non-Muslims in these specific historical contexts. Despite colonisation of his own country by Christian Europeans, 'Abduh is, however, secure enough in his faith to continue to recognise the soteriological potential in Christianity and Judaism, based on the inclusiveness that he clearly understands the Qur'an to be espousing. The possibility of genuine religious pluralism was rather slim in the pre-modern world with its severely demarcated political realms and sectarian identities, and it remains a fraught and debated concept in our own times. 'Abduh was without doubt much ahead of his time in his embrace of this concept (within an Abrahamic milieu), a concept he saw as naturally emerging through a faithful and holistic reading of the Qur'an and fidelity to its overall spirit and purport.[47]

Muslim relations with non-Abrahamic religious communities

Given its historical milieu, the Qur'an and the hadith literature are primarily concerned with Muslim relations with Arab polytheists and Jews and Christians. Muslims in the modern period, however, encounter adherents of other religious traditions and the inclusivists among them wish to develop a scripture-based hermeneutics of interfaith relations that recognises them as well, in addition to the traditional People of the Book. Recent efforts by Muslims to make dialogic overtures towards the adherents of two principal non-Abrahamic religious traditions – Hindusim and Buddhism – are briefly recounted below.

Muslims encountered Hindus and Buddhists already in Islam's formative period. In both cases, the status of *ahl al-dhimma* (protected people) was accorded to them, in parallel with a similar status being granted to the Zoroastrians in Persia in the seventh century, even though they are not specifically recognised in the Qur'an as Scriptuaries. The designation 'Protected People' therefore became a rather elastic concept in the hands of Muslim jurists who historically extended this status to members of religious communities who were willing to cohabit with Muslims peacefully, usually in exchange for a tribute paid to local Muslim authorities. But while a number of Muslim theologians engaged directly with especially Christian doctrine, and to a lesser extent with Jewish beliefs, there was not a similar concern expressed for engagement with Hindu and/or Buddhist religious tenets. The Arab Muslim scholar al-Biruni (d. c.1050) was a major exception in the pre-modern period who took a special interest in Indian religions. He left us a remarkably objective description of Hinduism and its practitioners, drawing parallels with Sufism and Greek philosophy. Al-Biruni's work may therefore be considered to be a very early work on comparative religion that was unprecedented in the pre-modern period.

It is not until the modern period (twentieth century onwards) that we find growing Muslim interest in articulating a specific hermeneutics of Hindu–Muslim and Buddhist–Muslim relations. The greatest numbers of Muslims and Hindus are found in India; therefore it is not surprising that Indian Muslims have taken the lead in finding a scriptural and historical basis for endorsing peaceful coexistence with Indian Hindus and Buddhists. In India, Muslims constitute about 15 per cent of the total population and therefore represent a sizeable minority. Globally, Indian Muslims represent the fourth largest Muslim community, behind Indonesia, Pakistan and Bangladesh. Islam has a long history in South Asia. By 711, an Arab Muslim expedition reached the banks of the Indus under a young Umayyad ruler called Muhammad b. Qasim. It was not until the tenth century, however, that military forays were made into the hinterland, especially under Mahmoud of Ghazni (r. 998–1030 CE). By the twelfth century, Turkish, Persian and Afghan warriors established their capital at Delhi in the Indo-Gangetic plain. The subsequent Delhi Sultanate (1211–1526) extended Muslim rule across much of the Indian subcontinent and was succeeded by the Mughal dynasty that ruled between 1526 and 1857, until the period of British colonisation.

Although Muslim rule was extended through conquest in India, the indigenous people were Islamised over a very long period of time through the agency of primarily pious Muslim preachers, teachers, mystics and traders who acclimatised themselves to their local environment. Muslim preachers, like Isma'ili missionaries in Sind and Rajasthan, often adopted the ways of local yogis and framed their Islamic message in language borrowed from Hindu religious terminology. Sufi practitioners established mosques, shrines and conventicles, which led to the formation of important points of contact between the Muslim elite and the general population. Some shrines were patronised by Muslims and Hindus alike and even commonly managed (with Buddhists, Jains and Christians), allowing for their transformation into major pilgrimage centres, such as that of Mu'in al-Din Chishti in Ajmer.[48]

One of the Mughal emperors, Akbar the Great (r. 1556–1605) as he was known, became fabled for his tolerance of all religions in his domain and sponsored Persian translations of Hindu epics, the Bhagavad Gita and books on Vedanta philosophy. He inaugurated a 'new' synthetic religion called 'Din Ilahi', which gathered together elements from Islam, Hinduism, Christianity, Zoroastrianism and Jainism. Akbar advocated for reconciliation between all religions and attempted to create common ground on the basis of shared, universal principles. His great-grandson, Dara Shukoh (1615–59) translated the Upanishads, established contact with Hindu learned men and attempted a synthesis of Sufism with Hindu Vedanta. Dara Shukoh was, however, executed for heresy by his brother, Aurangzeb (r. 1658–1707), who adopted more discriminatory practices towards his Hindu subjects after ascending to power. Among Indians, Akbar and Dara Shukoh remain revered figures who represent Hindu–Muslim rapprochement, while Mahmoud of Ghazni and Aurangzeb are invoked today as symbols of Muslim intolerance.[49]

Muslim encounters with Buddhism occurred at the same time as with Hinduism, when the aforementioned Umayyad general Muhammad b. Qasim reached Sind in 711. Sind was a largely Buddhist province at that time and Ibn Qasim is said to have extended the rights of the traditional People of the Book to the Buddhists by stating the following, as reported by the famous historian Abu al-Hasan al-Baladhuri (d. c. 892):

> The temples [lit. al-Budd, but referring to the temples of the Buddhists and the Hindus as well as the Jains] shall be treated by us as if they were the churches of the Christians, the synagogues of the Jews and the fire temples of the Magians.[50]

According to al-Baladhuri, Muhammad b. Qasim so endeared himself to the local population, that Hindus and Buddhists are said to have wept when he died and they created an image in his memory.[51]

In subsequent centuries, Muslims would continue to encounter Buddhists in Central Asia, Southeast Asia, Tibet and China among other places. As with Hindus, such encounters were both benign and violent, marked both by tolerance and persecution on the part of Muslim rulers. Where widespread Islamisation did occur, it was slow and usually occurred under the aegis of Muslim preachers and teachers. Until the Mongol conquests of the thirteenth century, Buddhism remained a significant presence in Central Asia and Iran.

These early examples of overall Muslim tolerance for a variety of religious traditions and practices are often recalled by modern Muslims to advocate for peaceful coexistence with religious practitioners who are not specifically mentioned in the Qur'an. Contemporary Muslim theologians who live with members of other non-Abrahamic religions, such as Confucianism, are the most enthusiastic proponents of deriving an inclusive theology of co-existence vis-à-vis such religious traditions. Chandra Muzaffar, a prominent Malaysian academic and advocate of a dialogue of civilisations and Islamic pluralism, has underscored the importance of stressing shared values, such as love and compassion, humility and modesty, patience and moderation, a high regard for moral education and the quest for knowledge, with Chinese citizens in his country.[52] Muzaffar is confident that given Malaysia's success already in crafting a largely peaceful multi-ethnic and multireligious society,

> it will emerge as another Andalusia, that illustrious civilization of learning and beauty that Islam created in Spain, which is widely regarded as perhaps the most successful example of multi-religious harmony in the pre-modern era.[53]

The stunning Crystal Mosque in Kuala Lumpur, Malaysia (featured on the dust jacket of this book) may be considered to be emblematic of this growing sense of inclusivity and receptivity among Malays towards the very modernity that makes such inclusivism imaginable and possible. The mosque with its post-modern angles and unusual exterior is boldly equipped with internet connections and incorporates features drawn from Chinese culture; yet it is nevertheless clearly recognisable as a mosque. While these aspects may be the source of dismay for the purist and conservative among Malay Muslims, to the confident, irenic Muslim, this house of worship signals harmony between this-worldly and other-worldly concerns and Islam's internal adaptability to variegated human cultures that may be understood to be part of the divine design described in the Qur'an.

An inclusive hermeneutic of interfaith relations for the twenty-first century

Muslim scholars who wish to develop a model for dialogue with Hindus and Buddhists and other non-Abrahamic religious communities draw upon past positive historical examples of interfaith tolerance and peaceful coexistence as the way forward. They also invariably look to scripture for guidance in this matter. Two Qur'anic verses (6:107–8) constitute a valuable proof-text in this regard. These verses state:

> Had God willed, they would not be idolaters; but We have not appointed you [addressing the Prophet] a watcher over them, nor are you their guardian. Do not abuse to whom they pray apart from God, or they will abuse God in retaliation without knowledge.

The most influential pre-modern commentators emphasise that these critical verses establish a protocol of interfaith dialogue with polytheists based on respect and consideration for their religious sensibilities. In the eighth century, Muqatil emphasises the message of religious freedom guaranteed in Qur'an 6:107 by noting that if God had so willed, He could have prevented the Meccans from being polytheists. Instead, the Meccans were given a choice between choosing to continue in their religion and opting to accept the truth of the Qur'anic revelation. Muhammad's role was primarily that of a messenger and not that of a guardian over the Meccans. The next verse clearly informs that the early Muslims used to curse the idols of the pagan Meccans, a practice which was forbidden by God lest the polytheists curse God in their ignorance.[54]

Al-Tabari similarly comments that Qur'an 6:107 affirms that if God had willed, the people of Mecca would have not have disbelieved in God and His messenger, but Muhammad was sent only as an emissary and summoner to people and not as an overseer of their actions or as one who is responsible for their maintenance and welfare. Qur'an 6:108 specifically forbids Muslims from reviling the idols of the polytheists for that would cause them to revile God in their ignorance, as has been reported by a number of very early scholars like Ibn 'Abbas, Qatada and others.[55]

Similar commentaries are given by al-Zamakhshari,[56] al-Razi[57] and Ibn Kathir.[58] Al-Zamakhshari notably provides a rationale for why this early practice of reviling idols was forbidden, in answer to the possible query that this prohibition appears to be contrary to the general ethical injunction to prevent what is objectionable (al-nahy 'an al-munkar); and polytheism, one may aver, is certainly objectionable from the Islamic perspective. The answer is that if an ostensibly moral act were to result in a greater wrong, then such an act should be proscribed.[59] A similar rationale is given by al-Razi in response to the same hypothetical question.[60]

The modern exegete Muhammad 'Abduh (d. 1905) reproduces many of the essential points made by his pre-modern predecessors in connection with these two verses. But he goes further than his predecessors in asserting that Qur'an 6:107 makes clear that God, despite being the Guardian and Overseer of humanity, does not force humans to believe in and obey Him. If He were to do so, humans would no longer be humans but become a different species; that is to say, humans by virtue of their humanness have freedom of choice in religious matters. This is therefore doubly true of the Prophet who was not sent as the guardian of humans. All the prophets through time, continues 'Abduh, have been 'summoners not overseers; guides not tyrants, obligated to not restrict even by an inch the God-given freedom of humans in matters of faith'. He dismisses the reported opinion (attributed to Ibn 'Abbas) that this verse had been abrogated by the so-called 'sword verse' Qur'an 9:5, saying this is not the opinion of the majority. This verse may have been revealed before the Medinan period when the Prophet became the ruler of the Muslim polity but its equivalent exists in Qur'an 9:79, a Medinan verse which states: 'Whoever believes in the Messenger has obeyed God, and whoever turns his back, we have not sent you as a guardian (hafizan) over them'.[61]

'Abduh further asserts that Qur'an 6:107 must be understood as containing a general prohibition against reviling any one's religion or article of belief. Thus Muslims may not insult Christians and vice versa, Sunnis may not revile the Shi'a and vice versa, and so forth. Those who revile other people do so, he says, out of 'love for one's self and culpable ignorance'.[62] It is noteworthy that 'Abduh quotes Qur'an 29:46 in this context. By invoking this verse here, he is clearly implying that the injunction contained in it to debate with the People of the Book with what is better has a broader applicability to all interreligious and intrareligious conversations. Considered together, these two verses – Qur'an 6:107 and Qur'an 29:46 – create for 'Abduh a moral imperative to conduct dialogue with all religious groups with congeniality and without recourse to offensive and harsh language.[63]

In this context, it is pertinent to point out that another verse from the Qur'an (49:13) is understood today in particular to contain a more general injunction to engage respectfully with all peoples everywhere, irrespective of faith, ethnicity, culture, and so on, so that mutual knowledge and understanding will ensue. The verse states:

> O humankind! We have created you from a male and a female, and made you into nations and tribes, that you might get to know one another. The noblest of you in God's sight is the one who is most righteous.

The Arabic verbal collocation li-ta'arafu contained in the phrase clearly advocates that humans should proactively get to know one another, irrespective of one's background, and reminds that individuals find esteem before God only on the basis of piety. Fazlur Rahman points to the verse's exhortation to different communities to 'compete with each other in goodness'.[64] As Khaled Abou El Fadl comments, Qur'an 49:13 (and other verses) 'can readily support an ethic of diversity and tolerance'.[65] This verse is therefore of great relevance in twenty-first-century discussions about deriving an authoritative scriptural mandate for positive dialogic encounters with people of all faith traditions (or of none). It is noteworthy that the verse and its interpretation was the topic of an extended international conference on interreligious dialogue, convened by the Council of Centers on Jewish–Christian Relations in Istanbul, Turkey, in 2010, indicating a growing recognition of its ecumenical potential in Abrahamic circles.

Because of the more parochial circumstances of their own time, medieval exegetes, however, tended to gloss the verb *ta'arafu* to mean primarily learning about each other's tribal and similar affiliational backgrounds in order to establish bonds of kinship and affection. In explanation of *ta'arafu*, al-Tabari, for example, glosses it as commanding people to get to know one another so that they may discover their bonds of kinship. He warns that knowledge of such kinship is not meant to induce any sense of superiority but rather 'to bring you closer to God, for indeed only the most pious among you is the most honorable'.[66] Ibn Kathir, in his exegesis of this term, cites a hadith in which the Prophet states, 'Learn about each other's pedigrees so as to establish your blood ties, for it is such ties which lead to love among people'.[67]

The inclusivists and pluralists among Muslims today insist that the exegetical purview of the verb *ta'arafu* can be extended to not just one's blood relatives but to all of humanity in its diversity. In contemporary circumstances, Qur'an 49:13 is understood by such Muslims as representing the overall objective of interfaith and intercultural conversations – to create a mandate for learning about one another as inhabitants of different countries, cultures and faith communities. The appreciation for such differences that exist due to God's plan for humankind can only enrich our lives, they say, and is an appropriate manifestation of the basic universalism of Islam.[68] Judgement of theological differences is a prerogative belonging to God alone, as unambiguously stated in a number of Qur'anic verses, including Qur'an 45:14–15, which state:

> Tell those who believe to forgive those who do not hope for the days of God; in order that He may reward people according to what they used to earn. Whoever does right, it is for his soul, and whoever does wrong, it is against it. And afterward you will be brought back to your Lord.

Such inclusivists also cite the famous early Meccan revelation (Qur'an 109:6) in which the Prophet is commanded to tell the pagan Arabs, 'To you your religion and to me mine', creating an explicit mandate for respecting the religious freedom of non-Muslims. Qur'an 17:70 is further invoked as a proof-text in this context; it states, 'We have granted dignity to all of humankind', with no exception implied. The well-known contemporary Mauritanian Muslim scholar Abdullah bin Bayyah has stressed the importance of this verse by commenting that 'The dignity of humanity precedes the dignity of faith and is subordinate to it.'[69]

The irenic–liberal interpretations of such critical verses in the Qur'an (which to some extent are sometimes already reflected in the exegeses of some pre-modern commentators like al-Zamakhshari, al-Razi, and are strongly stressed by 'Abduh in the nineteenth century) are admittedly more strikingly congenial to twenty-first-century sensibilities. After all, easier physical and intellectual access to other people's cultures and thought has made many Muslims in the contemporary period more receptive to different ways of looking at the world and to interaction with one another on a more egalitarian basis. As Reza Shah Kazemi, a prominent contemporary scholar of Islam and interfaith practitioner, remarks at the end of his path-breaking book *Common Ground between Islam and Buddhism*, the purpose of constructive interfaith dialogue is

> inviting into our tent the stranger who may not look, worship, or be like us in many ways, *because* [emphasis in text] he or she is a creation of God, here for a purpose, and someone to be honored as a fellow guest of God . . . The challenge before us is to understand our teachings better – from within and without – so we can engender a true celebration of humankind's diversity. For indeed, too many of us seem to have just enough faith to foment hatred, oppression, and fear among people, but not nearly enough to nurture kindness, compassion, and mercy.[70]

The capacious hermeneutics of interfaith relations adumbrated in modern works such as Kazemi's promises to provide the interpretive stimulus today for the emergence of a genuine inclusivism, and perhaps eventually pluralism, in Muslim ethical and moral thinking vis-à-vis all religions and peoples. Early signs of such modes of thinking are becoming quite evident, potentially inviting like-minded responses from people of goodwill from other traditions.[71]

Notes

1. Mujahid, *Tafsir*, 205.
2. Al-Tabari, *Tafsir*, 10:149–50.
3. Al-Tabari's polemical attitude towards Jews and Christians is discussed by Seth Ward in his article, 'A Fragment from an Unknown Work by al-Tabari on the Tradition "Expel the Jews and Christians from the Arabian Peninsula (and the Lands of Islam)"', *Bulletin of the School of Oriental and African Studies* 53 (1990): 407–20. As Ward suggests, the growing presence and influence of the *dhimmi*s in Islamic cities during al-Tabari's time contributed to the desire on the part of some jurists to firmly demarcate the theological and sociological boundaries between Muslims and non-Muslims.
4. Al-Zamakhshari, *Kashshaf*, 4:553.
5. Al-Razi, *Tafsir*, 9:63–4.

6. Ibn Kathir, *Tafsir*, 3:401.
7. Ibid.
8. Muqatil, *Tafsir*, 1:281.
9. See, for example, Martin Lings, *Muhammad: His Life Based on the Earliest Sources* (Cambridge: Islamic Texts Society, 1995), 302.
10. Al-Tabari, *Tafsir*, 3:300–2.
11. Al-Zamakhshari, *al-Kashshaf 'an haqa'iq ghawamid al-tanzil wa-'uyun al-aqawil fi wujuh al-ta'wil*, eds 'Adil Ahmad 'Abd al-Wujud and 'Ali Muhammad Mu'awwad (Riyad: Maktabat al-'ubaykan, 1998), 1:567.
12. For a quick overview of this event, see the article 'Mubahala' in the *Encyclopaedia of Islam*, second edition (Leiden: Brill, 1960–2007) which centres on Qur'an 3:61.
13. Al-Razi, *Tafsir*, 3:251.
14. Ibid. 3:252.
15. Ibid. 3:252–3.
16. Ibn Kathir, *Tafsir*, 1:351
17. Rida, *Tafsir*, 3:268–71.
18. See further my discussion of 'Abduh's views on abrogation in Afsaruddin, *Striving in the Path of God*, 238–9.
19. For a recent study of the Ibadis, see Valerie Hoffman, *The Essentials of Ibadi Islam* (Syracuse: Syracuse University Press, 2012).
20. This statement and responses from other Christian leaders and scholars are available at <http://www.acommonword.com/category/site/christian-responses/>; last accessed on 20 May 2014.
21. The full transcript of his address given at the University of Regensburg, Germany, 12 September 2006 is available at <http://www.religion.ucsb.edu/catholicstudies/resources/regensburg/pdf/TheSpeech.pdf>; last accessed on 20 June 2014. Pope Benedict is drawing upon common tropes of Christian European polemics against Islam that became prominent during the late nineteenth century. For example, in 1900, Gabriel Hanotaux (d. 1944), the French Minister of Foreign Affairs at the time, had similarly asserted that the belief of Muslims in the unity of God, as contrasted to Trinitarianism, had somehow contributed to their irrationality and backwardness. For an account of these initial claims and the subsequent exchange between Hanotaux and Muhammad 'Abduh, see Charles C. Adams, *Islam and Modernism in Egypt* (London: Routledge, 2000), 86 ff.
22. The full text is available at <http://www.acommonword.com/the-acw-document/>; last accessed on 19 May 2014.
23. Aref Nayed, 'The Promise of a Common Word', in *A Common Word Dossier*, 56, available at <http://www.acommonword.com/category/new-fruits/major-a-common-word-events/>; last accessed on 20 May 2014.
24. The full list of signatories is reproduced in Miroslav Volf et al. (eds), *A Common Word: Muslims and Christians on Loving God and Neighbor* (Grand Rapids, MI: Eerdmans Publishing Company, 2010), 214–37.
25. An impressive example of such a publication is the above-cited *A Common Word: Muslims and Christians on Loving God and Neighbor*, which contains a diverse array of articles explaining the significance of the commandment to love God and neighbour in both traditions and addresses a number of questions that have been directed at the Common Word initiative.
26. As a regular participant in these annual seminars for several years, I am happy to testify to the propitious results of such encounters.
27. Available at <http://www.isna.net/isna-celebrates-the-5th-annual-muslim-jewish-week end-of-twinning.html>; last accessed on 20 June 2014.

28. Quoted from its website <http://www.riifs.org/publications.html>; last accessed on 21 June 2014.

29. Ibid.

30. Quoted from its website: <http://www.kaiciid.org/en/the-centre/the-centre.html>; last accessed on 21 June 2014.

31. See the references to some of these events in Chapter Six.

32. From a comparative perspective, it should be remembered that this was at a time when Jews were usually given the choice between the sword and forced conversion to Christianity in Europe; a choice that was also extended to Muslims when Europeans more infrequently encountered them as minorities in Europe. For Jewish–Muslim relations in the pre-modern period, see, in general, Mark Cohen, *Under Crescent and Cross: the Jews in the Middle Ages* (Princeton: Princeton University Press, 1974), especially 30–74.

33. The main difference between Muslim minorities in North America and Europe and non-Muslim minorities in particularly the Arab world is that the latter have deep historical roots in the Middle East. The contributions of Arab Christians and Jews to the formation of the pre-modern Islamic civilisation are undeniable and speak to the chequered trajectory of Muslim and non-Muslim relations in this part of the world – mostly one characterised by tolerance infrequently punctuated by hostility and prejudice.

34. This point is stressed by the well-known Egyptian columnist and thinker Fahmi Huwaydi in his *Muwatinun, la dhimmiyun* (Citizens, not protected people) (Beirut and Cairo: Dar al-shuruq, 1985).

35. Majid Khadduri, *War and Peace in Islam* (Baltimore: Johns Hopkins University Press, 1979), 257–61.

36. Asghar Ali Engineer, *Rational Approach to Islam* (New Delhi: Gyan Publishing House, 2001), 149.

37. Asghar Ali Engineer, *On Developing Theology of Peace in Islam* (New Delhi: Sterling Publishers, 2005), 52.

38. Mohamed Talbi, *Al-Islam: Hurriya wa Hiwar* (Beirut: Dar al-nahar lil-nashr, 1999), *passim*. Talbi's views are described further by Ronald L. Nettler in his article, 'Mohamed Talbi on Understanding the Qur'an', in Suha Taji-Farouki (ed.), *Modern Muslim Intellectuals and the Qur'an* (Oxford: Oxford University Press, 2004), 225–39.

39. Mohamed Fathi Osman, *The Children of Adam: An Islamic Perspective on Pluralism* (Washington DC: Center for Muslim–Christian Understanding, Georgetown University, 1996), 13.

40. The Constitution of Medina does not mention the *jizya* in relation to the Jews of Medina since their males were expected to participate in the military defence of the polity.

41. Khaled Abou El Fadl, *The Place of Tolerance in Islam* (Boston: Beacon Press, 2002), 21–2.

42. For a recent detailed study of *naskh*, see Louay Fatoohi, *Abrogation in the Qur'an and Islamic Law* (New York: Routledge, 2012).

43. For a recent extensive discussion of this topic which shows a diversity of opinions among principal scholars of the pre-modern and modern periods, see Mohammad Hassan Khalil, *Islam and the Fate of Others: The Salvation Question* (Oxford: Oxford University Press, 2012).

44. The Islamic Studies scholar Abdulaziz Sachedina reads into Qur'an 3:85 a universalist understanding of true submission to God; see his *The Islamic Roots of Democratic Pluralism* (Oxford: Oxford University Press, 2001), 39, 44, and *passim*.

45. This discussion draws heavily on my article 'The Hermeneutics of Inter-Faith Relations: Retrieving Moderation and Pluralism as Universal Principles in Qur'anic Exegeses', *Journal of Religious Ethics* 37 (2009): 331–54.

46. Rida, *Tafsir*, 4:59.

47. See further Asma Afsaruddin, 'The "Upright Community": Interpreting the Righteousness

and Salvation of the People of the Book in the Qur'an', in Josef Meri (ed.), *Muslim-Jewish Relations in Past and Present: a Kaleidoscopic View* (Leiden: Brill, forthcoming).

48. See the monograph-length study of this shrine by P. M. Currie, *The Shrine and Cult of Mu'in al-Din Chishti of Ajmer* (Oxford: Oxford University Press, 2007).

49. Art. 'Hinduism and Islam' in Richard Martin (ed.), *The Encyclopaedia of Islam and the Muslim World* (New York: Macmillan Reference USA, 2004), 301–6.

50. Al-Baladhuri, *Futuh al-buldan* (Beirut: Maktaba al-Hilal,1988), 422–3; cited by Reza Shah Kazemi, *Common Ground between Islam and Buddhism: Spiritual and Ethical Affinities* (Louisville, KY: Fons Vitae, 2010), 8.

51. Al-Baladhuri, *Futuh*, 424; cited by Kazemi, *Common Ground*, 9.

52. Chandra Muzaffar, *Muslims Today: Changes within, Challenges without* (Islamabad: EMEL Publications, 2011), 207–24.

53. Ibid. 224.

54. Muqatil, *Tafsir*, 1:573.

55. Al-Tabari, *Jami' al-bayan*, 5:304–5.

56. Al-Zamakhshari, *Kashshaf*, 2:385.

57. Al-Razi, *Tafsir*, 5:108–11.

58. Ibn Kathir, *Tafsir*, 2:156.

59. Al-Zamakhshari, *Kashshaf*, 2:385.

60. Al-Razi, *Tafsir*, 5:110.

61. Rida, *Tafsir*, 7:548–9.

62. Ibid. 7:549.

63. Ibid. 7:550.

64. Fazlur Rahman, *Major Themes of the Qur'an* (Minneapolis, MN: Bibliotheca Islamica, 1980), 167.

65. Abou El Fadl, *Place of Tolerance*, 15.

66. Al-Tabari, *Jami' al-bayan*, 11:398.

67. Ibn Kathir, *Tafsir*, 4:218.

68. Another important Qur'anic verse cited in this context is 5:48, 'Had God so wanted, He would have made you one community; but He tries you by what befalls you, so race to do good works.'

69. Cited in Kazemi, *Common Ground*, 133.

70. Ibid. 136.

71. The Churches Education Commission, which is a conglomeration of European churches, adopted a statement in 2008 at a meeting held in Munich, Germany in which it expressed sentiments very similar to Kazemi's on the purpose of interreligious dialogue and the desirability of fostering religious pluralism. The pertinent remarks are: 'That God's saving will is universal: God wants to lead all people into fellowship with His truth; That the creaturely nature of human beings and their being in the image of God is the basis for respect a priori for all religious beliefs'. The statement is available at <http://cid.ceceurope.org/fileadmin/filer/cid/Doc_Various_Documents/CiDStatementonThR.pdf>; last accessed on 9 June 2014.

Epilogue: looking to the future

Predicting the future is a notoriously tricky, as well as risky, business. One may fall prey to making prognostications that may seem eminently sensible at the time but which an unexpected turn of events can speedily derail. One trend, however, seems to be practically guaranteed for the near and not-so-near future – Islam as an ethical, moral and social force will continue to be palpable on the world stage and perhaps only increase in its impact through time. This will be true – as it already is – not only for the traditional Islamic heartlands (the Middle East, South and South-East Asia, and parts of Africa) but for the West (especially Europe and North America) as well. Globalisation connects these broad swathes of the world and increasing transnational migration of Muslim populations has dissolved once sharply demarcated regional and national boundaries. The issues discussed in this book therefore have great resonance in all parts of the world where Muslims constitute a majority or a sizeable minority population.

The continued, if not enhanced, visibility of Islam into the foreseeable future, will be perceived as either a positive or negative development, depending on one's particular perspective on Islam and Muslims, while yet others may simply regard it as a neutral and inevitable development. For those who would view Islam's continuing and possibly escalating presence as positive, the focus is on the internal pluralism of the Islamic tradition, and on its rich moral, ethical and intellectual resources, its historical tolerance of religious and ethnic minorities, its non-ecclesial structure and even distrust of clerical rule, its strong emphasis on social justice and concern for the environment, among others. These historical orientations are understood by this group to configure Islam as a complex discursive tradition that can be, and already is, adaptable to the modern (or perhaps post-modern) world. Revitalisation and re-interpretations of key Islamic ethical and legal principles (embodied in the Sharia) demonstrate Islam's fit for the modern man and woman who still concede a role to religion in their private and public lives.

Those who regard this development with alarm are those who have become accustomed in a presentist vein to reflexively associate Islam and Muslims with everything retrograde in the modern period – above all, religious extremism, abuse of women, persecution of religious minorities, clericalism and political repression. While the first group is characterised by their detractors as overly optimistic and even 'apologetic', the second is criticised for their focus on the fringe elements of Muslim-majority societies and for conflating culture with religion.

Whether one likes it or not, it is abundantly clear in the second decade of the twenty-first century that Islam, like other religions, is not fading away. Religion of all sorts has made a dramatic comeback since the last quarter of the twentieth century and shows no signs of receding from public discourse and the public sphere where it appears most menacing to some. In the process, religion itself is becoming transformed even as it transforms societies in many parts of the world in the twenty-first century. Most religions are no longer of the 'old-time' variety, defined primarily by erudite men well versed in the intricacies of theology and legal casuistry. For better or for worse, religion is being reshaped by all kinds of unconventional actors today – engineers, doctors, politicians, human and gender rights advocates, women in general, and above all, by young people who often bypass the traditional religious authorities through recourse to the Internet and social media. We see such an internal ferment quite clearly underway in the Islamic milieu. Rather than an external clash of civilisations, this ferment has generated internal fault lines among Muslim populations globally, centred on the key issues discussed in this book. How Muslims resolve these issues among themselves will determine the kind of impact that Islam and Muslims will exert in the global arena in the future. This book has been an extended discussion of the hermeneutic and discursive strategies employed by contemporary Muslims to interrogate and negotiate some of the most burning issues associated with modernity.

But Muslims alone cannot determine the future. Non-Muslims, particularly the majority of Westerners, are willy-nilly implicated in this dialectical process. Just as the fiery rhetoric and violent actions of anti-liberal forces in Muslim-majority societies give rise to grave concern, so do the obscurantism and hatemongering of extremist right-wing factions in the West. The one is incomprehensible without the other. Economic disparities between the global North and South continue to generate socio-economic malaise and resentment on the part of the poor towards the wealthy, a resentment that cuts across religious, ethnic and national lines. Historical political injustices, especially those that occurred during the period of Christian European colonisation of much of the Islamic world, remain an open wound that continues to fester. The perpetration of violence on both sides shuts down communication and reinforces the political divide. While Muslims in the heartlands have the right to demand equitable solutions to grave political injustices inflicted on them by a powerful hegemonic West, including the latter's active support for local repressive governments, they are also responsible for addressing and rooting out the sources of religious and political militancy in their midst. While the United States in particular has a right to defend itself when attacked by terrorists claiming to act in the name of Islam, it must also be prepared to bear the brunt for the moral outrage generated by the continued killing of mostly Muslim civilians in Afghanistan, Pakistan, the Yemen and the Palestinian occupied territories by its own troops or those of its allies or through unmanned drone attacks.

As Muslim majority-societies are asked to transform themselves, so must Western polities. The best support for liberal societies – whether in the Islamic heartlands or in the West – is an unflagging commitment to socio-economic and political justice at a global level, a commitment that cannot be held hostage by nationalist concerns and narrow political agendas. Without this mutual commitment, which entails fundamental transformations in the moral, ethical and political comportment of Muslim and non-Muslim citizens of this planet, the current status quo does not portend a very congenial future.

Not all transformations can and must occur at the governmental level, of course. At the community and grassroots level, there are changes already occurring that are far more hopeful. Muslims in the traditional heartlands and in the West are forming social and political alliances with all kinds of partners in the name of a common adherence to social justice and commitment to building a more equitable and peaceful world. This was rather spectacularly evident in the Egyptian revolution when a popular coalition of Muslims, Christians and secularists brought down the government of Hosni Mubarak. This kind of partnership based on a shared world-view and principled opposition to injustice, wherever one may encounter it, was also evident when American Muslims, Christians, Jews and others attempted to stare down pastor Terry Jones when he threatened to burn a copy of the Qur'an in Florida and when extremist agitators tried to scuttle the building of the Park 51 Community Center in New York City. Change from below is perhaps more effective and enduring in the long run and civil and political friendships of this kind continue to pay rich dividends beyond the original event that brings such alliances into being. While the future remains the great unknown, these quiet and unheralded transformations allow for cautious optimism to emerge. In the remaking of our world today, Muslims play and will continue to play a critical role – as they make room for others in their midst and others make room for them – at the global table that grows (one hopes) ever more expansive and inclusive.

Select bibliography

'Abd al-Raziq, 'Ali. *Al-Islam wa-usul al-hukm*. Beirut: Dar maktabat al-hayat, 1966.

Abou El Fadl, Khaled. *And God Knows the Soldiers: The Authoritative and Authoritarian in Islamic Discourses*. Lanham, MD: University Press of America, 2001.

———. *Islam and the Challenge of Democracy*. Princeton: Princeton University Press, 2004.

———. *The Great Theft: Wrestling Islam from the Extremists*. New York: HarperOne, 2007.

———. *The Place of Tolerance in Islam*. Boston: Beacon Press, 2002.

———. *Speaking in God's Name: Islamic Law, Authority and Women*. Oxford: Oneworld, 2001.

Abu-Lughod, Lila. *Do Muslim Women Need Saving?* Cambridge, MA: Harvard University Press, 2013.

Abu-Nimer, Muhammad. *Non-Violence and Peacebuilding in Islam: Theory and Practice*. Gainesville: University Press of Florida, 2003.

Abu Rayya, Mahmud. *Adwa' 'ala al-sunna al-muhammadiyya*. Cairo: Dar al-ta'lif, 1958.

Adams, Charles C. *Islam and Modernism in Egypt*. London: Routledge, 2000.

El-Affendi, Abdelwahab. 'Democracy and Its (Muslim) Critics: An Islamic Alternative to Democracy?' in *Islamic Democratic Discourse: Theory, Debates and Philosophical Perspectives*. Ed. Muqtedar Khan. Lanham, MD: Lexington Books, 2006. Pp. 227–56.

Afsaruddin, Asma. 'Early Women Exemplars and the Construction of Gendered Space: (Re-) Defining Feminine Moral Excellence', in *Harem Histories: Envisioning Places and Living Spaces*. Ed. Marilyn Booth. Durham, NC and London: Duke University Press, 2010. Pp. 23–48.

———. 'The Hermeneutics of Inter-Faith Relations: Retrieving Moderation and Pluralism as Universal Principles in Qur'anic Exegeses', *Journal of Religious Ethics* 37 (2009): pp. 331–54.

———. 'Islamic Feminisms: Gender Egalitarianism and Legal Constraints', in *Social Difference and Constitutionalism in Pan Asia*. Ed. Susan Williams. Cambridge: Cambridge University Press, 2014. Pp. 292–315.

———. 'The "Islamic State": Genealogy, Facts, and Myths', *Journal of Church and State* 48 (2006): pp. 153–73.

———. 'Obedience to Political Authority: An Evolutionary Concept', in *Islamic Democratic Discourse: Theory, Debates, and Philosophical Perspectives*. Ed. Muqtedar Khan. New York: Lexington Books, 2006. Pp. 37–60.

———. *Striving in the Path of God: Jihad and Martyrdom in Islamic Thought* Oxford: Oxford University Press, 2013.

——. 'Theologizing about Democracy: A Critical Appraisal of Mawdudi's Thought', in *Islam, the State, and Political Authority: Medieval Issues and Modern Concerns*. Ed. Asma Afsaruddin. New York: Palgrave Macmillan, 2011. Pp. 131–54.

Allawi, Ali A. *The Crisis of Islamic Civilization*. New Haven: Yale University Press, 2010.

Ali, Souad T. *A Religion, Not a State: Ali 'Abd al-Raziq's Islamic Justification of Political Secularism*. Salt Lake City: The University of Utah Press, 2009.

Al-Alwani, Taha Jabir. *Fi Fiqh al-aqalliyyat al-muslima*. Cairo: Nahdat Misr, 2000.

——. *Towards a Fiqh for Minorities: Some Basic Reflections*. London and Washington DC: IIIT, 2003.

Asad, Talal. *The Idea of an Anthropology of Islam*. Occasional Papers, Washington DC: Center for Contemporary Arab Studies, Georgetown University, 1986.

——. *Formations of the Secular: Christianity, Islam, Modernity*. Stanford: Stanford University Press, 2003.

——. *Genealogies of Religion: Discipline and Reasons of Power in Christianity and Islam*. Baltimore: Johns Hopkins University Press, 1993.

Ayoob, Mohammed. *The Many Faces of Political Islam: Religion and Politics in the Muslim World*. Ann Arbor: University of Michigan Press, 2007.

Azmeh, Aziz. *Islams and Modernities*. London: Verso, 2009.

Al-Banna, Jamal. *al-'Awda ila 'l-qur'an*. Cairo: al-Ittihad al-islami al-duwali li 'l-'amal, 1984.

Badran, Margot. *Feminism in Islam: Secular and Religious Convergences*. Oxford: Oneworld, 2009.

Barlas, Asma Barlas. *'Believing Women' in Islam: Unreading Patriarchal Interpretations of the Qur'an*. Austin, TX: University of Texas Press, 2004.

Al-Baydawi, 'Abd Allah b. 'Umar. *Tafsir al-Baydawi*. Beirut: Dar al-kutub al-'ilmiyya, 1988.

Berger, Peter L. 'The Desecularization of the World: A Global Overview', in *Desecularization of the World: Resurgent Religion in World Politics: Resurgent Religion and World Politics*. Ed. Peter L. Berger. Grand Rapids, MI: Eerdmans Publishing Co, 1999. Pp. 1–18.

Binder, Leonard. 'Ali Abd al Raziq and Islamic Liberalism,' *Asian and African Studies* 10 (1982): pp. 31 – 67.

Bosworth, G. E. et al. (eds). *Encyclopedia of Islam*, new edition. Leiden: Brill, 1960–2005.

Brown, Daniel. *Rethinking Tradition in Modern Islamic Thought*. Cambridge: Cambridge University Press, 1996.

Brown, Jonathan. *The Canonization of al-Bukhari and Muslim: the Formation and Function of Sunni Hadith Canon*. Leiden: Brill, 2011.

——. *Hadith: Muhammad's Legacy in the Medieval and Modern World*. Oxford: Oneworld, 2009.

Bulliet, Richard. *The Case for Islamo-Christian Civilization*. New York: Columbia University Press, 2006.

Al-Buti, Muhammad Sa'id Ramadan. *Al-Jihad fi 'l-islam*. Damascus: Dar al-fikr, 1993.

Casanova, José. *Public Religions in the Modern World*. Chicago: University of Chicago Press, 1994.

Choueiri, Yousef. *Islamic Fundamentalism*. London: Pinter, 1990.

Dabashi, Hamid. *Being a Muslim in the World*. New York: Palgrave Macmillan, 2013.

Dallal, Ahmad. 'The Origins and Objectives of Islamic Revivalist Thought, 1750–1850', *Journal of the American Oriental Society* 113 (1993): 343–9.

Eisenstadt, Shmuel Noah. *Comparative Civilizations and Multiple Modernities*. Leiden: Brill, 2003. Vol. 2.

Enayat, Hamid. *Modern Islamic Political Thought*. Kuala Lumpur: Islamic Book Trust, 2001.

Engineer, Asghar Ali. *On Developing Theology of Peace in Islam*. New Delhi: Sterling Publishers, 2005.

Esposito, John L. 'Muhammad Iqbal and the Islamic State', in *Makers of Contemporary Islam*. Eds John L. Esposito and John Voll. Oxford: Oxford University Press, 2001. Pp. 175–90.

Esposito, John and John Voll (eds). *Islam and Democracy*. Oxford: Oxford University Press, 1996.

Euben, Roxanne L. 'Pre-Modern, Anti-Modern, or Post-Modern? Islamic and Western Critiques of Modernity', *Review of Politics* 59 (1997): 429–59.

Fadel, Mohammad. 'Is Historicism a Viable Strategy for Islamic Law Reform? The Case of "Never Shall a Folk Prosper Who Have Appointed a Woman to Rule Them"', *Islamic Law and Society* 18 (2011): 131–76.

——. 'Two Women, One Man: Knowledge, Power and Gender in Medieval Sunni Legal Thought.' *International Journal of Middle East Studies* 29 (1997): 185–204.

Fish, Steven. *Are Muslims Distinctive: A Look at the Evidence*. Oxford: Oxford University Press, 2011.

Gellner, Ernest. *Postmodernism, Reason and Religion*. New York: Routledge, 1992.

——. 'Marxism and Islam: Failure and Success', in *Power-Sharing Islam?* Ed. A. Tamimi. London: Liberty for Muslim World Publications, 1993. Pp. 33–42.

Gerth, H. H. and C. Wright Mills (eds). *From Max Weber, Essays in Sociology*, Oxford: Oxford University Press, 1946.

Al-Ghazali, Muhammad. *Ihya 'ulum al-din*. Ed. 'Abd Allah al-Khalidi. Beirut: Dar al-Arqam, n.d.

Göle, Nilüfer. 'Islam in Public: New Visibilities and New Imaginaries', in *Political Islam: A Critical Reader*. Ed. Frederick Volpi. New York: Routledge, 2011.

Gülen, M. Fethullah. *Key Concepts in the Practice of Sufism*. Fairfax, VA: The Fountain, 1999.

——. *Toward a Global Civilization of Love & Tolerance*. Somerset, NJ: Light Inc., 2004.

Habermas, Jürgen. 'Notes on Post-Secular Society', *New Perspectives Quarterly* 25 (2008): 17–29.

——. *The Structural Transformation of the Public Sphere: An Inquiry into a Category of Bourgeois Society*. Tr. T. Burger. Cambridge, MA: MIT Press, 1989.

Hallaq, Wael. *The Impossible State: Islam, Politics, and Modernity's Moral Predicament*. New York: Columbia University Press, 2012.

Hamid, Shadi. *Temptations of Power: Islamists and Illiberal Democracy in a New Middle East*. Oxford: Oxford University Press, 2014.

Hashemi, Nader. *Islam, Secularism, and Liberal Democracy: Towards a Democratic Theory for Muslim Societies*. New York: Oxford University Press, 2009.

Hassan, Rifaat. '"Made from Adam's Rib": the Woman's Creation Question'. *Al-Mushir* (1985): 124–55.

Al-Hibri, Azizah. 'A Study of Islamic Herstory?' *Women's Studies International Forum, Special Issue: Women and Islam* 5 (1982): 207–19.

Hofmann, Murad. 'Democracy or Shuracracy', in *Islam in Transition: Muslim Perspectives*. Ed. John J. Donohue and John L. Esposito. Oxford: Oxford University Press, 2007. Pp. 296–306.

Hourani, Albert. *Arabic Thought in the Liberal Age: 1798-1939*. Cambridge: Cambridge University Press, 1983.

Huda, Qamar-ul. *Crescent and Dove: Peace and Conflict Resolution in Islam*. Washington DC: United States Institute of Peace, 2010.

Husayn, Muhammad al-Khidr. *Naqd kitab al-islam wa-usul al-hukm*. Cairo: Dar al-shuruq, 1989.

Ibn Kathir, Isma'il b. 'Umar. *Tafsir al-qur'an al-'azim*. Beirut: Dar al-Jil, 1990.

Ibn Taymiyya, Taqi al-Din. *Majmu'at al-fatawa*. Ed. 'Amir al-Jazzar and Anwar al-Baz. Riyad: Maktabat al-'Ubaykan, 1998.

———. *Al-Siyasa al-shar'iyya*. Cairo: 'Ilm al-kitab, 1951.

Inglehart, Robert and Pippa Norris. 'The True Clash of Civilizations', *Foreign Policy* 135 (2001): 62–70.

Iqbal, Muhammad. *Iqbal: Manifestation of the Islamic Spirit, Two Contemporary Muslim Views: Ayatullah Sayyid Ali Khamene'i and Ali Shariati*. Tr. Mahliqa Qara'i and Laleh Bakhtiar. Markham, ON: Open Press, 1991.

———. *Speeches, Writings and Statements of Iqbal*. Ed. Latif Ahmad Sherwani. New Delhi: Adam Publishers, 2006.

Islamophobia, A Challenge to Us All. Report of the Runnymede Trust Commission on British Muslims and Islamophobia. London: The Runnymede Trust, 1997.

Jackson, Sherman. 'Jihad and the Modern World', *Islamic Law and Culture* 1 (2002): 1–26.

Jahanbegloo, Ramin. *Introduction to Nonviolence*. New York: Palgrave Macmillan, 2014.

Jamal, Amaney and Mark Tessler,. 'The Democracy Barometers: Attitudes in the Arab World', *The Journal of Democracy* 19 (2008): 97–110.

Jansen, Johannes J. G. *The Neglected Duty: The Creed of Sadat's Assassins and Islamic Resurgence in the Middle East*. London: Collier Macmillan, 1986.

Al-Jawziyya, Ibn Qayyim. *'Uddat al-sabirin wa-dhakirat al-shakirin*. Ed. Muhammad 'Ali Qutb. Beirut: Sharikat Dar al-arqam ibn abi al-arqam, n.d.

Juergensmeyer, Mark. *Terror in the Mind of God: The Global Rise of Religious Violence.* Berkeley and Los Angeles: University of California Press, 2003. 3rd edition.

Jum'a, Ali. *Al-Jihad fi 'l-islam.* Cairo: Nahdat misr li 'l-tiba'a wa al-nashr, 2005.

Juynboll, G. H. A. *The Authenticity of the Tradition Literature: Discussions in Modern Egypt.* Leiden: Brill, 1969.

Kazemi, Reza Shah. *Common Ground between Islam and Buddhism: Spiritual and Ethical Affinities.* Louisville, KY: Fons Vitae, 2010.

Khalil, Mohammad Hassan. *Islam and the Fate of Others: The Salvation Question.* Oxford: Oxford University Press, 2012.

Khan, Sayyid Ahmad. *Writings and Speeches of Sir Syed Ahmad Khan.* Ed. Shah Muhammad. Bombay: Nachiketa Publications, 1972.

Khan, Wahiduddin. *The True Jihad: The Concept of Peace, Tolerance and Non-Violence.* New Delhi: Goodword Books, 2002.

Kurzman, Charles. *The Missing Martyrs: Why There are so Few Muslim Terrorists.* Oxford: Oxford University Press, 2011.

Mahmood, Saba. 'Modern Power and the Reconfiguration of Religious Traditions'. *Stanford Electronic Humanities Review* 5:1 (1996).

Mahmoud, Mohamed. 'To Beat or Not to Beat: On the Exegetical Dilemmas over Qur'an, 4:34', *Journal of the American Oriental Society* 126 (2006): 546–9.

Mamdani, Mahmood. *Good Muslim, Bad Muslim.* New York: Doubleday, 2005.

Mandaville, Peter. *Global Political Islam.* New York: Routledge, 2007.

March, Andrew. 'Sources of Moral Obligation to Non-Muslims in the *Fiqh al-Aqalliyyat* (Jurisprudence of Muslim Minorities) Discourse', *Islamic Law and Society* 16 (2009): 34–94.

Mawdudi, Abul A'la. *First Principles of the Islamic State.* Tr. and ed. Khurshid Ahmad. Lahore: Islamic Publications Ltd, 1983.

——. *Political Theory of Islam.* Lahore: Islamic Publications Ltd, 1976.

——. *Towards Understanding the Qur'an.* Tr. and ed. Zafar Ishaq Ansari. Leicester: Islamic Foundation, 1988.

Mernissi, Fatima. *The Veil and the Male Elite: A Feminist Interpretation of Women's Rights in Islam.* Tr. Mary Jo Lakeland. Reading, MA: Addison-Wesley, 1991.

Modood, Tariq. 'Is There a Crisis of Secularism in Western Europe?' *Sociology of Religion* 73 (2012): 130–49.

Mottahedeh, Roy P. 'The Clash of Civilizations: An Islamicist's Critique', in *The New Crusades: Constructing the Muslim Enemy.* Ed. Emran Qureishi and Michael A. Sells. New York, Columbia University Press, 2003. Pp. 132–51.

Mujahid b. Jabr. *Tafsir Mujahid.* Ed. 'Abd al-Rahman al-Tahir b. Muhammad al-Surati. Islamabad: Majma' al-buhuth al-islamiyya, n.d.

Muqatil b. Sulayman. *Tafsir Muqatil b. Sulayman.* Cairo: Mu'assasat al-halabi wa-shuraka'uh, 1969?

Musa, Aisha. *Hadith as Scripture: Discussions on the Authority of Prophetic Traditions in Islam.* New York: Palgrave Macmillan, 2008.

Al-Muti'i, Muhammad Bakhit. *Haqiqat al-Islam wa-usul al-hukm*. Cairo: n. publ., n.d.

Nasr, Seyyed Vali. *Mawdudi and the Making of Islamic Revivalism*. New York: Oxford University Press, 1996.

Osman, Fathi. 'Shura and Democracy', in *Islam in Transition: Muslim Perspectives*, Eds John J. Donohue and John L. Esposito. Oxford: Oxford University Press, 2007. Pp. 296–306.

Parray, Tauseef Ahmad. 'The Legal Methodology of "Fiqh al-Aqalliyyat" and Its Critics: An Analytical Study', *Journal of Muslim Minority Affairs* 32/1 (2012): 88–107.

Peters, Rudolph. *Jihad in Classical and Modern Islam*. Princeton, NJ: Markus Wiener, 1996.

Al-Qaradawi, Yusuf. *Fi fiqh al-aqalliyyat al-muslima – hayat al-muslimin wasat al-mujtama'at al-ukhra*. Cairo: Dar al-Shuruq, 2001.

——. *Fiqh al-jihad*. Cairo: Maktaba Wahba, 2009.

Al-Qurtubi, Muhammad b. Ahmad. *Al-Jami' li-ahkam al-qur'an*. Ed. 'Abd al-Razzaq al-Mahdi. Beirut: Dar al-kitab al-'arabi, 2001.

Qutb, Sayyid. *Fi zilal al-qur'an*. Cairo: Dar al-shuruq, 2001.

——. *Ma'alim fi 'l-tariq*. Beirut: Dar al-shuruq, 1982.

Rahman, Fazlur. *Islam*. Chicago: University of Chicago Press, 1979.

——. *Islam and Modernity: Transformation of an Intellectual Tradition*. Chicago: University of Chicago Press.

——. *Islamic Methodology in History*. Islamabad: Islamic Research Institute, 1965.

——. *Major Themes of the Qur'an*. Minneapolis, MN: Bibliotheca Islamica, 1980.

Ramadan, Tariq. *The Arab Awakening: Islam and the New Middle East*. London and New York: Allen Lane, 2012.

——. *Radical Reform: Islamic Ethics and Liberation*. Oxford: Oxford University Press, 2009.

——. *Western Muslims and the Future of Islam*. Oxford: Oxford University Press, 2004.

Al-Razi, Fakhr al-Din. *Al-Tafsir al-kabir*. Beirut: Dar ihya' al-turath al-'arabi, 1999.

Rida, Rashid. *Tafsir al-Manar*. Beirut: Dar al-kutub al-'ilmiyya,1999.

Sachedina, Abdulaziz. *The Islamic Roots of Democratic Pluralism*. Oxford: Oxford University Press, 2001.

Saeed, Abdullah. *Reading the Qur'an in the Twenty-first Century*. London and New York: Routledge, 2014.

Said, Jawdat. *Non-Violence: The Basis of Settling Disputes in Islam*. Tr. Munzer A. Absi and H. Hilwani. Damascus: Dar al-fikr, 2002.

Sardar, Ziauddin. *Reading the Qur'an: The Contemporary Relevance of the Sacred Text of Islam*. Oxford: Oxford University Press, 2011.

Satha-Anand, Chaiwat, Glenn Paige, and Sarah Gilliat (eds). *Islam and Non-Violence*. Honolulu: University of Hawaii Press, 1993.

Al-Shafi'i, Muhammad. *Kitab al-umm*. Ed. Mahmud Matruji. Beirut: Dar al-kutub al-'ilmiyya, 2002.

——. *Al-Risala*. Eds 'Abd al-Latif al-Hamim and Mahir Yasin al-Fahl. Beirut: Dar al-kutub al-'ilmiyya, 2005.

——. *Al-Risala fi usul al-fiqh*. Ed. Ahmad Muhammad Shakir. Cairo: al-Halabi, 1940.

Al-Shawkani, Muhammad b. 'Ali. *Fath al-qadir: al-jami' bayna fannay al-riwaya wa-'l-diraya min 'ilm al-tafsir*. Beirut: Dar al-kutub al-'ilmiyya,1996.

Spellberg, Denise. *Thomas Jefferson's Qur'an: Islam and the Founders*. New York: Alfred A. Knopf, 2013.

Stepan, Alfred C. and Graeme B. Robertson. 'An "Arab" More Than a "Muslim" Democracy Gap', *The Journal of Democracy* 14 (2003): 30–44.

Stowasser, Barbara. *Women in the Qur'an, Traditions, and Interpretation*. Oxford: Oxford University Press, 1994.

Al-Tabari, Muhammad b. Jarir. *Tafsir al-Tabari*, also known as *Jami' al-bayan fi ta'wil al-qur'an*. Beirut: Dar al-kutub al-'ilmiyya, 1997.

Talbi, Mohamed. *Al-Islam: Hurriya wa Hiwar*. Beirut: Dar al-nahar lil-nashr, 1999.

Tepe, Sultan and Betul Demirkaya. '(Not) Getting Religion: Has Political Science Lost Sight of Islam?' *Politics and Religion* 4 (2011): 203–28.

Volf, Miroslav, Ghazi bin Muhammad and Melissa Yarrington (eds). *A Common Word: Muslims and Christians on Loving God and Neighbor*. Grand Rapids, MI: Eerdmans Publishing Company, 2010.

Voll, John O. 'The Mistaken Identification of "The West" with "Modernity"', *American Journal of Islamic Social Sciences* 13 (1996): 1–6.

Von Grunebaum, G. E. *Modern Islam: the Search for Cultural Identity*. Berkeley: University of California Press, 1962.

Wadud, Amina. *Qur'an and Woman: Rereading the Sacred Text from a Woman's Perspective*. New York: Oxford University Press, 1999.

Al-Wahidi, 'Ali b. Ahmad. *Al-Wasit fi tafsir al-Qur'an*. Ed. 'Adil Ahmad 'Abd al-Mawjud. Beirut: Dar al-kutub al-'ilmiyya, 1994.

Wali Allah, Shah. *Hujjat allah al-baligha*. Cairo: Dar al-turath, 1936.

——. *'Iqd al-jid fi ahkam al-ijtihad wa al-taqlid*. Cairo: al-Matba'a al-Salafiyya, 1385 AH.

Weber, Max. *The Protestant Ethic and the Spirit of Capitalism*. Ed. Talcott Parsons. London: Routledge, 1992.

Wildman, Wesley J. *Religious Philosophy as Multidisciplinary Comparative Inquiry: Envisioning a Future for the Philosophy of Religion*. Albany, NY: State University of New York Press, 2010.

Williams, Rowan. 'Civil and Religious Law in England: A Religious Perspective,' *Ecclesiastical Law Journal* 10 (2008): 262–82.

Yucesoy, Hayrettin. 'Justification of Political Authority in Medieval Sunni Thought', in *Islam, the State, and Political Authority: Medieval Issues and Modern Concerns*. Ed. Asma Afsaruddin. New York: Palgrave Macmillan, 2011. Pp. 9–33.

Al-Zamakhshari, Mahmud b. 'Umar. *al-Kashshaf 'an haqa'iq ghawamid al-tanzil wa-'uyun al-aqawil fi wujuh al-ta'wi*. Eds 'Adil Ahmad 'Abd al-Wujud and 'Ali Muhammad l. Mu'awwad. Riyad: Maktabat al-'Ubaykan, 1998.

Zebiri, Kate. 'The Redeployment of Orientalist Themes in Contemporary Islamophobia', *Studies in Contemporary Islam* 10 (2008): 4–44.

Al-Zuhayli, Wahba Mustafa. *Athar al-harb fi 'l-fiqh al-islami: dirasa muqarana.* Beirut: Dar al-fikr, 1981.

Index